Praise for *EMPOWERED*

"I recommend *INSPIRED* to every entrepreneur and burgeoning product person I talk to as the must read. That must-read list just doubled with *EMPOWERED*. It's destined to become a classic."

Shawn Boyer, Founder, GoHappy and Snagajob

"*EMPOWERED* dives deep into the tough organizational and cultural issues that get in the way of most companies I work with today. This is the experience and advice I've been waiting for in one book."

Jeff Patton, Product Process and Design Coach

"I've known Chris for well over a decade. He is one of the finest product leaders I know. The product managers who worked for him went on to become great product leaders themselves, in some of the best tech companies around. If you want to learn from the best, this book captures those lessons."

Doug Camplejohn, EVP and GM, Sales Cloud, Salesforce

"Once again, Marty's wisdom and unique perspective have synthesized best-in-class companies, cultures, and leaders into a thesis and set of principles that are transformational. Easy to consume and apply, *EMPOWERED* is a must read for product leaders and all leaders who are convinced there must be a better way."

Chuck Geiger, former CTO Chegg, IAC, PayPal, eBay, Wine.com, Travelocity

"If you're leading product people or even the whole product organization of your company, this book is for you. It's the first book to outline the underlying philosophy behind stellar product organizations from a leader's perspective, and its many examples make it easy to understand these concepts and apply them in your company's environment."

Petra Wille, Product Leadership Coach

"As one of the most respected leaders on product globally, Marty takes us for a fascinating ride that will help you become a better product leader so you can do what you do best—create satisfying, engaging experiences for your users and customers."

Simon Zhang, CEO, GrowingIO

"To thrive in this age of constant disruption, companies must accelerate innovation and continuously deliver products customers love. A higher level of consistent innovation can *only* come from truly empowered teams. Over the past several years, Marty's insights, practical advice, and wisdom have been immensely valuable during our transformation to a highly empowered product organization. In this book, Marty provides an essential blueprint for building empowered teams. If you are serious about achieving extraordinary business results and developing a product innovation culture you can be truly proud of, this is a must-read!"

Shamim Mohammad, SVP, Chief Information and Technology Officer, CarMax

"I've had the good fortune to work with Marty for many years, and yet, every time he comes out with a new book or article, I'm filled with both excitement and fear. What new product techniques are our competitors using that we are missing? EMPOWERED hits the mark dead on, and provides a recipe for creating great products. Marty has a knack for making difficult product techniques seem both necessary and tangible. Read the book and rejuvenate your company!"

Jeff Trom, CTO, Workiva

"The core challenge of all tech companies today is to be a truly product-led organization, with continuous product innovation resulting in sustainable competitive advantage. *EMPOWERED* gives executives and leaders the key to understand how they need to change their companies in order to survive and thrive."

Frerk-Malte Feller, COO, Afterpay

"If you are wondering what will ensure your company survives, or why your products are failing, read this book. This is the 'how to' manual for building great product companies that last."

Amanda Richardson, CEO, CoderPad

"I included *INSPIRED* as mandatory reading for anyone joining my product development teams. Now I'll add *EMPOWERED* to the list of mandatory reading."

Joca Torres, CPO, Gympass

"*INSPIRED* has been a manual for our team to build better products. *EMPOWERED* is now a manual to build a stronger team. Everything I've read from SVPG is spot on, and often feels like I can use it the same day."

Ian Cairns, Head of Product for Twitter Developer Platform

"*EMPOWERED* is first and foremost about permission. Companies have to give themselves the permission to orient around a culture of product centricity. Everything from org structure, to technology, to culture and coaching derives from this. And nothing embodies this idea more than Marty's writings."

Punit Soni, founder, CEO, Suki

EMPOWERED

The Silicon Valley Product Group Series

INSPIRED: How to Create Tech Products Customers Love, 2nd Edition
(Marty Cagan, 2017)

EMPOWERED: Ordinary People, Extraordinary Products
(Marty Cagan with Chris Jones, 2021)

TRANSFORMED: Becoming a Product-Driven Company
(Lea Hickman, 2021)

LOVED: How to Market Tech Products Customers Adore
(Martina Lauchengco, 2021)

MARTY CAGAN with CHRIS JONES
Silicon Valley Product Group

EMPOWERED

ORDINARY PEOPLE, EXTRAORDINARY PRODUCTS

WILEY

Library of Congress Cataloging-in-Publication Data is Available.

ISBN 9781119691297 (Hardcover)
ISBN 9781119691259 (ePDF)
ISBN 9781119691327 (ePub)

COVER DESIGN: PAUL MCCARTHY

Printed in the United States of America

SKY10035255_071522

This book is dedicated to Bill Campbell (1940–2016), known with affection as the Coach of Silicon Valley.

While I had met Bill a few times over the years, I was never fortunate enough to be coached by him. However, I count myself very lucky to have been managed and coached by several leaders who were coached by Bill.

Increasingly, I realize how many of the important lessons I've learned about leadership, empowerment, teams, and strong product companies can be traced back to Bill.

I hope he would approve of this book, and that he would be proud to see his teachings living on.

Contents

PART III   STAFFING   139

PART IV   PRODUCT VISION AND PRINCIPLES   187

I

Lessons from Top Tech Companies

My first book, *INSPIRED*, discussed how strong product teams at the best product companies use the modern techniques of product discovery to solve hard problems in ways their customers love, yet work for their business.

INSPIRED brought me and my SVPG Partners into many more organizations, well beyond Silicon Valley.

The most striking thing we learned was that in so many companies—even companies trying to do true, technology-powered products and services—product teams were too often not *allowed* to work the way they needed to.

We realized that it's not just the techniques that strong product teams use to discover successful products, but that the differences between how great product companies work and the rest run much deeper.

What we found in these companies was not pretty.

The Role of Technology

So many companies still have the old IT mindset when it comes to technology. It's viewed as a necessary cost rather than the core business enabler it needs to be. The people who work on the technology teams are literally there "to serve the business," and the technology managers and leaders are there to facilitate serving the business. Or it's shoved off to the side in some "digital" business unit. The technology teams are disconnected from the real customers—in fact, they're encouraged to think of their stakeholders as their customers.

Coaching

There is little if any active coaching of the people on the technology teams. And even if they wanted to coach, the managers often don't have the experience themselves. So the problems perpetuate.

Staffing

Most of these companies recognize that they don't have the staff they need, but they have very misguided ideas about how to correct that, and what to look for in product staff. So again, the problems perpetuate.

Product Vision

These companies rarely have an inspiring, compelling product vision. They may have had one during the early years of their company, but after the founders left, the vision faded. The people on the technology teams feel like they're just working in feature factories.

Team Topology

The technology people are divided up into teams where they feel like they aren't responsible for anything meaningful, they can't do much without depending on changes from several other teams, and that they're just a small cog in a giant wheel.

Product Strategy

It wouldn't be fair to say that most of these companies have a weak product strategy, because in truth, most have literally *no* strategy at all. They are just trying to please as many stakeholders as they can with the people and time and skills they have.

Team Objectives

Most of these companies have heard that Google and others use the OKR (Objectives and Key Results) technique to manage their work, and the CEO watched a video or read a book and thought it sounded easy. So they adopted the technique—layering it on top of their existing product roadmaps and culture—and every quarter there's a planning exercise that consumes a few weeks and is then largely ignored for the rest of the quarter. Most of the people on the teams say they get little if any value out of this technique.

Relationship to Business

The relationship between the technology teams and the rest of the business is not good. The stakeholders and executives have little or no trust in the technology teams. And the people on the technology teams feel like unappreciated mercenaries, subservient to the business.

Empowered Teams

Worst of all, the teams are not empowered to solve problems in ways customers love, yet work for the business. And as such, the teams can't be held accountable to results.

The product manager is really a *project* manager, shepherding the backlog items through the process. The designers and engineers are there just to design and code the features on the roadmap.

Motivation is low, sense of ownership is minimal, and innovation is rare.

It is easy to see why so many of these companies are ripe for disruption. And nothing at all like how product is done at strong product companies.[1]

What is especially shocking to me is that it is really no secret how the best companies work, and how financially successful they are. Which raises the question, why is this the case?

In my experience, it's not that these companies don't *want* to transform, it's that transforming is *hard*, and they just don't know *how*. Or even what it really *means* to transform.

What they need is to move to *empowered product teams*.

Now, you may not be using that term, and you may not even realize there are different types of technology teams.

But if what I described is similar to your organization, I need to share with you a few very hard truths:

- First, you have very little chance of getting meaningful business results, let alone actually innovating, from your way of working

- Second, your customers are big, ripe targets for a competitor that does not operate this way (e.g., Amazon), and knows how to provide products customers love, yet work for their business

- Third, you are largely wasting the talents and capabilities of the people you have hired, and your best people—the ones you desperately need to survive and thrive—will likely leave

- Finally, if you think that by moving to Agile you've already done some form of digital transformation, I am sorry to tell you, but you haven't even gotten started

I'm hoping that the reason you're reading this book is because you are convinced there must be a better way.

And there is.

---

[1] To be very clear, we have found exceptionally strong companies well beyond Silicon Valley, including in Shanghai, Melbourne, Tel Aviv, London, Berlin, Bangalore, and beyond, just as we have found very weak companies in the heart of San Francisco. It is the *difference* between the best and the rest that we focus on in this book.

CHAPTER

1

Behind Every Great Company

In this book, I want to share and highlight the differences between how *the best* companies create technology-powered products and how *most* companies create products.

The differences are both fundamental and striking.

The differences certainly include what many people think of as "product culture," but strong product companies often have very different cultures from one another, so it clearly goes beyond that.

For example, consider Amazon, Google, Apple, and Netflix. I would argue all four are very strong product companies, having consistently innovated for many years, yet they each have very different cultures.

I still believe culture is extremely important, but there is something about great product companies that is more fundamental.

It comes down to the views they have on the role of technology, the purpose of the people who work on the technology, and how they expect these people to work together to solve problems.

Moreover, I don't think it's an accident that, despite their different cultures, these four companies have the most important elements in common.

What I will try to do in this book is untangle the parts of the cultures of these companies that are more a reflection of their founders' personalities from those that are essential to consistent innovation.

I want to share the important lessons I've learned regarding what separates the best from the rest.

One surprising common thread among many of the best product companies is the legendary coach, Bill Campbell. During their formative years, Bill literally provided executive coaching to the founders of Apple, Amazon, and Google, as well as several others.

To get a sense of Bill's views and values, here is one of my favorite quotes about the role of leadership in a strong product company:

Leadership is about recognizing that there's a greatness in everyone, and your job is to create an environment where that greatness can emerge.

This book is all about identifying what makes such an environment, and I want to encourage you to consider adopting these important practices and behaviors.

Please note that I am not arguing that these strong product companies are models of virtue. All of them have been justifiably criticized about some of their policies and practices.[1]

But when it comes to the ability to consistently innovate, all four of these companies have demonstrated their skills, and I believe there is much to be learned from them.

At the core, I see three critically important differences between the strongest product companies and the rest:

The first is how the company views the role of technology.

The second is the role their product leaders play.

The third is how the company views the purpose of the product teams—the product managers, product designers, and engineers.

Let's take a closer look at each of these.

---

[1] For an unflinching critique of these companies when it comes to their policies, see the writings of Professor Scott Galloway (www.profgalloway.com).

The Role of Technology

There is a fundamental difference between how strong companies view the role and purpose of technology as compared to most other companies.

At its most basic level, the vast majority of companies view technology as a necessary expense. They know it's important, but they think of it more as a cost of doing business. If they can outsource the labor, even better. Fundamentally, they don't really consider themselves in the technology business. Instead, they think of themselves as in the insurance business, or the banking business, or the transportation business, or whatever. Certainly, they need some technology to operate, but it's viewed as a subservient role to "the business."

Because of that, in most companies, technology teams exist *to serve the business*. That is very often the exact phrase you will hear. But even if they aren't explicit about it, the different parts of "the business" end up driving what is actually built by the product teams.

In contrast, in strong product companies, technology is not an expense, it *is* the business. Technology enables and powers the products and services we provide to our customers. Technology allows us to solve problems for our customers in ways that are just now possible.

Whether the product or service is an insurance policy, a bank account, or an overnight parcel delivery, that product now has enabling technology at its core.

As such, in *strong* product companies, the purpose of the product team is *to serve customers by creating products customers love, yet work for the business*.

That is a profound difference, which impacts nearly everything about the company and how it works, and results in much higher motivation and morale. And most important, it results in a much higher level of innovation and value for customers and the business.

Strong Product Leadership

In *most* product companies, the role of true product leadership is largely missing in action.

Instead, they are mainly there as facilitators, responsible for staffing the in-house (or even worse, outsourced) feature factory, and keeping the trains running on time.

In *most* companies, there is no product strategy. Notice I didn't say a bad product strategy—I mean literally *no* product strategy. The feature teams are simply there "to serve the business."

The business certainly has reasons for what they request or put on the roadmaps, but they very rarely have a product strategy, or even the skills or data required to create one.

The stakeholders end up providing product teams with a prioritized list of features and projects that they need completed this quarter or this year. So, the "product strategy," if you could even call it that, is really about trying to please as much of the business as possible.

When technology product companies moved to Agile methods over the past 10–20 years, many managers and leaders questioned whether they were still necessary, since team members would be expected to take a much more active role in how they work.

I realize this is counterintuitive to many people, but while moving to truly empowered teams does require moving away from the old command-and-control model of management, it does *not* mean you need fewer leaders and managers. It means you need *better* leaders and managers.

It's actually easier for a manager to manage (often micromanage) in the old command-and-control style. It's not hard to assign a team a list of activities, or a list of features to build, and just tell them to do the work as fast as they can.

While this command-and-control style may be easier for the manager, it creates teams of mercenaries with no empowerment in any meaningful sense.

In contrast, in *strong* product companies, the product leaders are among the most impactful leaders in the company.

They are responsible for staffing and coaching the product teams; they are responsible for the product strategy and converting the strategy into action; and they're responsible for managing to results.

Empowered product teams depend on skilled product managers, product designers, and engineers, and it is the leaders and managers who are responsible for recruiting, hiring, and coaching these people.

Further, a focused and compelling product strategy—based on quantitative and qualitative insights—is among the most important contributions of product leadership.

Empowered Product Teams

In *most* companies, the technology teams are not *empowered* product teams, they are what I call here *feature teams*.

Feature teams look superficially like a product team. They are cross-functional, with a product manager, a product designer, and some number of engineers. The difference is that they are all about implementing features and projects (*output*), and as such are not empowered or held accountable to results.

The feature teams get to work first designing the features on the roadmap, maybe doing a little usability testing, and then proceeding to building, QA testing, and deploying the features (known as *delivery*).

These feature teams sometimes claim they're doing some product discovery, but they rarely are. They've already been told what the solution should be; they're not empowered to go figure out the solution themselves. They're just there to design and then code.

In these feature teams, there is usually a person with the product manager title, but they are mainly doing *project* management. They are there to ensure the features get designed and delivered. Necessary perhaps, but this is not *product* management.

Because the teams are provided, or are pressed to provide, roadmaps of features and projects, the focus of the team is *delivery*—delivery of these features. And features are output. Even if someone were to complain of lack of business results, who would you hold accountable?

In contrast, in strong product companies, teams are instead given *problems to solve*, rather than features to build, and most important, they are *empowered to solve those problems in the best way they see fit*. And they are then held accountable to the results.

In the empowered product team model, the product manager has a clear responsibility, which is to ensure that the solutions are *valuable* (our customers will buy the product and/or choose to use it), and *viable* (it will meet the needs of the business). Together with a product designer who is responsible for ensuring the solution is *usable*, and a tech lead who is responsible for ensuring the solution is *feasible*, the team is able to collaborate to address this full range of risks (value, viability, usability, and feasibility). Together, they own the problem and are responsible and accountable for the results.[2]

So, to summarize feature teams vs. empowered product teams:

Feature teams are cross-functional (a product manager doing mainly project management, a product designer, plus some engineers), and assigned features and projects to build rather than problems to solve, and as such they are all about output and not business results.

Empowered product teams are also cross-functional (a product manager, a product designer, and engineers), but in contrast to feature teams, they are assigned *problems to solve*, and are then empowered to come up with solutions that work—measured by outcome—and held accountable to results.[3]

Product Discovery

If you have not yet read *INSPIRED*, then you might be wondering: *What is so wrong with the business owners and stakeholders deciding what goes on the roadmap*, and therefore what the engineers should build?

This is considered the first and most important principle of product discovery: *our customers, and our stakeholders, aren't able to tell us what to build*.

It's not because our customers or stakeholders aren't smart or knowledgeable.

---

[2] To be clear, the designer and tech lead contribute much more than simply ensuring usability and feasibility respectively; what I'm referring to here is who we hold responsible and accountable for each risk.

[3] There is actually a third type of technology team, which is referred to as a *delivery team* (or "Scrum team" or "dev team"). A delivery team doesn't even pretend to be a true product team. They are not cross-functional, and they are not empowered. There is a product *owner* (responsible for administering the product backlog) and some number of engineers. They are purely about output (code and ship). If you're running a process like SAFe, then this is unfortunately you, and truthfully, I have no idea why you would want to read this book, since what I describe here is the polar opposite both philosophically and practically.

There are two fundamental reasons why our customers and stakeholders aren't able to tell us what to build:

First, the customers and stakeholders don't know what is just now possible—they are not experts in the enabling technologies, so they can't be expected to know the best way to solve the problems we're focused on, or even if the problem is possible to solve. It's often the case that innovations solve problems in ways that customers and stakeholders had no idea was possible.

Second, with technology products, it's very hard to predict in advance what solutions will work. There are many reasons why product ideas don't deliver the results we hoped. All too often we are excited about some idea, but our customers are not, so they don't buy what we thought they would. Or, we discover the idea has major privacy or security issues. Or we find out the idea will take much longer to build than anyone expected.

Empowered product teams understand these inherent issues, and product discovery is about *discovering a solution that our customers love, yet works for our business.*

We refer to this as product *discovery* to acknowledge that we understand what we can't know in advance, and to emphasize that our task is to *discover* a solution that is *valuable*, *usable*, *feasible*, and *viable*.

2

The Role of Technology

I promise that this book is very practical, and you'll be able to directly apply everything we discuss. But in this one chapter, if you'll bear with me, we need to get just a little philosophical.

It is plain to see the difference between feature teams and empowered product teams.

It is plain to see when companies view teams as there to serve the business, versus when they're there to serve customers in ways that work for the business.

It is plain to see when a company is just trying to please as many stakeholders as possible, versus when they have a clear and intentional product strategy.

But while these differences might be plain to see, that does not explain *why* these differences exist.

If we hope to close the gap between the best and the rest, we need to look at the root cause of this gap.

Roughly a decade ago, Marc Andreessen published what I consider one of the most important essays of our time, "Why Software Is Eating the World."[1] He described why he believed that technology was about to cause major disruption across virtually every industry. He gave voice to what I had been seeing in my own work—primarily with the disruptors, but occasionally with those under threat of disruption.

Ten years later, it's clear he was remarkably prescient.

That said, *most* companies seem to have not really understood his warnings.

Yes, they're all spending more on software now.

Yes, they've (mostly) moved to Agile methods.

But most have *not* transformed in any meaningful sense, and in particular most have *not* embraced technology as the business enabler it is.

The examples of this are unfortunately everywhere.

One of the clearest and most egregious recent examples has to be the absolute ineptitude of the leadership at Boeing with the software at the heart of the aircraft manufacturer's shocking 737 MAX crisis.[2]

Boeing's fundamental mistake was to consider this technology as just a necessary cost, rather than the core competency that enables them to provide the safest, most fuel-efficient, and most cost-effective airplanes available.

Rather than staffing an empowered product team—continuously working to provide the safest, most fuel-efficient, mission-critical control software—they decided to outsource this technology, thinking they could maybe save a few dollars.

It's not just the aerospace industry. The automotive industry has suffered from this mindset for decades,[3] until Tesla came along and proved what is truly possible when technology is at the core of the car, rather than treated as just a necessary cost. Going far beyond navigation and entertainment systems, using technology at its core and over-the-air updates, a Tesla actually *improves* over time rather than simply depreciating. Consider that for a moment.

---

[1] https://a16z.com/2011/08/20/why-software-is-eating-the-world/.
[2] https://www.bloomberg.com/news/articles/2019-06-28/boeing-s-737-max-software-outsourced-to-9-an-hour-engineers.
[3] Bob Lutz, *Car Guys vs. Bean Counters: The Battle for the Soul of American Business* (New York: Portfolio/Penguin, 2013).

Pixar has shown the film industry what is truly possible when technology is at the core of an animated feature film, rather than just a necessary cost. Pixar uses technology in ways far beyond traditional film-making, and the technology teams are as valued as the creative teams.

As you may know, Pixar is now part of Disney, and look at how Disney has embraced technology to completely reimagine so many of their existing businesses. This includes everything from their legacy theme parks to what they've recently done with the Disney+ video streaming service.

The same story is playing out in the insurance, banking, health care, telecommunications, education, agriculture, transportation, and defense industries. I could keep going.

Often, when I am having dinner with one of the CEOs from a company that doesn't get this, they'll tell me how they're *not* a technology company—they're an insurance company, or a health care company, or an agricultural company. I'll say, "Let me tell you what I would do if I was a product leader at Amazon or Apple, and we've decided to go after your market because we believe it is large and underserved, and that technology is available that enables dramatically better solutions for your customers."

After describing how we would set up our teams around the enabling technology to optimize for true innovation, I also point out that, competitively, we would be betting on them *not* being able to respond because they would be too busy trying to protect their old business.

It's not that these CEOs don't admire what companies like Amazon and Netflix and others have done—they generally do. It's that they don't see how these lessons apply to them. They don't understand what Marc was trying to warn them about.

Of course, there are many possible reasons why the CEOs of these companies have been so slow to grok this. Sometimes, they have worked in the old world of business so long that they need more time to wrap their head around the changes. Sometimes, I can't help but feel like they are fearful of technology. Sometimes, they just seem to be resisting change. But, ultimately, these are all just excuses. The board is supposed to be there to ensure the CEO is able to effectively lead the company.

What is especially ironic is that these companies are almost always spending far *more* on technology than they need to. In fact, I've never seen more wasted technology investment than I find in these companies that don't understand the true role of technology.

Rather than outsourcing hundreds or even thousands of mercenary engineers—and providing them roadmaps of features from their stakeholders which rarely generate the necessary business results—I explain to them that they will receive a much greater return from a significantly smaller number of the *right* employees. Employees who are given business and customer problems to solve and are held accountable to the results.

One way or another, becoming one of the *best* companies today requires senior leaders who understand the true and essential role of technology.

The Technology Leader

One very common manifestation of how a company views the role of technology is whether the engineers building the company's products report up to a CIO (chief information officer)/head of IT, or whether they report up to a CTO (chief technology officer)/head of engineering.

This may seem like a minor issue, but I've come to realize it's a much more significant impediment to transformation than most companies realize.

With the big caveat that each individual CIO is a unique person, I share this not as an absolute, but as something to seriously and honestly consider. Also, it is important to realize that the core CIO job (managing the IT function) is both important and difficult.

But here's the problem: the CIO truly *is* there *to serve the business*.

The very traits that make for a strong CIO can easily end up undermining the company's attempts to transform.

That's my theory for why I've found it very difficult to get CIOs—even strong CIOs—to appreciate, much less adopt, the mindset, methods, and practices of product engineering organizations.

(continued)

(continued)

What's especially problematic is that product engineers—the type the future of your company depends on—are rarely willing to work for a CIO because they know this difference in mindset is extremely important.

Engineers in a CIO's organization play a very different role than engineers in a CTO's organization. It's the difference between feature teams and empowered product teams.

In some cases, I've encouraged the CIO to retitle as CTO (because I believed the person was up to the challenges of this much larger role), and in other cases I've strongly encouraged the CEO to hire a true CTO to lead product engineering.

3

Strong Product Leadership

The heart of this book is the importance of strong product leadership.

To be clear, by "product leadership" I mean the leaders and managers of product management, the leaders and managers of product design,[1] and the leaders and managers of engineering.

For this discussion, I will distinguish between leaders and managers. Certainly, many leaders are also managers, and many managers are also leaders, but even if both roles are covered by the same person, there are different responsibilities.

Overall, we look to leadership for inspiration and we look to management for execution.

---

[1] In this book I refer to the role of product design, and the title product designer. Many companies use the terms user experience design or customer experience design. What's important is that I am including service design, interaction design, visual design, and, for devices, industrial design.

The Role of Leadership—Inspiration

The subject of strong leadership, is of course, a major topic, but it is a clear and visible difference between *strong* product companies and *most* companies.

The purpose of strong leadership is to inspire and motivate the organization.

If product teams are to be empowered to make good decisions, they need to have the strategic context necessary to make those decisions.

Part of the strategic context comes from the senior leaders of the company, such as the purpose of the business (the mission) and critical business objectives, but the product leadership has four major explicit responsibilities:

Product Vision and Principles

The product vision describes the future we are trying to create and, most important, how it improves the lives of our customers.

It is usually between 3 and 10 years out. The product vision serves as the shared goal for the product organization.

There may be any number of cross-functional, empowered product teams—ranging from a few in a startup, to hundreds in a large enterprise—but they all need to head in the same direction and contribute in their own way to solving the larger problem.

Some companies refer to the product vision as their "North Star"—in the sense that no matter what product team you're on, and whatever specific problem you're trying to solve, you can all see and follow the North Star. You always know how your piece contributes to the more meaningful whole.

More generally, the product vision is what keeps us inspired and excited to come to work each day—month after month, year after year.

It is worth noting that the product vision is typically the single most powerful recruiting tool for strong product people.

Product principles complement the product vision by speaking to the nature of the products that your organization believes it needs to produce. The principles reflect the values of the organization, and also some strategic decisions that help the teams make the right decisions when faced with difficult trade-offs.

Team Topology

The "team topology" refers to how we break up the work among different product teams to best enable them to do great work. This includes the structure and scope of teams, and their relationship to one another.

Product Strategy

The product strategy describes how we plan to accomplish the product vision, while meeting the needs of the business as we go. The strategy derives from *focus*, then leverages *insights*, converts these insights into *action*, and finally *manages* the work through to completion.

Product Evangelism

Another critical role of leaders is communicating the product vision, principles, and product strategy—both to the internal product organization, and also across the company more broadly.

John Doerr, the famous venture capitalist, likes to explain that "We need teams of missionaries, not teams of mercenaries."

If we want teams of missionaries, it's essential that every person in the organization understands and is convinced—they need to be *true believers*.

This requires an ongoing crusade of evangelizing—in recruiting, onboarding, weekly 1:1 coaching, all-hands meetings, team lunches, and everything in between.

The larger the organization, the more essential it is to be *very good* at evangelism, and it's important for the leaders to understand that evangelism is something that is never "done." It needs to be a constant.

We want to ensure that every member of the product organization has joined because they sincerely believe in the larger purpose.

Normally, it is the product vision that describes what people are signing up for, but one way or another, we need to ensure the people on the team are true believers.

For example, if your vision is to deliver mass-market electric cars, then we need people that are willing to take the leap of faith that this is both possible and worthy. Note that it is not a problem if the person you hire has different views on what might work to get us to mass-market electric cars, but it is not helpful, for example, to hire a passionate advocate for internal combustion engines.

The Role of Management—Execution

There are of course many types of "managers" in a company. I'm most interested here in those people responsible for hiring and developing the actual members of the cross-functional product teams.

Normally, this includes the director of product management, the director of product design, and the managers and directors of engineering. I'm not focused here on more senior-level managers (managers of managers), or non-people managers (such as product managers or product marketing managers).

If you want to have truly empowered product teams, then your success depends very directly on these first-level people managers.

If you are wondering why there are so many weak product companies in the world, this would be the primary culprit. And until and unless this is corrected, there's little hope for transformation.

It is important that these managers understand—and can effectively communicate—the product vision, principles, and product strategy from the senior leaders. Beyond that, these managers have three critically important responsibilities:

Staffing

These are the people we hold responsible for staffing the product teams. This means sourcing, recruiting, interviewing, onboarding, evaluating, promoting, and when necessary, replacing the members of the teams.

If you have an HR function at your company, they are there to *support* managers with these activities, but they are in no way a substitute for the manager in these responsibilities.

Coaching

Probably the single most important, yet most often overlooked, element to capable management is coaching. At the very minimum, this involves a weekly 1:1 with the people who report to you as their people manager.

It is the most important responsibility of every people manager to develop the skills of their people. This most definitely does not mean micromanaging them. It does mean understanding their weaknesses and helping them to improve, providing guidance on lessons learned, removing obstacles, and what is loosely referred to as "connecting the dots."

For example, let's say you are the manager of product design, and you meet each week for an hour or so with each of the six product designers from six different product teams that work for you.

These six product designers are each first-class members of their cross-functional product teams (because design is a first-class activity, and as such it needs to partner closely with the product manager and engineers as they tackle and solve hard problems). But even if that designer is exceptionally skilled, how can she be expected to keep track of what is going on with all the other product teams? What if the design she is working on right now for her situation is in some way inconsistent or incompatible with solutions underway with other teams? The design manager is expected to flag these conflicts and get the relevant designers together to consider the bigger picture and the impact of the different solutions on the user.

More generally, every member of a product team deserves to have someone who is committed to helping them get better at their craft. This is why, in the vast majority of strong tech product organizations, the engineers report to experienced engineering managers; the designers report to experienced design managers; and the product managers report to proven managers of product management.

Team Objectives

The third responsibility of the people managers is to ensure that each product team has one or two clear objectives they have been assigned (typically quarterly) which spell out the problems they are being asked to solve.

These objectives derive directly from the product strategy—it's where insights are turned into actions.

This is also where empowerment becomes *real* and not just a buzzword. The team is given a small number of significant problems to solve (the team objectives).

The team considers the problems and proposes clear measures of success (the key results), which they then discuss with their managers. The managers may need to iterate with their teams and others to try and get as much coverage as possible of the broader organization's objectives.

The litmus test for empowerment is that the team is able to decide the best way to solve the problems they have been assigned (the objectives).

It takes strong managers to be self-confident and secure enough to truly empower the people that work for them, and to stand back and let the team take credit for their successes.

Empowered Product Teams

What is most surprising to me is that the virtues of truly empowered product teams are not a secret. In fact, there are plenty of books and articles out there that describe why these types of teams are so much more effective at innovation and in solving hard problems.

While quite a few these books are inspiring and well worth reading, most companies have not been convinced to empower their teams in any meaningful sense. Why is that?

When I ask this question of CEOs and other key leaders of these organizations, the answer typically boils down to one word: *trust*.

The leaders don't trust the teams. Specifically, they don't believe they have the level of people on their teams they need to truly empower them. So, along with the other key business leaders from across the company, they believe they need to very explicitly direct the teams themselves. This is also known as the "command-and-control" model of management.

When I ask these leaders why they don't put people in place that they do trust, they usually argue that they either can't find, can't afford, or can't attract the level of people that Google, Amazon, Apple, and Netflix hire.

I then point out to them the many people I know who have moved from companies like theirs to one of these leading companies, and how their performance dramatically improved in the process.

And further, having worked with many people at each of these companies, I point out how ordinary the vast majority of the people on these teams actually are. Maybe the important difference lies elsewhere?

Maybe these strong companies have different views on how to leverage their talent in order to help their ordinary people reach their true potential and create, together, extraordinary products.

Leadership in Action

This book argues that the key to building strong product companies is having strong product leaders.

After all, these are the people responsible for staffing and coaching the members of the product teams, and they are responsible for the product vision, principles, and especially the product strategy, which determines the specific problems we need product teams to solve.

So, what do these strong product leaders look like? And what are they like to work for?

In *INSPIRED*, I profiled six product managers who were all responsible for iconic products, yet were largely unknown, and I told their stories—including the challenges they faced and how they overcame them.

In *EMPOWERED*, I want to do the same, but this time with product leaders. I profile here eight product leaders. Each has had an exceptional career at iconic product companies. Yet again, most of them are largely unknown.

I highlight two leaders of product management, two leaders of product design, two leaders of engineering, and two leaders of companies.

I'm not trying to provide full biographies here, but rather, I asked them each to share, in their own words, their journeys to leadership. My hope is that their words will give you a good sense of their approach to leadership, and most of all, what it is like to work with and for a strong and experienced product leader.

CHAPTER

6

A Guide to
EMPOWERED

Who This Book Is For

This book is intended for anyone interested in creating a strong product organization—from a startup founder to the CEO of a major technology-powered company.

Specifically, the book is aimed at *product leaders* and *aspiring product leaders*. Especially the leaders of product managers, product designers, and engineers.

When you see a reference to "product person," that is normally anyone in product management, product design, or engineering. The person might be an individual contributor or a manager.

While there are many other roles you may find within a given product team—delivery manager, user researcher, data analyst, data scientist, and product marketing manager being the main ones—this book focuses on the three core roles of product manager (PM), product designer (designer), and engineering tech lead (tech lead).

When you see a reference to a "product leader," that is normally a manager/director/VP/CPO of product management, manager/director/VP/CDO of product design, or a manager/director/VP/CTO of engineering.

Unless stated otherwise, the advice in the book is aimed at *product leaders*.

If some advice is aimed at a specific role, such as a product manager, product designer, tech lead, or data scientist, then this will be called out explicitly.

While there is some role-specific information for product designers and their leaders, and engineers and their leaders, there is more information for product managers and their leaders. This is because, when moving to empowered product teams, the product manager role and the product management leadership role are usually furthest from where they need to be.

Who Is Speaking?

Unless otherwise noted, the author's voice is either Marty Cagan or Chris Jones. Both of us are partners at the Silicon Valley Product Group.

We don't call out which person wrote each chapter because we both agree with everything written here, and both of us were involved in the many iterations required to get from the first draft of each chapter to the resulting book.

Further, the lessons shared in this book are drawn from the broader set of SVPG partners. Between all of us, we have well over 100 years of experience leading product organizations at many of the top tech companies.

We are intentionally writing in the first person because we want to come as close as possible to the experience of sitting down with you, the reader, for a series of one-on-one coaching sessions, where our only goal is to help you become an exceptionally strong product leader.

How This Book Is Organized

So that you know the range of topics that are coming, here's an overview of the book:

- In Part II, we focus on the most important responsibility of strong product leaders, which is *coaching* and development of the people on the product teams.
- In Part III, we discuss *staffing* these product teams—how to identify, recruit, and onboard these people and ensure they are effective.
- In Part IV, we discuss the *product vision and principles*, which define the future we are trying to create.
- In Part V, we look at how we structure the product teams into a *team topology* that best meets the company's needs.
- In Part VI, we discuss the *product strategy*, which is how we decide which are the most important problems for these product teams to solve.
- In Part VII, we convert our product strategy into action through *team objectives* (problems to solve) for each product team.
- In Part VIII, we provide a detailed *case study* that shows how each of these concepts plays out in practice in a complicated, real-world situation.
- In Part IX, we discuss how to establish the necessary *collaboration* between the product organization and the rest of the business.
- In Part X, we tie everything together and give you a plan for *transforming your organization* to work the way the best teams and companies do.

While the type of change that is necessary is by no means easy, it is absolutely possible. This book is specifically designed to give you the knowledge and the skills you'll need to succeed.

II

Coaching

Coaching is no longer a specialty; you cannot be a good manager without being a good coach.

—*Bill Campbell*

Bill made this statement years ago, but one of the major learnings of our industry post-pandemic, is that coaching is more essential than ever. If you hope to innovate at scale, it is simply not optional. Problems escalate faster, relationships are damaged much more easily, and collaboration is harder.

Which is why you'll notice that the longest part of this book is on coaching. That is no accident.

In the technology industry, we focus so much on the core skills and competencies used by product managers, designers, and engineers, but so little on the skills and competencies of managers and leaders. Yet it is these managers and leaders who are responsible for molding people into effective teams.

The logic is simple: Your company depends on successful products. And successful products come from strong product teams.

Coaching is what turns ordinary people into extraordinary product teams.

If a product team is not effective, we need to look hard at the people on that team and see where we can help them improve as individuals, and especially as a team.

The chapters in this part highlight the most important areas of coaching and development for members of product teams. Unless you've been personally coached by an experienced manager, many of the topics may be new to you. Certainly, if you can speak from experience on these topics, so much the better, but if not, it is still valuable to be able to discuss the topic openly. You can learn and improve together.

More than anything, good coaching is an ongoing dialog, with the goal of helping the employee to reach her potential.

7

The Coaching Mindset

Coaching might be even more essential than mentoring to our careers and our teams. Whereas mentors dole out words of wisdom, coaches roll up their sleeves and get their hands dirty. They don't just believe in our potential; they get in the arena to help us realize our potential. They hold up a mirror so we can see our blind spots and they hold us accountable for working through our sore spots. They take responsibility for making us better without taking credit for our accomplishments.

—Bill Campbell

In this chapter, I'd like to focus not on the people you are trying to coach, but rather, on the necessary mindset of *you* as coach.

The wrong mindset may lead you to apply these tools in ways that actually undermine their intent.

For example, you may be committed to having regular one-on-one meetings with each of your team members, but if these meetings consist primarily of you allocating and prioritizing tasks, they are not helpful—and likely even harmful—as a coaching tool.

A coaching mindset provides a foundation of intent. It is the framing that directs your application of coaching techniques, and your guiding principle for taking action and making decisions around developing a team.

If you are an experienced coach or manager, you may have already developed your own set of principles. If not, or if you are new to management, or if you are responsible for developing a new manager, this chapter attempts to describe the most important guidelines for coaching and management.

Developing People Is Job #1

It's amazing and distressing how few managers actually subscribe to this principle—that developing people is job #1. Most say the right things about the importance of the team, but their actions tell a very different story. They see their accountability for aggregate product outcomes as their most important job and treat their teams as a means to an end.

If you are a manager, you should be spending most of your time and energy on coaching your team. This means expending real effort on things such as assessing your team, creating coaching plans, and actively helping them improve and develop.

You should measure your own job performance on the successes of your team members, even more than the success of your products.

Empowering People Produces the Best Results

Many new managers see their job as driving their team's task list.

This may result in a few short-term tactical successes, but your product will never reach its full potential if the team is only asked to execute *your* ideas and actions. More important, you will find it very hard to retain strong people when they have so little sense of ownership over their work.

Empowering means creating an environment where your people can own outcomes and not just tasks. This doesn't mean *less* management—it means *better* management.

You must step back to create this space, while stepping in to remove impediments, clarify context, and provide guidance.

Remember that we need teams of *missionaries*, not teams of *mercenaries*.

Beware Your Own Insecurities

Insecure managers have a particularly hard time empowering people.

The insecure manager is so worried about being recognized for their contribution, they can see their team's success as a threat to that recognition, rather than the confirmation of the contribution that it truly is. They may deal with this by closely controlling how the team works, or by controlling the team's visibility to leadership. Truly bad managers may actively undermine their own team.

Be aware of your insecurities and understand how your behavior can interfere with empowering your team.

I want to be clear that this is not about being arrogant. If anything, arrogance itself is frequently a manifestation of insecurity. Most good managers have a healthy level of humility and are always exploring and working to improve their own performance and growth. They can have these feelings without micromanaging or undermining their team.

You might be wondering what you can do if you, as a leader in the organization, don't personally have the necessary experience to coach and develop others. If this is the case, at least you are aware of this major gap in your qualifications for the job, but it will be essential for you to immediately find some product leader coaching for yourself. Find someone that has been there and done that at a strong product company and engage them to coach you—and help you in coaching your people.

Cultivate Diverse Points of View

An insecure manager may suppress opinions that are different from her own. This obviously impedes the development of the team, but it also stifles her effectiveness as a leader. Good leaders know that they will get the best results when they are able to consider diverse points of view. They also know that they don't have a monopoly on good ideas and that the best ones may come from others.

Nurturing a team that allows for diverse points of view begins with the hiring process where you consider your team as a portfolio of strengths and backgrounds.

It continues with creating a space where alternative points of view can flourish. In some cases, this means empowering a product person to approach her work in a way that is different from yours. In others, it means collecting a diverse range of opinions so that you can make the best decision.

Note that I'm not suggesting you encourage consensus of opinion within your team. Rather, as a manager, you are helping your team learn how to make good decisions collaboratively—leveraging the skills and expertise of each person.

Seek Out Teaching Moments

Many, if not most, people are not aware of their own potential. As a coach, you are in a unique position to help them see it.

Reaching potential requires working through adversity. As a coach, you are always looking for opportunities that encourage your people to stretch beyond their comfort zone. Use judgment to right-size the opportunity for the person and development area. You shouldn't ask someone to try something that you know they aren't ready for, but you need to find things that create some discomfort. It's through pushing through the discomfort that people overcome their fears and realize what they're truly capable of.

Reaching potential doesn't just mean addressing gaps in competence. It also means recognizing and developing inherent strengths. This is particularly important for more seasoned product people who already have a good grasp of the job.

Continually Earn the Trust of Your Team

None of your coaching efforts will be effective without trust.

This is not something you can demand or expect to happen on its own. It comes from continually demonstrating through your actions your genuine commitment to the success and development of each member of your team.

Of course, it's important that you support your team both privately and publicly. Even more important is being honest with them in both praise and criticism. Don't hold back if someone is doing particularly well. Similarly, don't sugarcoat areas that need improvement. Always remember to praise publicly but criticize privately.

I have found that you can help establish personal rapport and trust by sharing some of your own personal challenges. Trust also comes from expressing a genuine interest in the person as a *person*, and not just a member of the team.

Of course, you must use judgment here and not pry or insert yourself where you're not wanted. That said, I've always found that trust grows whenever a working relationship is humanized.

Have the Courage to Correct Mistakes

Sometimes, despite your best efforts, you can't find a path for a team member to become successful. When you reach this point, it's important that you act decisively.

For many managers, this is the hardest principle to follow. Coaching is about development, so you are necessarily looking at people's problems as opportunities to develop. More than this, telling someone they are not working out is one of the most painful conversations you can have. It can feel easier to just avoid it altogether and soldier through.

This hurts you, your team, and the person herself. First, you are likely spending much more time on this person than you should, at the expense of others. You're also signaling to the rest of the team that you're willing to tolerate mediocrity while at the same time asking them to work hard—a reliable path to undermining trust and killing motivation. Finally, the person with the performance issue is not getting the opportunity to move to another situation where she may have a better shot at success.

Note that I'm not suggesting you be cavalier about firing people or moving people into different jobs. You should always treat these decisions very seriously. I am saying that when you know, don't wait. You're not doing anyone any favors.

I (Chris) was fortunate in my early career to work for a company that was deeply committed to the values of coaching. The leaders didn't just "talk the talk" about team development, they took real action every day that communicated their commitment to these ideals, baking them firmly into the culture of the company. This meant that, as I grew into progressively larger management and leadership responsibilities, I had a solid framing for approaching my job, and I did my part to pass the ideas along—both in words and actions.

Unfortunately, most companies today are not so committed to coaching and development of their people, and you may have to be the one who models this approach. This starts with having a clear understanding of, and commitment to, a strong coaching mindset.

Alternatives to Manager as Coach

In the majority of tech companies, the organizational structure is very typical. It's a functional organizational model, which means that product managers work for a manager or director of product management; the designers work for a manager or director of design; and the engineers work for a manager or director of engineering.

In this organizational model, the manager is expected to serve as the coach of her reports.

However, there are a few alternative organizational structures out there, and in these alternative structures the manager might not have the necessary experience in the role to be able to provide effective coaching.

An example of this might be that we have a person in a product team leadership role—similar to the general manager of a small business unit—and that person might come from any number of backgrounds. Let's say for the purposes of this discussion that she comes from business development.

Now let's say the members of the cross-functional product team all report to her. But she has never been a product manager, or a designer, or an engineer. How can she coach her reports?

While it is our first choice to have the manager be the coach, when this is not possible, we can still provide effective coaching. The key is that someone in the organization needs to be tasked with providing the necessary coaching.

So, for example, there may be a design manager from another part of the organization that is asked to provide the necessary coaching to the designer. Similar for the product manager, and for the engineers.

The key is to ensure that, one way or another, coaching is considered a top priority, and that every person on a product team knows who is specifically assigned to help her develop and reach her full potential.

8

The Assessment

In this chapter, I will describe a coaching tool for helping managers of product people raise the level of performance of the people that report to them.

I want every product leader to feel considerable urgency and importance around this need.

Empowered product teams depend on competent product people, and if you don't develop your people and provide growth opportunities, there are usually other companies that will. I have always been a big believer in the old adage that "people join a company but leave their manager."

This chapter explores the technique that I use and advocate for assessing a *product manager*. It is easily adjusted for product designers or tech leads.

It is the foundation for then coaching the person to success (the *coaching plan*, which we'll discuss next).

This assessment is structured in the form of a gap analysis. The purpose is to assess the product person's current level of competence along each of several necessary dimensions, and then compare that with the level of competence that's expected for this particular role.

This format acknowledges that not all skills are equally important, not all gaps are equally significant, and expectations change with the level of responsibility. This tool is intended to help focus the attention where it is most needed.

People, Process, and Product

As readers of *INSPIRED* know, the taxonomy I like to use when talking about product is the three pillars: people, process, and product.

For purposes of the assessment tool, I like to cover *product* first because product knowledge is the foundation for everything else. Without competence in product knowledge, the rest doesn't really matter.

Product Knowledge

- User and customer knowledge—Is the product manager an acknowledged expert on her target users/customers?
- Data knowledge—Is the product manager skilled with the various data tools and considered by her product team and her stakeholders as an acknowledged expert in how the product is actually used by users?
- Industry and domain knowledge—Is the product manager knowledgeable about the industry and domain? Does she understand the competitive landscape and the relevant industry trends?
- Business and company knowledge—Does the product manager understand the various dimensions of your company's business, including marketing, sales, finance (both revenue and costs), services, legal, compliance, privacy, and so on? And do the stakeholders believe that the product manager understands their concerns and constraints?

- Product operational knowledge—Is the product manager considered an acknowledged expert on how her product actually works? Would she be able to effectively demo to a prospective customer, train a new customer on how to successfully use it, and handle live customer support inquiries?

Product knowledge really is table stakes. A new product manager typically requires two to three months to ramp up to speed on product knowledge, assuming she dives in aggressively and spends several hours per day learning.

Process Skills and Techniques

- Product discovery techniques—Does the product manager have a strong understanding of the product risks and how to address each of them? Does she understand how to tackle risks up front, before engineers are asked to build? Does she know how to solve problems collaboratively? Does she focus on outcome? Does she understand and utilize both qualitative and quantitative techniques?
- Product optimization techniques—Once a product or new capability is live and in production, does the product manager know how to utilize optimization techniques to rapidly improve and refine her product?
- Product delivery techniques—While the product manager's primary responsibility is discovery, she still has an important supporting role to play in delivery. Does she understand her responsibilities to the engineers and to product marketing?
- Product development process—Does the product manager have a solid understanding of the broader product-development process including discovery and delivery, as well as the product manager's administrative responsibilities as the team's product owner?

New product managers are expected to know the basic techniques, but strong product managers are always developing their skills and learning new and more-advanced techniques. Much like a good surgeon is constantly following the latest learnings on surgical skills and techniques, a strong product manager always has more to learn in terms of skills and techniques.

People Skills and Responsibilities

- Team collaboration skills—How effectively does the product manager work with her engineers and product designer? Is it a collaborative relationship? Is there mutual respect? Is the product manager involving the engineers and designer early enough and providing them direct access to customers? Is the product manager fully leveraging her team's skills and minds?

- Stakeholder collaboration skills—How good is the product manager at collaborating with her stakeholders across the company? Do they feel like they have a true partner in product that is genuinely committed to their business success? Has she established mutual respect and mutual trust with each stakeholder, including the senior leadership of the company?

- Evangelism skills—Is the product manager able to effectively share the product's vision and product strategy, and motivate and inspire her product team as well as the various stakeholders and others in the company who must contribute to the product in one way or another?

- Leadership skills—While the product manager does not actually manage anyone, she does need to influence and inspire people, so leadership skills are important. Is she an effective communicator and motivator? Do her team and stakeholders look to her for leadership, especially in stressful situations?

People skills are similar to product knowledge in that if you don't have a solid foundation, it is very hard to do the PM job at all. Yet, as with process skills, strong product managers constantly work to improve and develop their people skills.

Note that the taxonomy above is the set of skills and techniques that I generally use. However, in certain situations, I customize this list based on the company's culture or the company's industry.

As an example, in media companies there is a special and critically important relationship between product and editorial, and I like to call out this relationship explicitly and not leave it bundled in with other stakeholders. Which is to say, if you as the product leader think you should adjust this taxonomy of skills, then by all means you should do that.

The Gap Analysis

Now that we have the skills taxonomy, the core of this technique is a gap analysis. The way this works is that the manager should review the set of criteria above and assign two ratings to each skill.

Expectations vs. Current Capability

The first rating is an assessment of where the employee needs to be in this skill (i.e., *expectations* rating), and the second rating is an assessment of where the employee currently performs on this scale (i.e., her *capability*). I typically rate these on a 1–10 scale, with 10 being a skill that is absolutely essential to the job.

So, for example, if you consider a skill such as "Product Discovery Techniques" an 8 in expectations, yet you assess your product manager's current capability as a 4, then there is a significant gap for a critical skill, and you'll need to get to work coaching the product manager on her knowledge or skills in this key area.

Note: Normally, the difference between a product manager and senior product manager, for example, is captured in the expectations of where the level of skills should be (the expectations rating). As just one example, I usually rate stakeholder collaboration skills a 7 in expectations for a standard product manager-level person, yet I consider this skill a 9 for a senior product manager.

Note: The level of *expectations* is always set by the manager, if not the organization as a whole. Most of our effort is in determining the *capability rating*. Normally, the assessment of the product manager's capability level is done by the manager. However, there is no reason why the product manager can't also do a self-assessment, and in fact I encourage that. But be aware that it is not at all uncommon for the self-assessment to expose some significant differences with how the product manager assesses her own capabilities. A manager that only relies on the self-assessment because she is uncomfortable confronting these differences in perception is, in my view, abdicating her responsibility as a manager.

The Coaching Plan

Now that we've done a skills assessment and subsequent gap analysis, we are looking for the areas with the biggest gaps. That's the purpose of this assessment.

For the coaching plan, I like to limit the initial focus to the top-three areas. After progressing on these, the product person can move on to the next most important areas.

As the manager, you can now provide this product person with coaching, training, reading, or exercises intended to develop her skills in each area.

In the next chapter, I will share what I typically recommend in a coaching plan for developing each skill in the taxonomy described above. But many of you already know how to coach a product manager in a specific skill, so all you really need is the assessment and gap analysis described here.

Also, once an employee has successfully closed the gaps, it is the ideal time to show her how the expectation ratings move for the next-level position, and she can set about developing and demonstrating the skills necessary for a promotion.

Be sure to sit down with each of your product people no less than once a week to discuss progress on the coaching plan.

Assessments vs. Performance Reviews

Finally, you might be wondering how this sort of skills assessment and coaching plan relates to performance reviews. We will discuss performance reviews in more detail in the next part of the book on Staffing.

In general, I find the way most companies implement performance reviews to be of little use in terms of developing people. Sadly, they are more about HR compliance and salary administration.

You may have to comply with your HR department's requirements in terms of annual reviews, but just realize that these are in *no way* an adequate substitute for active, ongoing, engaged coaching and development of each team member's skills.

One thing to be careful of is that your ongoing efforts to coach your employees to be ready for promotion are not the same as being able to grant that promotion. Many companies have policies regarding when promotions can be granted, so you don't want to set expectations with your employee that you can't deliver on. The way I phrase this with the employee is that I will make every effort to prepare the employee for promotion, and then I will advocate for that promotion, but I can't always guarantee if and when that promotion will happen.

The good news is if you actively manage the skills assessment and the coaching plan as I describe here, then the annual review fire drill will be much easier.

The Coaching Plan

In the previous chapter, I defined a tool to assess the current skill level of a product person in order to identify skill gaps.

In this sequel chapter, I would like to share how I coach product people on each of these specific gaps.

In truth, the full version of this coaching plan is really this entire book, but I am hopeful that I can provide enough examples and suggestions in this chapter to help most managers give useful guidance and coaching.

Note that I am using the same people, process, and product taxonomy of skills that I spelled out in the previous chapter, so if you are unsure what any of these topics are about, please refer back to that chapter. And also, as with the assessment chapter, I am using the example of the *product manager* here, although much of what is written here will also be helpful for product designers and tech leads.

Product Knowledge

To set your expectations, product knowledge is where a new product manager spends most of her time in the onboarding process. It usually requires two to three months of time to ramp up, assuming she is provided the necessary coaching and she aggressively focuses on this for several hours per day.

But to be clear, a product manager that does not have this level of knowledge has no business serving as product manager for her team. And the responsibility for ensuring this level of competence is squarely on her manager.

User and Customer Knowledge

There really is no substitute for getting out of the office and visiting users and customers. That said, there is much to be gained by first taking advantage of the knowledge of your colleagues.

As you go about this learning, remember that each person you speak with brings their own perspective, and you're looking to understand that perspective and learn as many perspectives as possible.

If your company has a user research team, that's my favorite place to start, and it is a valuable relationship for the product manager to establish. User researchers are there to educate you—they know if you don't truly grok the issues, then you won't fix them.

Next, if you have a customer success or customer service team, that is a terrific resource. You want to learn who their favorite customers are, and their least favorite, and why. You will also want to spend quality time with this team to understand more about how customers perceive your product. But for now, you want to learn what they can teach you about your users and customers.

Product marketing is another valuable perspective on users and customers, and another important relationship for the product manager to establish. Product marketing will also have good insight into the broader sales and marketing organizations and the people you should talk with who will have useful perspectives.

In many companies, the founders or CEO have had more customer exposure than anyone, and they are another great resource.

Ask the founders which customers they consider the most helpful for you to truly get to know and understand. You're not only looking for happy customers, just as you're not only looking for unhappy customers. You're after as many perspectives as you can get.

At this point, you're ready to go out there and meet real users and customers.

To set your expectations, when I (Marty) first took responsibility for a new B2B product, my manager wanted me to visit 30 customers (and further, he insisted that half be from outside the United States) before making any meaningful decisions. I don't think that the number 30 is special, but I can tell you it's not just 2 or 3. I typically recommend at least 15 customer visits as part of new PM onboarding.

When I returned from that trip, I had progressed from knowing virtually nothing to knowing as much as anyone in our organization. I leveraged what I learned—and the people I met and the relationships I established—for years.

Once you're actually sitting down with users and customers, a whole other topic is the techniques we use to learn, but that's the discovery techniques topic. With every interaction, at the very least, you're looking to learn: Are the customers who you think they are? Do they have the problems you think they have? How do they solve that problem today? What would it take to get them to switch?

Note that there are some obvious differences between customers that are businesses versus consumers, but the principle is the same in either case.

Note also that if you are joining an existing team with a skilled product designer and tech lead, then you absolutely want to learn as much from them as possible. And if you're joining a new team, then you want to include these two key people with you during your learning.

Data Knowledge

There are generally three types of data and tools that the new product manager will need to achieve competence on. There is typically one tool that contains the data about how users interact with your product—user analytics. Another tool typically contains data about the sales cycle for your product—sales analytics. And a third typically shows how this data is changing over time—data warehouse analytics.

Realize that achieving competence for each of these tools means two things. First, that you know how to answer questions with that tool—you're learning how to operate it. Second, you need to understand what the data in the tool is trying to tell you.

Your go-to resource for coming up to speed on the data (tool operation and data semantics) is usually one of the company's data analysts. This is another key relationship for the new product manager to establish. But to be clear, unless you have a full-time data analyst or data scientists embedded in your product team, they are not there for you to delegate work to them. They are there to educate and empower you to answer questions with data.

This topic is intertwined with the topic below about understanding your business. Every product has a set of key performance indicators (KPIs) that collectively describe your product's health, and while data tools will help you understand where you're at, your business will dictate which KPIs are most important for you to focus on.

Industry and Domain Knowledge

In general, the product manager is expected to become competent on the domain. This is, of course, different for every product. Media products are different from developer products, which are different from advertising-technology products. Fortunately, in most cases, there is a wealth of easily accessible knowledge just an internet search away.

However, with certain products in very specialized domains (such as taxation, surgical devices, and regulatory compliance), there will usually be an in-house resource available to all of the product managers who is an acknowledged expert on the domain. These people are sometimes called *subject matter experts* or *domain experts*, and this person is another important relationship for the product manager to establish. The PM is not expected to become as knowledgeable about the domain as these experts, but she does need to learn enough to engage and collaborate effectively.

In terms of broader tech industry knowledge, there are many industry analysts that provide analysis and insights.[1]

---

[1] I've long been a fan of www.stratechery.com and recommend this resource to all product managers and product leaders.

Key to industry knowledge is identifying which industry trends are expected to be relevant to the PM's product. The first step is to identify the trends, and then there may be some education needed to understand what the trend or technology enables and what the capabilities and limitations may be.

Also included in industry knowledge is competitive analysis. Product marketing is a good resource to get started here, but the product manager will need to have a deeper understanding of the offerings, vision, and strategy of each of the major players in the landscape.

When I coach product managers on competitive analysis, I like to ask the PM to evaluate the top three to five players in the space and to write up a narrative comparing and contrasting the strengths and weaknesses of each player—highlighting opportunities.

Business and Company Knowledge

For most new product managers, understanding how their own business works requires the greatest amount of work. But this is often the essential difference between competent product managers and those who are not.

One way I like to get started on this is to have the new product manager fill out a business model canvas (any of the variants are fine for this) for their product. It is a quick and easy way to help the product manager quickly realize the areas she may not yet understand.

Sales and Marketing—Go-To-Market

The go-to-market strategy is an essential aspect of every product. This describes how our product makes it into the hands of users and customers. It applies to every type of product—from consumer to enterprise—but it's usually most involved when selling to businesses. Your product may get sold through a direct sales force, or an indirect channel such as resellers, or directly to your customers.

The sales process starts with marketing, which itself has many different strategies and techniques. Ultimately, there's always some type of funnel starting with people becoming aware you exist, and hopefully proceeding through to the point where they are an active user and customer.

The new PM needs to understand the entire funnel from awareness to trials to onboarding. It's especially important to understand the capabilities and limitations of the sales channel. Your colleagues in product marketing are normally your go-to resource for learning about your go-to-market strategy.

Finance—Revenue and Costs

It's also essential for the new product manager to gain a deep understanding of the financials regarding her product. This involves both the revenue side as well as costs.

I've long advocated making a friend in finance for this purpose. There is a set of financial-related KPIs for every product, and you need to first understand what those KPIs are (e.g., lifetime value of the customer), and what they mean (e.g., how is lifetime value calculated?). Finally, you need to learn where your product stands (e.g., is your lifetime value sufficient compared to your cost to acquire new customers?).[2]

Legal—Privacy and Compliance

Another critical aspect to your business is legal. These issues mainly relate to privacy, security, compliance, and increasingly, ethics. As with finance, establishing a relationship with someone in legal who can help the new PM understand legal constraints is important—not just in coming up to speed, but also when considering new product ideas.

Business Development—Partnerships

Most products today involve some number of partnerships. It may be a technology partner that's used to deliver your products or services, or it may be a sales or marketing partnership to acquire new customers.

---

[2] I often recommend the book http://leananalyticsbook.com/ to help the new PM learn more about which analytics are important to their type of product.

Whatever the purpose, these agreements usually come along with constraints about what we can do, so it's important for the product manager to understand these contracts and constraints.

Additional Areas

The areas above are common to almost every product, but it's also true that many products have one or more additional areas, depending on the nature of the company.

If the company is structured around multiple business units, then these business unit leaders (e.g., GMs) are critical stakeholders.

Similarly, media companies have editorial/content; e-commerce companies have merchandising; hardware or device companies have manufacturing; and companies that sell globally have international, as just a few examples.

Product Operational Knowledge

This topic really should be obvious, but I can't tell you how often I meet a product manager who doesn't actually know their own product beyond how to give a basic demo. But hopefully it's clear that a product manager must be an expert user of her own product in order to be trusted.

For consumer products, it is not usually very hard to become expert on the product's use, but for products for businesses this can be much more difficult—especially when the product manager lacks the domain knowledge.

Coming up to speed on this typically involves reading whatever user or customer documentation exists, taking whatever training classes may exist, spending time with customer service staff, and if at all possible, using your own products on a daily basis (this is known as *dogfooding*).

As a clear litmus test, if an important industry analyst were to offer to come visit your company to discuss your product, either the product manager would give the briefing herself, or at a minimum she would be spending significant time preparing the person who would be giving the briefing (usually the product marketing manager).

Process Skills and Techniques

There are countless process-related skills and techniques, and new techniques are always emerging. The main objective for those of us responsible for coaching product managers is to make sure the PM is knowledgeable about techniques that are suitable for the tasks at hand.

Product Discovery Techniques

At a minimum, the new PM must understand the four different types of product risk (value, usability, feasibility, and viability), the different forms of prototypes to tackle these risks, and how to test those risks qualitatively and quantitatively.

There are many online resources and training classes, and the book *INSPIRED* goes into detail on these product discovery techniques.

When I coach PMs, I typically have them read the book, and then I like to make sure they understand the techniques by describing different scenarios and asking the PM how she would address them. I'm looking to make sure she is thinking about risk appropriately, and that she understands the strengths and limitations of each technique.

Product Optimization Techniques

For products that are in production and have significant traffic, there are important techniques referred to as *product optimization techniques* that the product manager needs to understand and know how to effectively utilize.

This typically involves learning one of the commercial tools and then running an ongoing series of A/B tests—mostly to optimize the product funnel, but it could be used for other purposes as well.

Product Delivery Techniques

In general, product delivery techniques are the focus of the engineers on the team. However, it's important for the product manager to understand the delivery techniques that are being used (e.g., continuous delivery), and in some cases—such as release planning—to take a more active role.

For example, for certain large product changes, a parallel deployment may be called for. The product manager needs to know what these techniques entail—especially the additional engineering costs—to make suitable decisions regarding delivery.

Product Development Process

The decision as to which development process the engineers use to develop and deliver software is up to the engineers and engineering leadership. However, the PM does play a role in the process, and she must understand what her responsibilities are.

Most teams use some form of Scrum, Kanban, and/or XP (Extreme Programming) techniques. Often, teams use a blend of these.

I usually recommend that the new PM take a CSPO (*Certified Scrum Product Owner*) course if she has not already done so. That simple and short course will explain her responsibilities as the product owner for the team.

Most companies have also standardized on a tool for managing the product backlog, so the new PM will need to learn this tool as well.

Note that I have long complained that too many product managers have only had CSPO training, and then they don't understand why they fail as a product manager. Hopefully it is very clear at this point that the CSPO responsibilities, while important, are just a very small subset of the responsibilities of the product manager of an empowered product team.

People Skills and Responsibilities

Thus far, we have mainly discussed areas (product knowledge and process skills and techniques) where just about anyone who's willing to put in the time and effort can succeed. And I would argue that, without that foundation, nothing else matters.

That said, the difference between being just a competent PM, and a truly effective PM, is often their skills with people.

There has long been a debate in the product world about whether these people skills can be effectively taught or coached. In my experience, for most but not all people, you can significantly improve and develop their people skills. But they do have to want to improve.

If the person is not good at these skills, and shows no sincere interest in improving, then that's when the manager needs to help the person find a more suitable job.

Team Collaboration Skills

Modern product management is all about true collaboration between product, design, and engineering. This begins with ensuring the product manager is knowledgeable about the real contribution of product design and engineering.

The PM does not need to be personally skilled in either design or engineering (most aren't, although many PMs believe they're great designers), but they do need to understand and appreciate their contributions to the point where they understand that what design and engineering bring to the table is just as essential as what the PM brings.

Next, the PM needs to establish the relationships necessary for true collaboration, which is built on trust and respect.

In my own coaching of PMs, once they've learned the basics we've discussed above, most of the coaching I do has to do with collaboration.

When I sit down with a product team to talk about a problem they're trying to solve, I rarely spend time with just the PM. Almost always, it is with the PM, the product designer, and the tech lead.

Again, that's just the nature of product today. But during these sessions, I am witness to countless interactions. And afterward, if I've observed something, I often pull the PM aside and try to point out how her interactions during that meeting either helped or hurt her efforts to build trust.

A one-hour meeting discussing a problem or objective will usually yield many good examples I can use as a coaching opportunity for the PM. How engaged is the rest of the team? Are they acting like they are empowered to solve the problem, or are they acting like order takers? Is the designer and engineer bringing potential solutions to the table or just pointing out issues with whatever the PM proposed? Are they spending too much time talking (e.g., planning) and not enough time trying (e.g., prototyping)? How are they resolving differences of opinion?

Stakeholder Collaboration Skills

Many of the points regarding team collaboration skills also apply to stakeholder collaboration skills, but it's actually easier to build trust and relationships with your own teammates (e.g., your designer and engineers) because you interact with them every day—focused on solving the same problem.

There are additional dynamics at play with stakeholders. First of all, while most PMs are individual contributors, most stakeholders are company executives. They are often very knowledgeable about their part of the business, and they are often used to giving orders.

The key to successful working relationships with stakeholders is establishing mutual trust.

For the PM, that starts with putting in the time and effort to understand what each of the stakeholder's constraints are. We discussed this under *Business and Company Knowledge* above.

But once the PM has put in that effort, she needs to personally convince each stakeholder that she understands what they are concerned with, and that she'll make every effort to come up with solutions that work for them.

And in any case, whenever she identifies something that might be of concern, she will preview those solutions with that stakeholder before the team builds anything.

Building this trust takes time, as there are less interactions, and each interaction carries more weight.

Again, in my work with product teams, I often observe PM/stakeholder interactions and there are many good coaching opportunities. I try to reinforce the actions that helped build trust and point out alternative approaches for actions that diminish trust.

Evangelism Skills

Especially in medium to large-sized companies, so much of product involves persuasion. This involves convincing your team and your stakeholders that you understand what you need to do, and you've got a solid plan to deliver.

My favorite technique for developing a strong and compelling argument is the written narrative, which is discussed in Chapter 11, The Written Narrative.

I also encourage PMs to take a presentation skills class where your presentations are video recorded and you are provided professional critiques. I've personally taken this class twice over my career and consider it invaluable.

Leadership Skills

Finally, so much of strong product management is actually about leadership.

Leadership skills are especially important for the PM because the product team and the stakeholders don't report to you, so you must depend on persuasion and leadership.

Which is to say, for the PM, leadership must be earned. It does not come with the title.

But this is also why so many strong product managers go on to become successful heads of product and CEOs.

So, how do you develop these leadership skills? The prerequisites are the items above. If you've done your homework and demonstrated your knowledge and skills, and you have earned the trust and respect of your team and your stakeholders, you are well on your way.

Beyond this, I encourage all product managers to become life-long students of leadership. Most of us know people we consider terrible leaders. Some of us are lucky enough to know people we consider exceptionally strong leaders. Discussing the defining characteristics of each makes for excellent coaching discussions.

Coaching Tech Leads

I absolutely love coaching tech leads. More often than not, these are the people behind the world's most impressive innovations.

A tech lead is essentially a senior-level engineer who has taken on the additional responsibility of participating in the ongoing product discovery work. The tech lead is the key partner to the product manager and product designer.

They are asked to care not just about building and delivering reliable products, but also to care about *what* gets built.

Tech leads bring deep knowledge of the enabling technologies, and when that knowledge is combined with a direct understanding of the customer's pain and problems, magic can result.

If you've spent any real time with engineers, you know that not all engineers are interested in anything beyond coding, and that's fine. We don't need every engineer to become a tech lead.

I will say that many of my favorite product companies try to screen for this when they interview engineers—they want engineers who care just as much about *what* they build as *how* they build it. But even these companies make exceptions. It's only a problem if you don't have at least one such person on a product team, especially if you hope to be an empowered product team.

A surprising percentage of the tech leads I've coached have told me that, ultimately, they would like to one day start a company of their own. I strongly encourage this and point out to them the many successful CEOs in tech who started as engineers. When this is their goal, I often encourage the tech lead to consider the product management role for a year or two. Even if they go back to engineering, this experience is invaluable and positions them much better for a startup co-founder role.

No matter what their career goals, the real potential of a tech lead comes from combining their understanding of technology with an appreciation for the issues customers struggle with.

I always encourage tech leads to visit as many customers as they can. But I also try to make a point—after visiting an interesting customer myself—to stop by and chat with the tech leads about what I saw and learned, and what they might think about that.

The bottom line is I have found that every single minute you invest in coaching a tech lead on either customers or business context will be among the best possible uses of your time.

Coaching Product Designers

Product designers have an especially difficult job. There are many design-related skills, and while the product designer does not need to be an expert in all of them, she does need to have a considerably broad range of knowledge and skills:

- Service design
- Interaction design
- Visual design
- Industrial design (for physical devices)
- Prototyping
- User research

Most successful product designers are very strong in at least prototyping and interaction design, and they know enough about service design, visual design, and user research to leverage the relevant techniques and people where necessary.

As a design manager, your product designers often come from different backgrounds, so much of your coaching time will be spent helping the product designer address the gaps.

The other important responsibility to keep in mind for design managers is that they are the frontline for ensuring a holistic view of design. This means that, while there may be many product teams—each with a skilled product designer—the design managers need to ensure that the experience works as a whole, across teams.

Design managers ensure a holistic view by reviewing designs at the weekly one-on-ones and by holding design sessions with the broader group of product designers, especially to discuss difficult design problems.

One challenge when moving to empowered product teams is that most product managers and engineers coming from feature teams have never worked with a professional product designer, so they don't even know yet what they are missing. As a result, design leaders often need to raise the bar and educate product managers and tech leads about what strong product design is and how product designers contribute to successful products.

LOVED

SVPG Partner Martina Lauchengco is publishing another book in the SVPG series, LOVED, *discussing the critically important topic of product marketing. As many know, product marketing is adjacent to product management, but what most don't know is that product marketing has changed dramatically and has become more critical than ever. What follows is an excerpt from her upcoming book:*

Let me be blunt.

Most product marketers aren't great at what they do. They are good at getting a lot of stuff done, but it's not always clear it's making a difference. The talent of the people in the role is also uneven, contributing to its reputation—somewhere between ho-hum and occasionally great.

Product marketing is not: managing a checklist of everything needed to get done for launch, project management, or just being a facilitator between product and sales. The classic understanding of product marketing is first you build a product, then bring it to market. The failure in this approach is companies just explain what their product does and why it's different and assume people care.

Great product marketing requires understanding the market first. It pressure-tests assumptions based on what the market tells you so you can adapt, position, and market into customers' true reality. It makes clear why your product matters and should be loved using customers' language, experience, and needs.

The real indicators of successful product marketing are market adoption and momentum. But most people don't know what to look for or when is the right time to start doing product marketing.

Take Company Z. They're real, but I'm not using names so you can think about all the startup stories you know just like theirs. They were a brainchild of a team of PhDs who collectively had

(continued)

(continued)

decades of expertise among them. After being selected as a finalist at a well-respected technology competition, they decided it was time to bring their idea to market.

Their technology was impressive. A prominent analyst wrote about its effectiveness, noting they had never seen anything like it. They showed a demonstration to a top C-suite executive at a Fortune 100 company, and he said "This is amazing." They got venture capital funding based on all this and were off to the races.

Or so they thought.

As is common at these early stages, one of their technical founders was the front man for everything: sales, product, marketing, people. But after six months of meetings with dozens of executives, they didn't have any buyers. So they stopped trying to pitch their product at every meeting and instead started asking every executive they met what their most pressing priorities were.

It turned out the problem their technology solved didn't make the top-five, and in some cases, even the top-10 priorities. You might wonder why Company Z didn't start there, but remember, they got some early data points that made them think they were on a path to create something of value.

The team realized with a little bit of rework, they could pivot their product into a more nimble solution to a problem that was much higher on these executives' priority list.

Their new product intersected with a well-established, decades-old category with very mature incumbents. They created an easy-to-use setup that could much more quickly give teams answers. Armed with this new approach, Company Z created a demo that showed what their product could do. They figured since the product did so many things, they would show a demo. But this made them skip the crucial step of figuring out how to talk about what they did succinctly and why people should care.

Without the right mental anchors, prospective customers still struggled to understand why they should pay attention. Company Z asked, "Should we talk about the regulatory environment which makes what we do more relevant? Do we point out what's broken with the older, incumbent software even if we only do a piece of what they do much better?"

Company Z tried to answer these questions by hiring salespeople to sell their product. Since they now had salespeople, they hired someone who could "generate demand" because the salespeople needed more names to call. This was a mistake. Without repeatable messages, the sales team couldn't effectively communicate the product's value. Despite a growing go-to-market team, very little changed. Less than a handful of customers signed on. At this point, nearly two years had gone by.

Enter "Josie," their newly hired director of product marketing. She positioned them into the existing category by carving out a niche they named that made their focus clear. Within three months, here's what happened:

- A white paper articulated what wasn't working with the existing category and introduced the need for the niche they had named. A prominent analyst company was so intrigued by this white paper, the analysts in the category all asked to be on a call to learn more.

- She created all new product collateral, bringing more consistency between the sales deck and the website so they all messaged the same thing everywhere customers looked.

- She partnered equally well with product and sales, working in lockstep adapting materials as frequently as was necessary. She was immediately seen as incredibly valuable by everyone in the small company.

- They declared and agreed on a marketing strategy. This meant even if Josie wasn't the one doing all the work, the rest of the team knew the 'why' behind everything they were doing in marketing.

Company Z eventually got some great customers and market momentum ... but way more slowly and painfully than was necessary. Had they brought in product marketing earlier, they could have

(continued)

(continued)

discovered—and solved—go-to-market gaps sooner. Instead they spent a lot of time, money, and resources on things that weren't working.

Marketing can be very esoteric to people who spend their lives building products. Product marketing creates the bones around which the body of marketing and sales work takes shape. This is why if you're a technology company and only have one person doing marketing, it should be a product marketer. It's simply how you'll get to your goals faster. But *who* does the work and *how well* they do it is more important than the work itself. If you're investing in creating great products, it's imperative to also invest in great product marketing.

CHAPTER
10

The One-on-One

I'd be surprised if you haven't at least heard about the coaching technique known as the "one-on-one" (aka "1:1") and you've probably experienced some version of it yourself. But judging from my discussions with countless product managers and product leaders, you may have never experienced this technique done well. Yet this is the foundation of coaching.

As I (Marty) wrote this, I was trying to remember where I learned these points and the key people who influenced my views. After so many years, it's tough to say, but it represents the best of more than a dozen managers that helped me during my own development—either directly as my manager, or indirectly as a colleague that I learned from. Ben Horowitz is an example of the latter, as he made a big impression on me regarding this technique.

This chapter is written for the manager of individual contributor product people. The people responsible for hiring and developing product managers, product designers, and engineers.

Keys to Effective One-on-Ones

The Purpose

The primary purpose of the 1:1 is to help the product person develop and improve. Yes, you will get an update. Yes, you will be able to discuss work. But this is first and foremost about helping the person to first reach competence, and then to reach her potential. If you lose sight of the purpose, the real value of this session is quickly lost.

The Relationship

This is a relationship that depends on trust. The product person must understand and believe that you as the manager are genuinely and sincerely committed to helping her reach her full potential. That is your primary job as the manager. If the product person is effective and gets promoted, you did your job. Likewise, if the product person is not able to reach competence, you have failed. And the product person needs to understand that for you both to succeed, you'll need to be able to trust and depend on each other, and most important, to be able to speak honestly and frankly.

The Onboarding

With most new product people, there is a necessary and critical onboarding period where the person acquires the skills and knowledge required to get up to speed (reach competence).

Every person is different, bringing different experience and knowledge to the job. In Chapter 8, The Assessment, I discussed a tool I use to quickly assess a new product person to determine which areas to focus on. But, until the product person is strong enough to be considered competent, it is your responsibility to ensure the person is not doing harm to her team and is making reasonable decisions.

Normally, this period of close oversight lasts on the order of two to three months, and it is a much more intense coaching relationship than the ongoing coaching that happens once the product person is deemed capable.

The Frequency

This is one of those areas where there's a range of opinions out there, but I feel strongly that the 1:1 should be no less than 30 minutes, once per week, and that this session is sacred and not to be another one of those "You okay with skipping this week?" kind of meetings. You may need to occasionally reschedule, but don't cancel. Please consider the message this sends.

For new PMs in the onboarding period who are not yet competent, it may be two to three times per week, or even daily.

Once the trust between manager and employee is established, 1:1 coaching works well with video calls. The key is to establish an environment conducive to developing the relationship and having honest, constructive discussions.

Sharing Context

If you are to empower your product person to solve problems in the best way her team sees fit, as a leader and manager you must provide her with the strategic context.

This means making sure she understands the company's mission and objectives for the year, the product vision, the product strategy for the broader product, and the team objectives for her particular product team.

The bulk of this discussion happens during onboarding, but each quarter you'll need to discuss the upcoming quarter's specific team objectives. Sometimes, those are fairly complicated discussions.

Homework

There's simply no substitute for the product person doing her homework. It is the foundation for competence, and it's the main activity during the onboarding period. You can guide the product person to the right resources, and answer questions about the material, but it's on the person to spend the time and effort to do her homework and gain this knowledge.

What does homework really mean? For a product manager, it means learning the product inside and out. Learning about the users and customers. Learning the data. Learning the capabilities of the enabling technologies. Learning the industry. Learning the various dimensions of the business, especially financial, sales, go-to-market, service, and legal.

Thinking and Acting Like a Product Person

Beyond doing homework, coaching is mainly about helping the product person learn to think and act like a *strong* product person.

What does it mean to think like a product person? It means focusing on outcome. Considering all of the risks—value, usability, feasibility, and business viability. Thinking holistically about all dimensions of the business and the product. Anticipating ethical considerations or impacts. Creative problem solving. Persistence in the face of obstacles. Leveraging engineering and the art of the possible. Leveraging design and the power of user experience. Leveraging data to learn and to make a compelling argument.

What does it mean to act like a product person? Listening. Collaborating. Shared learning. Evangelizing. Inspiring. Giving credit and accepting blame. Taking responsibility. Knowing what you can't know and admitting what you don't know. Demonstrating humility. Building relationships across the company. Getting to know customers on a personal level. Leading.

Holistic View

Also known as "connecting the dots." You can't expect every product person to be able to stay on top of what all the other product teams are doing. One of the important benefits of the 1:1 is that you are aware of what activities and issues are occurring in the various teams, and you may very likely be the first one to see an issue brewing or duplication occurring. It is your job to point out these potential areas of conflict or impact and encourage the product person to collaborate with the relevant colleagues to resolve, and if necessary, for you to make a decision to remove the conflict.

Providing Feedback

Also known as "tough love" or "radical candor," honest, constructive feedback is the main source of value you provide as manager. Feedback should be frequent and as timely as possible (at the first opportunity to discuss privately). Remember to praise publicly but criticize privately.

Many managers mistakenly believe that the only time they should collect and deliver feedback is at an annual performance review, but in truth there are opportunities every day to collect feedback, both directly and indirectly. There is usually no shortage of meetings with the opportunity to observe the product person's interactions directly.

Moreover, as the manager, you should always be seeking constructive feedback on the person—asking the other members of the product team about their interactions and asking senior executives, stakeholders, and business owners about their impressions and suggestions.

After a while, giving constructive feedback moves from awkward to second nature. But until then, force yourself to come up with some helpful constructive feedback *every week*.

Continuous Improvement

Hopefully, it's clear to you that product jobs are very hard. It is a journey not a destination. You can have 25 years of hands-on product experience and you will still be learning and improving. Every product effort has its own risk profile. New enabling technologies constantly emerge. Today's services are tomorrow's platforms. Markets develop. Customer behaviors change. Companies grow. Expectations rise.

The best product leaders measure their success in how many people they've helped earn promotions, or have moved on to serve on increasingly impactful products, or to become leaders of the company, or even to start their own companies.

Anti-Patterns

I could end the chapter here, but I have seen so many managers who think they understand and do all this, yet fail to develop their people. In my experience, here are the most common reasons for that:

Manager Just Doesn't Care

By far the biggest reason I see that people don't develop and reach competence is because so many managers either don't like developing people, or they don't view it as their primary responsibility. So, it's pushed off as a secondary task, if that, and the message to the employee is clear: You're on your own.

Manager Reverts to Micromanaging

It's actually easier for you to simply issue specific instructions and micromanage—to just give the person a list of tasks to do, and if any real decisions need to be made, to bring them to your attention and you'll make the call. It's beyond the scope of this chapter for me to list all the reasons why this results in disappointment, but in any case, it won't develop the people we need, and it's not a scalable solution.

Manager Spends Time Talking and Not Listening

While there's nothing wrong with preparing for the session by jotting down some notes of items to discuss, it's critical to keep in mind that this session is primarily for the product person and not for you. It's all too easy for you to talk for 30 minutes straight, and then you're out of time. Moreover, it's important to recognize that people learn in different ways, and you'll learn that by listening not talking.

Manager Doesn't Provide Difficult Feedback

It's true that learning to give frank, honest, constructive feedback is hard for many people. But if it's not done, the person doesn't grow and improve at the pace we need. This usually becomes very clear at the next performance review, where the employee is surprised by the negative feedback.

Just to be perfectly clear here, at the performance review, *nothing should be a surprise*—everything should have already been discussed in depth, likely for months. The performance review is discussed in an upcoming chapter, as it's the source of lots of grief and angst for all parties. But, for now, the important thing to keep in mind is that it is never the key tool for developing people—the weekly 1:1 is.

Manager Is Insecure and/or Incompetent

This technique is predicated on you as manager being competent yourself (otherwise, how would you be able to coach others to competence?), you are secure enough in your own contributions and value that you are happy to shine a light on others when they do well, and you don't feel threatened by their success. But sadly, we all know of managers where, for whatever reason, this is not the case. The person responsible for ensuring strong people managers is the head of product in a larger company and the CEO in a startup.

As we discussed earlier, if you don't personally have the necessary experience to coach and develop others, it will be essential for you to immediately find some product leader coaching for yourself. Please don't take this responsibility lightly.

Manager Doesn't Cut Losses

I hesitate to include this one because to me this is the last resort. But sometimes we have a manager that has been working sincerely, tirelessly, and capably for several months to coach the person, yet she can't seem to get the product person to competence.

It's important to realize that not everyone is cut out to be a product person. When I find this to be the case, it's usually because the person was simply reassigned from a different role at the company—maybe because this person used to be a customer and knew the product or the domain, or knew the CEO, or whatever—but she simply doesn't have the core foundation to succeed in the role.

Moreover, hopefully it's clear that the product roles of product manager, product designer, and tech lead are not "junior" roles.

Someone who needs to be told what to do every day is not cut out for the product person role. And this is also not scalable. You need people that can be developed into capable and competent product people—that can be given an objective and then counted on to find a way to get it done.

My view in this case is that you are responsible for getting the new product person to competence. If you're not able to accomplish this in a reasonable period of time (usually three to six months), then you need to take responsibility to help that person find a more suitable job where they *can* be successful.

Summary

If you're a product leader and you have not been focused on coaching, I hope you come to realize that this is what your job is really all about, and you'll use this as a framework for giving coaching an honest effort.

For product leaders, the product team *is* our product, and this is how we develop a great product.

If you're a product person, and you have not been receiving this type of ongoing, intense coaching, then I hope you'll bring this up with your manager and see if she would be willing to invest the time to help you reach your potential.

If you're entering a career as a product person and evaluating companies and positions, then the single most important thing you can do in the interview process (once you've convinced the company that you have the potential and are worth investing in) is to try to determine if the hiring manager is willing and able to provide you this level of coaching.

CHAPTER
11

The Written Narrative

In the previous chapter, I talked about the importance of the 1:1 coaching session between a manager and her employee. That technique is about providing an ongoing mechanism for helping the product person reach her potential.

In this chapter, I'd like to discuss my single favorite coaching tool for helping product people become exceptional: the written narrative.

But first I need to admit that of all the various coaching techniques I have and use, this one gets more resistance than any other technique. In fact, with more than a few people I have had to essentially force them to use it.

It's not so much that people doubt the effectiveness, it's just that it can often be painful. And I've found that the people who need this technique the most are often the ones who resist it the most.

Product people, especially product managers, have to make arguments all the time. Not so much for minor things, but once things become costly and risky—good examples include large features and projects, and especially significant new efforts—there will naturally be many people who will question and challenge the work. Usually, it's the executives from across the company, but it often starts with convincing your own team.

The technique I'm talking about is writing out a narrative explaining your argument and recommendation.

To be clear, I am not talking about a spec of any sort. A spec is not intended to be a persuasive piece—it's just a document describing the details of what you want built.

Rather, I'm talking about a roughly six-page document that describes in narrative form the problem you're trying to solve, why this will be valuable for your customers and for your business, and your strategy for solving the problem. If this narrative is done well, the reader will be both inspired and convinced.

One company that has made this written narrative the core of how they operate and innovate is Amazon. They have embraced this technique more than any other company I know, and I don't think it's a coincidence that they are one of the world's most consistently innovative companies.

Here's the thing. It's not hard for you as product person, in some kickoff meeting, to show a PowerPoint presentation, wave your hands, toss out some data points, and sound enthusiastic and confident. And then watch as the meeting degenerates into design by committee, or just as bad, everyone gets frustrated and just turns to the highest-paid person in the room for direction.

When this happens, it's clear to me that the product person did not do the necessary homework. The person doesn't truly know the topic. The argument is weak. The person has not sufficiently considered and addressed the various perspectives and constraints.

What the written narrative does is make this obvious.

We've all seen product people stand up and bluster, and pretend to know what they're talking about. But with the written narrative, there is no faking it.

As former Netscape engineer and longtime Amazonian Brad Porter puts it, "Speed and scale are weapons, and Amazon has already told everyone its secret … if only they have the discipline to implement it."[1]

---

[1] Brad Porter at https://www.linkedin.com/pulse/beauty-amazons-6-pager-brad-porter/.

Despite Amazon's 25-year record of consistent technology-powered innovation, most product people I know would do nearly anything to avoid having to write out this type of narrative analysis and recommendation. Yet, it's one of the most valuable things they could do to both move faster *and* make better decisions.

This is why I emphasized the one-on-one technique first. Very few product people have the discipline to do this written narrative and confront the glaring holes in their arguments alone. However, the manager can coach the product person through this process.

The structure is to write the narrative itself in a few pages and then follow this with an FAQ. The idea is to anticipate the different concerns and objections that might come from key executives and stakeholders, take the time to consider and write up clear answers to these objections, and then review these responses with the people that have these concerns. When the executive later reads this narrative, she can see that you anticipated the issues and considered the response, and she knows that you have done your homework.

You might use this narrative to kick off decision meetings like Amazon does. Or, even if you decide you want to do that PowerPoint presentation, I promise you that if you first do a good job on the written narrative, then your presentation will be very easy to create and will flow directly from the narrative. The presentation will be much better for it, and your visible preparation on the material will leave your audience justifiably impressed.

I had to be convinced of this myself early in my career, and I'm just grateful that I had a manager who pushed me well outside my comfort zone to do this. I've been a convert ever since.

I still use this technique frequently. When I am working on a new keynote presentation, I force myself to write out a full narrative first, iterate until it's logical and compelling, test the narrative with people I respect and know will tell me the truth, and only then do I create the actual presentation.

If you've never tried this technique before, on your next significant effort, I hope you'll give the written narrative technique a try. Expect it to be uncomfortable. Be sure to incorporate the perspectives of the members of your team and key stakeholders. Spend the time to make it clear, concise, and compelling. I'm confident you'll be a much stronger product person as a result.

12

Strategic Context

To continue with our series on coaching, in this chapter I cover a different aspect of coaching: ensuring the product team has the necessary understanding of the broader business context in which they are operating.

I refer to this information as the *strategic context*, and as you'll see, this includes several important and major topics, all of which I will discuss in depth elsewhere. But, together, these topics form the understanding necessary for teams to make good choices.

If product teams are to be empowered to make decisions, they need to have the context necessary to make these decisions. This strategic context typically comes from the product leaders of the company but needs to be deeply understood by the product team, especially the product manager.

Normally, the strategic context is part of the onboarding for any new product person joining the organization.

Note: In this chapter, I use the term "company" to represent the larger business entity, but in very large companies, there may be several business units or divisions where this strategic context may be different

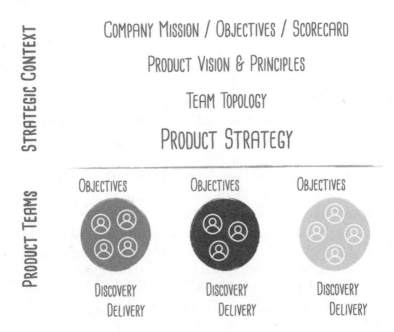

for each. As an example, Google's YouTube business unit has a very different strategic context than their AdWords business unit.

Generally, there are six types of strategic context.

Company Mission

Simply put, this is the *purpose* of the company. It is meant to communicate to everyone involved *why* we are here. This is usually a simple statement, and it's intended to be durable—usually lasting for a decade or more, if not the life of the company.

If any employee does not know the mission of the company, then that would be an obvious sign that something is seriously wrong in the culture and/or the leaders.

But, while it's common that everyone knows the purpose of the company, many people may not know how they personally are able to contribute to that mission.

Company Scorecard

Every product and every company have some key performance indicators (KPIs) that help provide an understanding of the overall picture and health of the business, referred to here as the *company scorecard*, but sometimes called the *company dashboard* or the *health metrics*. In some cases, these may be fairly straightforward, and other times they can be quite complex.

As an example, in a two-sided marketplace, there are usually some critical KPIs that tell us whether our marketplace is healthy, meaning that both sides receive value, and the marketplace is in balance.

As an obvious example of an unhealthy marketplace, suppose you had a jobs marketplace with employers posting jobs and job seekers searching for work. But imagine you had thousands of people coming every day to search for jobs, but almost no jobs were available. The job seekers would be frustrated and likely would leave to go elsewhere.

And, of course, in a two-sided job marketplace, we would have at least two funnels—one to bring in job seekers and one to bring in employers—and we'd closely watch the key metrics for each funnel.

The company scorecard captures these business dynamics. It does not focus on every metric, but it focuses on the most important and informative metrics. It is how the leaders of the company judge the overall health and performance of the company.

Company Objectives

Once we understand the company scorecard, we can discuss the specific objectives the company is focused on for this year.

These objectives are selected by the senior leadership team, usually with the participation of the board, as the most important areas of focus. They might be related to growth, expansion, profitability, or customer satisfaction. And for each of these areas of improvement, there are typically specific business targets the company hopes to achieve (the key results).

Hopefully everyone understands that these company objectives must be *outcomes* (business results), and not *output* (such as delivering on specific projects).

The key results are nearly always KPIs that are on the company scorecard. If they're not yet on the scorecard, then they would typically be added.

In this way, the company can track progress on the objectives and at the same time ensure there are no negative unintended consequences to the health of the business.

Product Vision and Principles

Ultimately, the way we deliver on a company's mission is to develop products and services for our customers. The product vision is how we hope to do that.

Normally, the product vision is somewhere between 3 years and 10 years out and describes the future we are trying to create, and why that future will improve the lives of our customers.

The mission may provide the purpose, but it's the vision that begins to make this tangible. It's worth noting that the product vision is also our single best tool for recruiting strong product people.

This is what these people will be working on every day for several years, so it needs to be inspiring. Yet it's also important that the product vision not be too specific because we know we can't yet know the details.

We will be going deep into product vision in Part IV, but this is what empowered product teams will be figuring out: how to make this vision a reality.

The product principles complement the product vision by stating the values and beliefs that are intended to inform the many product decisions that will need to be made.

So many decisions revolve around trade-offs, and the product principles help to illuminate the values we prioritize when we make these trade-offs.

The product teams need to understand these principles and the reasoning behind each one.

Team Topology

The team topology (covered in Part V) describes what each product team is responsible for. It's important for each of the product teams to understand where they sit in the larger picture, and how their team relates to the other teams.

Product Strategy

The product strategy is where things start to become more specific.

We have a set of company objectives that we are all here to help achieve this year, we have a product vision that we need multiple years to achieve, and we also generally have multiple product teams—each with different skills and areas of responsibility.

The product strategy connects these concepts. It is the product strategy that will drive each specific product team's objectives.

How product strategy does this is a major topic of this book (Part VI).

Once each product team has their objectives, they can get to work tackling the problems they need to solve.

The strategic context provided by the company mission, company scorecard, company objectives, product vision and principles, and product strategy is meant to apply to *all* product teams in the company.

Each product person, and especially each product manager, needs to understand this strategic context, and she needs to demonstrate in her statements, actions, and decisions how her team is contributing to the common goals.

CHAPTER

13

Sense of Ownership

The previous several chapters have provided a set of coaching tools and techniques designed to help you get your product managers to competence.

However, in this and the next several chapters I would like to explore coaching behavior and mindset.

A strong product person is not just competent in terms of knowledge and skills, she also has an effective product mindset and consistently demonstrates good judgment in her decisions and her interactions.

In this chapter, I discuss an important mindset for a product person, which is the difference between thinking like an owner versus thinking like an employee.

I want to acknowledge up front that this chapter touches on a sensitive subject for many people, because the topic can quickly get personal—especially for those who have grown up in countries with different attitudes toward work and its role in one's life.

But this is why I need to remind everyone that I'm all about sharing the practices and techniques from what I consider the best tech product teams in the world.

I'm not trying to share what *most* companies do (you learned in the preface what I think of how most companies work). I'm trying to share *best* practice. I'm also trying to judge *best* by objective results and not by subjective standards.

With those caveats, many product leaders have heard the phrase "we want to hire product people that think like an owner and not like an employee," but what does that really mean? And just how important is this really?

In Jeff Bezos's original 1997 letter to shareholders, he stated:

We will continue to focus on hiring and retaining versatile and talented employees, and continue to weight their compensation to stock options rather than cash. We know our success will be largely affected by our ability to attract and retain a motivated employee base, each of whom must think like, and therefore must actually be, an owner.[1]

He reiterated this critical point yet again in his most recent shareholder letter.[2]

Jeff Bezos is trying to tell us all something extremely important, and that one of the most important things a good manager can help develop in her product people is an owner's mindset.

So, let's consider this "think like an owner" concept.

This is similar to the missionaries not mercenaries concept, but in truth, it's not too hard to get excited about something meaningful—like a compelling product vision—yet not think like an owner.

So, while I think most owners act like missionaries, not all missionaries act like owners.

You know now that creating empowered product teams involves giving product teams *ownership* of a problem to solve, so that they have the ability to solve problems the best way they see fit.

---

[1] http://media.corporate-ir.net/media_files/irol/97/97664/reports/Shareholderletter97.pdf.
[2] https://blog.aboutamazon.com/company-news/2019-letter-to-shareholders.

The empowered product team model depends on product people who think like an owner, but it doesn't usually happen just because the product person is working on an empowered team.

I (Marty) still remember how this concept was first explained to me when I was considering expanding from a tech lead to take on the product manager responsibilities, along with the rationale I was given to my inevitable questions of "Why?"

I was told that, as product manager, to think like an owner meant I needed to feel a real obligation and responsibility to my customers, my product team, my stakeholders, and my company's investors.

Why? Because the product team takes their lead from the product manager, and the team and the company executives will judge me by my words and actions.

I was told that my product team was counting on me to provide them the strategic context necessary for the designers and engineers to come up with the best possible solutions.

Why? Because teams do much better work when given the context and a problem to solve, rather than describing to them the so-called requirements of a solution.

I was told that, in order to do this, I'd need to "do my homework"—customers, data, business, and industry (a phrase I've repeated literally thousands of times).

Why? Because the designer and engineers need someone on the team with this knowledge and context and this would be my direct contribution to solving the problems the team has been assigned.

I was told I had to commit to figuring out a way over whatever obstacles would arise, and to expect that many would indeed arise.

Why? Because technology products are never easy. I remember the actual phrase: "There will always be many good reasons not to ship, and it's your responsibility to figure out a way over, around, or through each obstacle."

I was told that my performance would be measured by results (a phrase popular again today, but that was literally the tagline for HP in the 1980s).

Why? Because we need to be careful never to confuse output with outcome. Our customers care about results, not effort or activity.

I was told that to succeed meant that I'd have to work hard to establish and maintain relationships with people from all across the company whom I'd need to depend on—and who would depend on me.

Why? Because in a company, especially a large company, there are many people there to ensure that the assets are protected—the sales force, the revenue, the customers, the reputation—and getting things done in a company means understanding and respecting these constraints by coming up with solutions that work for the business.

I was told that the leaders of the company would be continuously judging me to decide if they felt I had done my homework, if I was thinking and acting like an owner, and if the product team was in good hands.

Why? Because executives of companies with the empowered team model learn that the product manager is the canary in the coal mine.

I was also told I'd have to take responsibility when things didn't go well, yet give credit to the team when things did go well.

Why? Because that's what good leaders (and good owners) do.

I was told that it was my responsibility to motivate and evangelize my team.

Why? Because we want a team of missionaries not mercenaries.

Finally, as most product people have heard many times before, I was told that I'd have the responsibility to ensure success but not the authority to direct people.

Why? Because innovation depends on true collaboration with design and engineering, which is a peer relationship and not a reporting relationship (there are other reasons as well, but that's for another chapter).

Now, I'm not claiming this is verbatim, but I do think it is a fairly reasonable recollection. And in terms of thinking like an owner versus an employee, it's very much the same message I try to pass along to product people I coach.

If I had to boil it all down, I'd say that thinking like an owner versus thinking like an employee is primarily about taking responsibility for the outcome rather than just the activities.

Interestingly, I often try to convince exceptional designers and engineers to consider moving to product management. And while I've had some good success with that, the single most common objection I hear is an unwillingness to take responsibility for outcomes (and the pressure that implies).

I understand and respect their choice on that, but I do agree with Jeff Bezos that this is an important mindset, especially for product managers.

The Power of Equity

When discussing thinking like an owner, it's important to acknowledge that this entire discussion is directly related to the stock compensation topic.

Stock compensation is designed so that you are *literally* an owner, not just thinking like one.

I believe it's not at all an accident that the top tech product companies in the world use equity, either in the form of stock options or grants, to spread ownership.

It's no secret that this is a big contributor to the innovation engine that powers Silicon Valley. Many people think the equity topic only applies to startups, but it applies to companies of all sizes, including some of the largest and best product companies such as Amazon, Google, Netflix, and Apple.

However, less well known is that, in many parts of the world, the local tax laws make awarding equity difficult. I can't help but notice that I hear a lot more of the dreaded refrain "that's not my job" at these companies.

There are other ways besides equity to have your key employees share in the actual rewards of product success. The most obvious is a company profit-sharing plan.

But I do think if CEOs want their key people to think and behave like owners, they should compensate them like owners. Nobody expects that an individual contributor engineer will get the same level of equity as a senior vice president, but it doesn't take much to be material if the company does in fact do well.

Similarly, it's important to evergreen the equity. What this means is that you don't want people to leave once they have fully vested, so you continue to award additional stock to your strong performers every year.

An evergreen strategy with equity means that your best people will always feel like they would be leaving behind substantial compensation if they exit before they are fully vested.

(continued)

(continued)

To me, this is an example of a clear win-win. It's very good for the employee and very good for the company (and hence the company's shareholders).

However you accomplish it, as a manager, I have always found it immensely powerful to be able to point out that the employee is a part owner in the company just as I am. We need to be thinking about creating value for the company over the long term and not just focusing on our specific daily issues.

14

Managing Time

I've long said that, to get the critically important work of a product manager done, you need on the order of four solid hours a day.

If the person is a product designer or tech lead and is not able to spend most of the day doing actually creative work, then you have a larger problem. So, this is mainly an issue with product managers.

To be clear, I'm not talking about email or Slack or meetings. I mean quality time working on coming up with solutions to the difficult problems we're trying to solve—otherwise known as *product discovery*.

Still, that doesn't sound too bad, until you look at your calendar and realize that your only chance for those four hours is from 6:00 p.m. until 10:00 p.m. at night (and hence the infamous 60-hour workweek of so many product managers).

You've all seen the frenzied product manager that spends her time rushing from meeting to meeting, constantly complaining about not having any time to do "real product work."

So, it's no surprise that one of the most common, and most important, coaching topics is helping a new product manager learn to manage her time.

When I start coaching on this problem, I begin by looking at how she is spending her time, and in the vast majority of cases, I find that the product manager is spending most of her day doing *project* management work, rather than *product* management work.

Now, they don't necessarily call it that, but I try to point out to them that's actually what's going on.

So, why is this?

Partly because the work *does* need to be done—especially when it's urgent—and the product manager may not believe there is anyone else available or able to do it.

Partly because a lot of product managers have never been trained or coached on what product management is really all about, and they think that's what the job is.

And partly because I think many people are actually more comfortable with the project management tasks, as they are tangible and much more straightforward, and it can feel productive to check lots of things off the list every day.

Now, it's important to acknowledge that there's always some amount of project management in every leadership role—engineering managers, marketing managers, CEOs—they all need to "herd the cats" at times. But that is not what defines those jobs, and that's not what defines the product manager job either.

Your highest-order contribution and responsibility as product manager is to make sure that what the engineers are asked to build will be worth building. That it will deliver the necessary results.

This means working with designers and engineers to come up with solutions that are valuable, usable, feasible, and viable. That is product discovery, and that is what takes on the order of four solid hours a day.

I encourage product managers to block off this time for the week, and protect that time, and then you still have half a day for other stuff.

Of course, the project management work doesn't go away. Which is why my favorite answer to this problem is for the product manager to team up with a delivery manager who can take on the project management, so the product manager can actually focus on her job.

But I also know that many product managers, even many good ones, aren't comfortable giving up that responsibility.

One way or another, if you can't manage to clear four hours a day during your workday, then I only know of two possibilities: either you extend your workday, or you fail to deliver results and so you fail at your job.

Some argue that it's about working smarter, not harder. I would absolutely agree with this. In fact, if you read my book *INSPIRED*, you know it's all about sharing techniques that allow us to work smarter and faster rather than harder. I think I've published as much as anyone on how product managers can work smarter not harder. That said, even with a skilled product manager, using the very latest techniques, you still need those four hours.

Others will argue that work will always expand to fill whatever time is available, and while this is true in general, and certainly applies to the product management role as well, this is not the key issue here. If the product manager thinks like an owner and not like an employee, and commits to an outcome rather than just a list of activities, then this is really about delivering results.

Please note that I am only talking about product managers of empowered product teams here. There are several all-too-common situations where "product management" is a very different job:

- If you are the product *owner* of a delivery team, then I'm not referring to you.
- If you are the product manager of a *feature* team, then your job would be more accurately characterized as a project/delivery manager, and I'm not referring to you either.
- In a true startup, where the number of people at the company is small, typically the project management burden is also small, and is not a problem to be covered by the product manager.

Taking control of your time may be harder than ever, but it is also more important than ever. If your job is to manage or coach product managers, then this very likely will be one of your most important coaching topics.

CHAPTER

15

Thinking

So far in this series of chapters on coaching, I've described a tool for assessing a current or prospective product person, and then provided detailed examples of how to craft a coaching plan to help the product person first reach competence, and then to reach her full potential.

We've discussed the importance of the 1:1, and we've discussed the written narrative technique.

We've also looked at coaching not just her skills and techniques, but also her mindset, including thinking like an owner rather than an employee.

In this chapter, I'd like to tackle another aspect of mindset, which admittedly can be a little awkward to discuss, but is perhaps the single most important behavior of a capable product person—the ability to *think*.

Often people refer to this with the shorthand phrase of looking for people that are "smart." I'm guilty of this too. But the term "smart" is ambiguous and can obscure the real issue.

When people say "smart," they are mostly referring to intelligence.

First, we need to acknowledge that intelligence and thinking are not at all the same thing.

I do believe that in order to think effectively (and more generally, to succeed in a career in product), you do need to have a certain level of intelligence.

However, I meet countless people who are clearly intelligent, yet waste their minds because they don't know how to (or are unwilling to) actually solve hard problems by thinking.

Second, we also need to recognize that *acquiring* knowledge and *applying* knowledge are two different things.

Google, and the wealth of resources it provides easy access to, has made knowledge easier to acquire than ever before, but has done little to help people actually learn to think and apply that knowledge.

Why is thinking so important? Because at its core, product teams are all about problem solving.

One of the reasons that I love working with designers and engineers so much (and also why I love to recruit designers and engineers into product management) is that thinking is at the very core of what they do.

Yes, they are makers. But in order to design an experience or craft an implementation, they must essentially be problem solvers. Designers and engineers are skilled at solving for problems with many constraints. It is literally what they do every day.

Similarly, product managers must be problem solvers as well. They are not trying to design the user experience, or architect a scalable, fault-tolerant solution. Rather, they solve for constraints aligned around their customer's business, their industry, and especially their own business. Is this something their customers need? Is it substantially better than the alternatives? Is it something the company can effectively market and sell, that they can afford to build, that they can service and support, and that complies with legal and regulatory constraints?

Moreover, one of the special challenges with technology-powered products and services is that we must solve simultaneously for all three types of constraints—product, design, and engineering. Hence the need for true collaboration (the subject of the next chapter).

Obviously, some degree of thinking and problem solving is required for any job. But for product managers, designers, and engineers, it is the core.

It's not hard to spot when a product person is weak when it comes to thinking. While I am a big believer in encouraging questions, this presumes the person has done their homework and put in the intellectual effort to actually consider the issue first. All too often, it is obvious they have not.

Good product companies try to determine how well the candidate can think and solve problems during the interview process. The issue is not whether the candidate actually knows the answer to a question. The issue is what does she do when she doesn't know the answer?

Which is why critical thinking and problem-solving skills are so important.

My favorite technique for developing good thinking skills is the written narrative that I described earlier. In that chapter, I warned you that for someone who is not used to actually thinking through hard problems, this technique can be truly painful. But those are the people that need this technique the most. And for some people, it is here that you'll realize they are not cut out to be a product person.

But as long as the person has the necessary intelligence, and is willing to put in the intellectual effort, I believe that the ability to learn to think and solve hard problems is absolutely something that can be developed. However, it will require active coaching and sincere effort by the manager and the product person.

CHAPTER

16

Team Collaboration

I n this chapter, I continue the series on coaching product people by talking about another critically important skill that is so often misunderstood or underappreciated, and that is team collaboration.

Collaboration is one of those words that is used so often in so many different ways that it has lost its meaning for many people. Of course, they think they're collaborative. Few people view themselves as anti-collaborative.

But in the context of an empowered, cross-functional product team, being collaborative has a very specific meaning, and it is most definitely not how many people, especially product managers, are inclined to work. So, this is often a critically important area for the manager to focus on during coaching.

It's also worth pointing out that when your product team has remote employees, this collaboration often suffers, so your coaching of collaboration needs to increase for your remote workers.

In *INSPIRED*, I talk about the three critical characteristics of strong product teams, no matter what processes they use: the first is tackling risks early; the second is solving problems collaboratively; and the third is being accountable to results.

Regarding the second critical characteristic—solving problems collaboratively—it is no longer the old, waterfall process of a product manager defining requirements, and handing them off to a designer to come up with a design that meets those requirements, and then handing that off to engineers to implement the design.

So, what do we really mean by collaboration?

Let's start by talking about what collaboration is not.

First, collaboration is not about *consensus*. While we like it when the product team agrees on the best course of action, we do not expect or insist on this. Rather, we depend on the expertise of each member of the product team. Generally speaking, if the tech lead feels a specific architecture is called for, we defer to the tech lead. If the designer feels a specific user experience is called for, we defer to the designer. Occasionally there will be conflicts and judgment calls, and normally we'll run a test to resolve them.

Second, collaboration is not about *artifacts*. Many product managers think their job is to produce some form of document capturing "requirements," or, at the least, they are there to write user stories. It is true that sometimes we need to create artifacts (especially when team members are remote), but that is certainly *not* how we collaborate. In fact, these artifacts more often get in the way of actual collaboration.

Why is that? Because once the product manager has declared something is a "requirement," it pretty much ends the conversation and moves the discussion into implementation. At this point, the designer feels like she's there to ensure that the design conforms to the company style guide, the engineers feel like they are there just to code, and we're back to Waterfall.

Third, collaboration is also not about *compromise*. If you end up with a mediocre user experience, slow performance and limited scalability, and dubious value for customers, as a team you lose.

We need to find a solution that *works*. By that we mean that it is *valuable* (valuable enough that target customers will actually buy it or choose to use it), it is *usable* (so users can actually experience that value), it is *feasible* (so we can actually deliver that value), and it is *viable* for our business (so the rest of our company can effectively market, sell, and support the solution).

In order to do this, we need to know what we can't know, admit what we don't know, and focus on discovering a solution that works.

And that requires true collaboration.

Remember that our job in product is to solve the problems we are asked to solve, in ways that our customers love, yet that work for our business. That's our job as an empowered, cross-functional product team, and each member of the team is there because they bring necessary skills.

This all starts with true and intense collaboration between product management, product design, and engineering.

My favorite way to actually do this is to sit around a prototype (usually created by the designer) so as a team you can consider and discuss the proposed solution on the table. The designer can consider different approaches to the experience, the engineers can consider implications of different approaches and the potential of different enabling technologies, and the product manager can consider the impacts and consequences of each potential direction (e.g., would there be privacy violations, or would this be something that would work with our sales channel?).

Note that while doing product discovery, certain tools and techniques serve both to facilitate collaboration as well as to provide an artifact as an output of that collaboration. Two very popular examples of that are prototypes and story maps.

The very act of creating and discussing prototypes and story maps facilitates true collaboration. And if you are diligent about keeping your prototype or story map up to date, then they can also serve as an artifact—capturing the learning and decisions from the discovery work.

The real benefit and purpose of the tools in this case are in fostering the collaboration. However, it is a nice side benefit to have an artifact at the end.

It's not really the prototype that's critical here, as much as the nature of the collaboration that it facilitates.

Notice that the product manager and engineers aren't trying to tell the designer how to do her job. And the product manager and designers are not there to tell the engineers how to do their jobs. And the designers and engineers aren't there to tell the product manager how to do her job.

Rather, in a healthy and competent team, each member of the team is counting on the others to have done their homework and bring the necessary skills to the table.

But please don't misunderstand this as designers are only responsible for usability and engineers are only responsible for feasibility, because this would miss the real point of collaboration.

Designers often have insights based on deep understanding of our users and their behaviors that lead us in a different direction in terms of the problem we're solving, or our approach to the problem. These insights will often have a big impact on value, and indirect impacts on things like performance.

Similarly, strong engineers have deep insights into the enabling technology that often leads us to entirely different solutions to the problems we were assigned—often much better than anything the product manager, the designer, or especially the customer could have imagined.

If I had to pick the one thing I love most about the feeling of true collaboration on an empowered product team, it is the form of magic that happens when you have people who are a) motivated and b) skilled in their respective discipline—product management, product design and engineering—and they sit around a prototype or watch a user interact with a prototype. The engineer points out new possibilities, the designer points out different potential experiences, and the product manager weighs in with the sales- or financial- or privacy-related implications, and after exploring a bunch of approaches, they find one that actually works. It's valuable, it's usable, it's feasible, and it's viable.

In my experience, there are two situations where this most often goes wrong.

The first is that the product manager has not done her homework and she doesn't know the various aspects and constraints of the business—sales, marketing, finance, legal, privacy, and so on—so the product team really doesn't have the information it needs to solve the problems it has been assigned (which usually means they're back to implementing features on a roadmap).

That's why we discussed early in this part on coaching that, as a manager, your first priority is to assess the product manager and create a plan to get her to competence.

The second situation is arrogance. If the product manager believes the solution she already has in mind is clearly the best, even if she is right, collaboration is stifled, and she probably now has a team of mercenaries rather than missionaries.

Another important form of collaboration, especially in companies with a direct sales force, is engaging with prospective customers to determine if your product can meet their needs.

It is natural for the prospect to try to dictate requirements for features, but your job is to work to understand their underlying issues and constraints, and then work collaboratively with your prospective customers to determine if there's a general solution that will meet their needs. This form of collaboration is at the heart of the customer discovery program technique.[1]

Collaboration means product managers, product designers, and engineers working together with customers and stakeholders and executives to come up with a solution that solves for all of our constraints and risks. This is what we mean by solutions that our customers love, yet work for our business.

Getting good at true collaboration is at the heart of how strong product teams work. It's a combination of skills and mindset, and it often takes active coaching by the manager to help new product people develop this capability.

---

[1]This technique is described in detail in *INSPIRED* and is one of the most powerful and effective discovery techniques.

17

Stakeholder Collaboration

People on feature teams dread the topic of stakeholders, especially product managers and product designers. They view these people as at worst dictatorial, or at best as obstacles to deal with.

This is yet another very clear example of the difference between feature teams and empowered product teams.

In companies with the feature team model, those features are usually coming from stakeholders, so the stakeholders view themselves as "the client," and they view the product teams as "the hired IT resource."

It's another way of saying that the purpose of a feature team is to "serve the business."

Yet, in an empowered product team, the purpose of the product team is "to serve the customers in ways customers love, yet work for the business."

So, in an empowered product team, while we still can't ignore the business, it is a very different relationship. Our job is to find a solution that works for customers *and* for the various parts of the business.

While it's true that the majority of the actual collaboration for a product team is happening between the product manager, designer, and engineers, a healthy relationship with stakeholders is based on true collaboration as well.

The product manager is not there to "gather requirements" from stakeholders, but the product manager is also not there to dictate solutions to stakeholders. Rather, the strong product manager understands that each stakeholder is responsible for some key aspect of the business, and they are a key partner in helping to come up with a solution that works.

A common and clear example of this is that often what we are trying to do has legal implications, maybe around privacy or regulatory compliance. The legal stakeholder is your partner in understanding these constraints and helping to evaluate the suitability of various approaches.

Again, a constructive, collaborative relationship with stakeholders is predicated on the product manager having done her homework so she can be that effective partner with the stakeholder, and not just some form of facilitator or project manager.

Everything I said above is doubly important when we're talking about collaborating with company executives. In general, the more senior in the organization, the more the executives care about everything—customers, brand, revenue, compliance—and the more important it is for the product manager to have done her homework.

Collaborating with stakeholders and executives involves listening carefully to try to understand the constraints, and thinking hard about solutions that would work for our customers and our business.

Good product work is never easy, but it is much more enjoyable when you have a strong, collaborative relationship with your key stakeholders.

This begins by the manager coaching her product people on the role of each stakeholder, and why they are there, what they are concerned about and why, and what they need to succeed at their jobs.

Building the Foundation for Trust

Modern product work is all about relationships. This is particularly true for product managers.

Even if you leave out external parties like vendors, analysts, press, and customers, the list of internal people a PM must work with is still very large. It ranges from product team collaborators (engineers, designers, data analysts, user researchers, other product managers, etc.) to all manner of executives and stakeholders (sales, marketing, legal, risk, founders, business leads, etc.).

In modern product organizations, a PM's effectiveness depends on her ability to effectively navigate a range of personalities. She needs to understand the multiple agendas of others while simultaneously advancing her own.

PMs sometimes need coaching to realize that trust is most easily built if you do it *before you need it*. This requires deliberate effort.

Try this exercise: Have the PM write down the list of people with whom she regularly collaborates. Add to the list any stakeholders whose input she regularly needs. Next, circle the three to five names that are most important to her having a successful outcome in her work. Finally, circle the names of the one or two people she most dreads having to deal with. Congratulations! You've identified the list of relationships in which this PM needs to invest.

So how does she do this?

Have her start by simply getting to know these people one on one. If she can meet face to face for a coffee or lunch, do that. If not, schedule a video call.

Encourage her to get to know their interests outside of work, and if it's comfortable, to share her own. This is a time to be genuine. It's about creating a foundation for trust.

Not everyone will be comfortable with this, so don't force it. But remind her that putting in a little effort can go a long way toward establishing trust.

For those people who are particularly important to her job, she may consider having a regular chat, perhaps every one to two weeks.

This shouldn't include a work agenda. Instead, she should use the time to build rapport and trust.

Of course, this is much harder when the people she works with are in different cities or countries. In those cases, she can invest in trust by having extra time on calls dedicated to nonwork topics.

With mutual trust, interactions go more smoothly. It's easier to disagree professionally without either party taking it personally. Everyone's job becomes more enjoyable when they're working with people they care about.

CHAPTER
18

Imposter Syndrome

I have a bit of a contrarian opinion on imposter syndrome.

First, I want to be clear that I'm not talking here about people who have a debilitating mental illness. I know people in this situation, and none would use the mild term "imposter syndrome" to describe the severe level of anxiety they deal with.

That said, let me be clear that I believe imposter syndrome, as most people use that term, is a very real thing. In fact, I think most mentally healthy people (at least those that aren't egomaniacs) doubt themselves and can feel insecure about asserting their opinions on others. I (Marty) like to emphasize to the people I coach that this is a normal and healthy fear, and I share that I absolutely still feel the same way.

Second, I think it's important to acknowledge that imposters are also a real thing. I find it very frustrating, especially in the product and design spaces, how many people on social media, authors of articles and books, and conference speakers are, at least in my personal opinion, advocating nonsense.

I think imposter syndrome is a very healthy and necessary emotion, and an important signal from our minds. But most people misunderstand that signal. They think it's just natural fear and insecurities, everyone has them, and they need to simply overcome their worries and push past them.

But I interpret this signal very differently. It is my mind warning me of the consequences if I don't do my homework and truly prepare. The fear of looking clueless is what keeps me up late preparing, studying, thinking, writing, rehearsing, and iterating.

Most important, the fear of looking clueless is also what pushes me to try out my article/talk/presentation beforehand on some people that I highly respect and I know will tell me honestly if I am not solid in my thinking or my delivery.

The reason I know that my worries are not unfounded is because, more than a few times, those people have indeed saved me from myself.

When I go to conferences, I too often hear speakers who, if they have imposter syndrome, clearly did not take the warning seriously.

Should they be praised for overcoming their stage fright fears and getting in front of a group?

To me that's like giving a child a trophy just for showing up to the game.

More generally, I see this as yet another example of where we need managers and leaders who care enough about their people that they are willing to devote the time and energy to coaching them.

Whenever I see some product person deliver an underwhelming presentation to an executive team or a conference, my frustration is centered not on the product person, but rather on that person's manager.

Why didn't she ensure the product person was prepared? Did she provide relevant, actionable, honest feedback? Did she insist on reviewing a draft or a rehearsal? If the topic was not in her area of expertise, did she ensure the product person had access to some people who could be counted on to provide useful and honest feedback? If the product person is especially nervous speaking in front of a group (many are), did the manager provide the product manager with several progressive opportunities to get used to public speaking? Or enroll the product person in presentation training?

Empowered product teams are predicated on trust—especially the product manager having earned the trust of the executives. When a product manager appears unprepared or naive in front of the executives, that trust is diminished, and it will take a long time to regain it.

Moreover, this is why I tell managers and leaders of product that they are only as strong as their weakest employee.

Whether you're a product person or a product leader, there's no reason to be an imposter. Listen to your mind warning you of the consequences of not preparing, seek out people you trust to give you honest and expert feedback, and iterate until they are satisfied that you are truly adding value.

19

Customer-Centricity

I n this chapter we'll discuss how to help develop the critical trait of customer-centricity.

If you ask a CEO or a product person if they care about their customers, you'll usually get some sort of indignant "Of course I do!" response, sometimes followed with a defensive "Are you suggesting I don't?"

Pretty much everyone talks about how much they care about their customers. But when you actually get inside the company and you see how they handle a situation such as an outage, or when a product change causes customer confusion or frustration, or the infrequency that they actually sit down with real users and customers, it's easy to see the difference between those who claim they care about their customers and those who demonstrate their care every day.

This trait is very much related to company culture and is, of course, heavily influenced by the words and actions of the company's leaders.

I'll say up front that if your leaders don't demonstrate this sincere care for your customers, then it will be very hard to develop this in your product people or anyone else. In each and every case I know of where the company truly cares about their customers, it's clear that it comes from the very top.

But assuming this is something that is central to your company's core values and not just lip service, then we need to talk about how we develop this trait in your product people.

Clearly some people are more naturally empathetic than others, but in my experience people often tend to assume the worst about people they don't know. The most common manifestation of this is the horde of product people who tend to think of their customers as not very bright.

The first thing I like to emphasize is to be very specific and protective over the term "customer."

It is an all-too-common problem where a product person thinks she has many different "customers." In addition to the actual paying customers, she views each stakeholder as a customer, and she views the customer service team as her customer, and she views the CEO as one of her customers too.

I see this as just a remnant of the old role of technology to "serve the business." But more important—and I personally feel very strongly about this—besides confusing the relationship with stakeholders, this seriously dilutes the role of the *true* customer.

So, I talk with the product person about the various constituencies involved with her product. Besides the users of our customer-facing products as our true customers, there may be internal users of our customer-enabling products, and there may be developers using platform services. All of these may be necessary to provide value and are therefore important, but none have the weight or importance of the true customers.

I see the same problem in consumer-internet companies where there is a tendency to view our advertising partners as customers, but again they are *not* the customer, and it's important to realize that. We work with our advertising partners to develop products for our true customers. If the true customer does not like the product, they won't engage, so we fail, and our advertising partners fail as well.

I prefer to keep the term "customer" almost sacred, and I believe this helps the product person understand the role the customer necessarily plays in our actions and decisions.

I am a big fan of using storytelling to drive home what caring for customers really means in practice. A few of my favorites are the early FedEx Wedding Dress story,[1] the REI Hiking Boot Replacement story (described in the movie *Wild*),[2] and many great stories from early Zappos, which you can read about in the book, *Delivering Happiness*.[3]

I also recommend a minimum of three, one-hour customer interactions each week, *ongoing*, and during the weekly 1:1, I love to ask about these customer interactions and see what the product person has learned. I also encourage the product person to share with me stories of what they experienced during these visits, and then to share these stories widely around the company. I explain that my purpose is to establish the reputation of this product person as someone who has a deep and personal knowledge of the company's users and customers.

The true test of customer-centricity is how the product person handles difficult or especially stressful decisions. When a customer is at a standstill (often referred to as a "showstopper") because of some problem with our product, how does the product person respond? Is it business as usual? Or is the product person ensuring a sense of urgency (not panic) and leading by example to come up with an effective solution?

One of the behaviors I love in companies that are truly customer-centric is that leaders will usually proactively reach out to the product team and offer to help in any way they can. This sends a very clear message to the team as to their importance without resorting to micromanaging them.

Be aware, however, that in companies that are truly customer-centric, if the product team is not prioritizing solving the customer problem as highly as the executives do, then the executives may lose confidence in the product team, and they will often step in. They might be very supportive of the concept of empowered teams, but if you make them choose between empowered teams and taking care of customers, you probably won't like what they decide.

Finally, while I need to make certain the product person genuinely likes and respects her customers, I don't want her to think her job is to

---

[1] https://www.informit.com/articles/article.aspx?p=28294&seqNum=4.
[2] https://time.com/3620359/the-true-story-behind-wild/.
[3] Tony Hsieh, *Delivering Happiness: A Path to Profits, Passion and Purpose* (New York: Hachette Book Group, 2013).

ask her customers what to build. I am always careful to emphasize that the job is to innovate on *behalf* of our customers, and I explain the difference between how a strong product manager works and how, for example, focus groups work.

In my experience, sincere and consistent customer-centricity takes a while to develop in a new product person—on the order of a year or more. There will be mistakes in judgment along the way, but with active and constructive coaching, you can help the product person learn how to embody this trait and communicate its importance to the rest of her product team and beyond.

20

Integrity

This chapter and the next tackle two of the toughest, yet most crucial, aspects of successful product teams.

In this chapter, I address integrity, and in the one that follows, we'll explore decision making. These two topics are distinct, but interrelated. I tackle integrity first because it is the foundation for good decision making in an empowered product team.

Especially for product managers of empowered product teams, integrity is not some sort of lofty aspirational goal. As I explained earlier, empowered product teams are predicated on *trust*—with executives, stakeholders, customers, and your own product team. I also explained how this trust is based on both competence and character. And integrity is at the heart of the necessary character.

The first thing I want to acknowledge is that developing, demonstrating, and preserving your integrity is in no way easy.

Forces are constantly conspiring to challenge your integrity.

Just imagine you've just come out of a meeting with the CEO in which she has impressed upon you just how critically important it is to be able to deliver something urgently. Yet your team has explained to you how they absolutely need more time.

Or you are sitting with a customer who is frustrated and angry because the product your team provided is not what they were led to believe they would receive.

Or one of your stakeholders has confided in you that she's looking at leaving the company because she feels unable to do her job with the level of support she receives from the product and technology organization.

Or one of your business development partners is investing heavily in their side of your relationship, and you know that the product is unlikely to provide the value they are depending on.

I could go on, but I'm guessing you can relate. Most product people have experienced these situations and have struggled to determine a course of action that addresses the immediate issue, yet doesn't derail your longer-term efforts and also manages to keep your integrity intact.

An experienced manager can coach a product person through these many types of situations and make all the difference to the career of a new product person: identifying and avoiding the landmines, understanding the priorities and the larger context, and navigating the personalities.

As with so many topics, tackling these challenges is different when coaching a product manager for an empowered product team versus a product manager for a feature team, which as I've discussed before, is much more of a *project* manager role.

The feature team product/project manager role is still difficult, and integrity is still important, but in this case the product manager is fundamentally a messenger. She passes along requirements, constraints, and dates to the product team, and passes back concerns, status, or bad news up to management.

However, if you're coaching a product manager of an empowered product team, the expectations are much higher: you're expected to try and figure out a solution that works for the customer and works for your business. While that's not always possible, you are expected to have the necessary knowledge and understanding of the business, and the ability to come up with creative solutions to tough problems.

I want to emphasize that what I'm about to share is what I've found has worked for me, and for many of the people I have coached. I am not arguing that this is the only path to integrity. In fact, I suspect there are differences based on the values of your company's and your country's culture. But if my list causes you to seriously consider what is important to demonstrating ongoing integrity in your company, I would call that a useful outcome.

When I coach product people on integrity, there are three essential behaviors I focus on: dependability, the company's best interests, and accountability.

Dependability

Integrity begins with impressing upon the product person how her word and her commitments need to be taken very seriously. You need to explain that if she misleads the executives, customers, or stakeholders—even with the best of intentions—she may permanently damage her reputation in the company and prevent establishing the trust that is so essential to effective product teams.

At the heart of demonstrating and preserving integrity is the concept of a *high-integrity commitment* (talked about in depth in Part VII).

First, if she gives her word on something—to a customer, stakeholder, executive, partner, or her own team—she needs to first be sure she is basing her commitment on informed judgment. And second, she absolutely needs to do everything possible to then deliver on what she or her team has promised.

This means not making a commitment unless and until her product team has had the opportunity to do sufficient product discovery to reasonably consider the risks of value, usability, feasibility, and viability. And just to be explicit, that means leaning on the expertise and experience of the designer and engineers.

Moreover, with an empowered product team, it's not sufficient just to ship something when promised. What you ship must actually work—it must solve the problem for the customer and/or the business. This is much more difficult.

Getting good at managing these high-integrity commitments is key to building a dependable reputation for her team.

The Company's Best Interests

The product manager needs to be perceived as always acting in the best interests of the company—not only protecting her or her team's interests.

In larger companies, especially those perceived as highly political, people are often suspected of having personal agendas or "fiefdoms." But for a product team to be entrusted and empowered, it's essential that the product team, and especially the product manager, be perceived as not only understanding the overall objective of the company, but as sincerely committed to doing everything in her power to help the company succeed.

(As an important side note, this is a major reason why equity-based incentive and compensation plans are so effective—*none* of us wins unless the *company* wins.)

It's not unusual for a new product manager to wonder how she can demonstrate this understanding of the company's best interests when she's the product manager of just a single team. But there are many opportunities: helping out another product team on one of their critical objectives, going above and beyond for a customer or a stakeholder, or publicly giving credit to others. And most common of all, making or supporting a decision that is not necessarily optimal for her product team, but is clearly better for the customer or the business.

Another difference between a feature team and an empowered product team is how engaged and committed the team is. It's not hard for leadership to tell if a team is engaged and passionate about the mission of the company and their part in making that happen. While *project* managers often resort to imposing deadlines, if you hope to have an empowered team of missionaries, the *product* manager needs to instead share the overall purpose of the work.

Accountability

An empowered product team signs up to achieve results. But with that empowerment necessarily comes the responsibility of accountability for those results.

But what does accountability really mean in practice? Thankfully, it doesn't usually mean that people get fired when results don't materialize.

Accountability for a product manager of an empowered product team means a willingness to take responsibility for mistakes. Even when fault may lie with others, she always asks what she could have personally done to have better managed the risk or achieved a better outcome.

You may have heard the old saying, "If a product team succeeds, it's because everyone on the team did what they needed to do, but if a product team fails, it's the product manager."

Some people think this saying is facetious, but not really.

Consider the case where the engineers take much longer to deliver something than expected. Well, did the product manager fully appreciate the feasibility risk here? Did she elicit and then listen to the engineers' concerns? A quick feasibility prototype very likely would have uncovered the true cost during product discovery.

Or suppose there turned out to be serious legal obstacles—putting the product in jeopardy. Legal considerations are a core component of business viability and normally something the product manager would have explored and addressed during discovery.

Yet it's also important to explain that integrity does not mean perfection. Mistakes will happen. But the product manager's career will survive these mistakes if she is on the whole dependable in her commitments, always works toward the company's best interests, and takes responsibility for her mistakes.

21

Decisions

I n the previous chapter, I discussed the importance of integrity and
how it is the basis for decision making in an empowered product
team. In this chapter, I'd like to focus on how I coach product teams in
making good decisions.

Remember that in feature teams most of the meaningful decisions
have been made upstream by executives and stakeholders. In contrast,
an empowered product team is all about pushing decisions down to the
product team level.

When I say, "good decisions," I'm not just referring here to logical, data-informed business decisions. I mean decisions that the rest of
your product team, your executives, your stakeholders, and your customers can support and understand, even if they disagree.

You might wonder why we need to worry about all of these constituencies. You may think that if it's the right thing for the product and
the customer, then this will all work out in the end. But this ignores the
realities and complexities of people and companies, especially if you're
striving for an empowered team of *missionaries* rather than *mercenaries*.

While making decisions is what empowered product teams do literally every day, *how* they make these decisions is often what separates the best from the rest.

First, we need to keep in mind that good decisions rest on a foundation of integrity—you are perceived as being dependable in your commitments, you are believed to be acting in the best interests of the company, and you're willing to be accountable to the results.

Second, we need to constantly keep in mind the outcome we are striving for when we make a decision. We certainly want this to prove to be a successful decision—that is to say, one that is timely and contributes to a good outcome. But, beyond that, we want the leaders and stakeholders to understand and respect our rationale, even if they might have chosen differently. And we want the parties to feel genuinely heard and respected, even if the decision ended up not going their way.

With these two points in mind, here are the five key behaviors that I coach product teams on when it comes to decision making.

Right-Size Decision Analysis

It's critical to acknowledge that not all decisions are equally important or consequential. We make decisions every day—ranging from selecting what bugs to fix, to choosing the best approach to solving a hard problem.

I encourage the product team to consider the level of risk and the associated level of consequence.

Consequence means, if you make a mistake, how big of a deal is it? In many cases, we can recover from a mistake literally in a few hours. In other cases, the consequence may very well put the product or even the company's future at risk.

Depending on the level of risk and consequence, you may feel there is critical information you absolutely need to collect before you can make a decision, and in other cases you may feel comfortable making the decision based on the imperfect information you have today.

Consider also the people who will be impacted by this decision. Maybe there are revenue implications, or sales, or legal. If you need the support of other key people—executives or stakeholders or customers—then you'll need to elicit their concerns or constraints and also bring them along on the decision.

Good decisions, especially in risky, consequential situations, begin by creating a plan of attack. This is also where I spend a good deal of my coaching time because here my experience as a manager and coach can help the product team get started in the right direction.

As an example, it's normal for a novice product manager to either seriously underestimate or overestimate risk. She ends up spending too much time in discovery on items that don't really matter, and then doesn't have time for the risks that do.

Collaboration-Based Decision Making

Almost every product person I've ever coached has struggled with the question of what decisions she "owns" and what decisions others "own." And I have to work hard to try to change this mindset.

I've written earlier about how important it is to coach product teams on what we really mean by collaboration.

In terms of specific decisions, I want the product manager to depend on, and usually defer to, the expertise and experience of her team—especially regarding design/usability and technology/feasibility.

Good decision making is not about getting everyone to agree (the consensus model), and it's not about pleasing the most people (the voting model), and it's also not about having one person who is expected to make all the decisions (the benevolent dictator model).

If the decision is primarily about enabling technology, if at all possible, we defer to our tech lead. If the decision is primarily about the user or customer experience, if at all possible, we defer to our product designer. And if the decision is primarily about business viability, we will depend on the product manager collaborating with the relevant stakeholders.

The hardest decisions are usually around value, as value is a function of the whole.

Resolving Disagreements

While collaboration-based decisions cover most cases, we will still face situations where there is disagreement.

For example, suppose your tech lead and your product designer disagree on the best approach to solving a problem. Or perhaps your CEO or another executive disagrees with your team.

It's important to realize that, in good organizations with strong, empowered product teams that genuinely care about their work and their customers, disagreements like these are normal and healthy. And especially since we often have imperfect information to make decisions, opinion and judgment play a necessary role.

Suppose, for example, the tech lead and the designer disagree on an approach because the tech lead considers the design unnecessarily difficult to implement, yet the designer considers this design necessary to the experience.

This is where it's critically important for the product team to know when and how to run a test.

This is another area where an experienced manager can coach the product team on the least expensive and most appropriate discovery technique for running this particular test and collecting the necessary data.

It usually involves the creation of a specific type of prototype, and then using this prototype to collect evidence or, if warranted, statistically significant results or proof.

Note that if you make collaboration-based decisions, and run tests for cases with disagreements, there will be very few situations of the product manager needing to override her team or escalate a decision up to senior management.

Transparency

Keeping in mind our goal of bringing our team and our leaders along with us in understanding the rationale for our decisions, it's important that we be transparent in making them. We don't want anyone to think we are making uninformed decisions, or ignoring important concerns, or pursuing our own agendas.

For minor decisions, it is often sufficient just to explain clearly and simply in a note why a decision was made. For major decisions, I am a very big fan of the written narrative we discussed earlier. Especially with the FAQ section where each anticipated objection or concern is spelled out and addressed.

This is yet another very good coaching opportunity, and I try to warn managers that many product people initially resist the rigors of a written narrative, but this is precisely what is warranted for consequential decisions.

Disagree and Commit

As I said above, it's important to acknowledge that in good organizations with empowered teams, we will often disagree, and sometimes passionately—even after running a test and collecting evidence. Please keep in mind that this is not a bad thing, and a clear sign of missionaries.

However, it's also important to emphasize to the team that, while disagreement and debate are necessary and good, at the end we may need to agree to disagree. Most people understand this, and as long as they genuinely feel like they were heard and their views considered, they are fine with this. But this is not enough.

We need the team—especially the product manager—to go one step further and agree to commit to the decision that was made, even if they disagree with it.

This can be hard for a new product manager to learn, especially because they are rightly concerned with their integrity.

But imagine how toxic it is to the team if the product manager were to say to leadership, for example, that she deferred to her tech lead but doesn't agree with the decision. Or suppose leadership makes a significant decision that the product manager doesn't agree with, and then she complains about that decision to her product team.

Compare that to the situation where the product manager shares the various views and opinions that were considered, and then explains the reasoning for the decision and details how she intends to make that decision successful.

There is no need for her to hide what her personal opinion was, but she must demonstrate that she understands the various options and the reason for the eventual decision, and that she can and will do everything she can to make that decision successful.

Decision making is a skill that will continue to develop over a career, especially as the product manager progresses in her career and becomes responsible for progressively more difficult, more important, and more consequential decisions and judgments. This topic alone can usually fill up the weekly 1:1 with good, constructive discussions and coaching.

A final note on decision making: Jim Barksdale, former CEO of Netscape Communications—and a very big influence on me (Marty) and the many others who worked for him—was famous for voicing his three rules of decisions:

1. If you see a snake, kill it.[1]
2. Don't play with dead snakes.
3. All opportunities start out looking like snakes.

---

[1] For those not familiar with Southern colloquialisms, a "snake" refers to an important decision that has to be made. So, the first rule is to identify the issue as such and make the decision. The second rule refers to not continually going back and revisiting earlier decisions (snakes can still bite you even if they're no longer alive). Finally, remember that opportunities can often start out looking like difficult problems or decisions.

22

Effective Meetings

I need to confess up front that I have never been a fan of meetings. I know that my experiences sitting in countless poorly prepared, ineptly run, slow moving, wastes of time that prevented me from doing something I considered infinitely more important have permanently biased me against them.

That said, I have also been in some meetings that were very different. Where the organizer was prepared, and information was clear and logical, a solid decision was made, and everyone in the room at least understood—even if they didn't personally agree (the all-important *disagree and commit*).

The result is that, when I coach people, I'm very particular about how they run meetings, or even if they really need to hold a meeting. Meetings are a very easy way for other executives to form judgments about the people on the product team, especially the product manager.

An important caveat before we jump into this.

I'm not talking here about meetings between members of the product team, such as a standup or retro, or any number of daily interactions. If the product manager and product designer sit down over a video call or in person to look at a prototype, while they are literally meeting, that's just daily work and not the subject of this chapter. We are talking here about gatherings that go beyond the product team. It may include the stakeholders or the executives, or partners, or members of other teams.

The first thing to understand is that the biggest pain about meetings is that they are *synchronous*. This means that every attendee needs to stop whatever they are doing, wherever they are, and meet—either in person or over a videoconference or the phone. That is rarely easy, or even welcome, so the meeting organizer needs to keep this in mind at all times.

If there's a way to serve the purpose *asynchronously*, then that's generally a better path. A status update or communicating information about a new release are great examples.

While there are, of course, an infinite number of possible reasons for a meeting, in practice, in product organizations, there are generally three types: communication, decisions, and problem solving.

Communication

In this case, we have some nontrivial information that the organizer believes is too important or too complex to be sent via an asynchronous means such as an email. An example might be an all-hands or a session where the leaders explain the product strategy.

Decisions

The second type of meeting requires a decision, usually because it's beyond what the product team can decide on its own. This is usually because the impact reaches into other parts of the company or there is substantial risk.

In this case, I am a very big advocate of the written narrative. We start the meeting with each member reading the narrative, and then we discuss and make an informed decision.

Problem Solving

The third type of meeting is fundamentally for problem solving. We don't know what the best course of action is (otherwise we probably would have written that up in a narrative and presented it for a decision). But we believe that, if we can get the right minds in the room, that together we may be able to solve an especially difficult problem.

An example might be a postmortem after an outage, where we consider what we could do differently going forward to avoid this type of problem in the future.

Organizing Effective Meetings

Here's how I coach product teams on meetings.

Purpose: First, being very clear on the purpose of the meeting is an important start for the meeting organizer.

Attendees: Next, it's important to decide on the attendees. I encourage the organizer to make two lists. One list with those people that are absolutely essential (if they have a last-minute conflict would you need to postpone?), and one list with those that are optional.

Preparation: In all three types of meetings, preparation is essential.

If it's a *communication* session, do you have clarity on the content? Do you have the right medium to communicate this content? Necessary images or visuals?

If it's a *decision* meeting, do you have the written narrative, and has it been reviewed by someone who understands the space?

If it's a *problem-solving* session, how will you explain the situation or context to the attendees? Have you already gathered the relevant data? Are you prepared to answer the various questions that will come up?

Facilitation: Assuming you've prepared, your job as the organizer is to facilitate an effective meeting. The nature of the facilitation will be different depending on the type of meeting. You are not there to police the meeting—you are there to ensure you get to the necessary decision or solution.

Follow-up: Once the meeting has reached a conclusion, there is usually some follow-up that needs to be done. This may involve notifying interested parties of the decision or next steps, but it's important to close the loop.

So, the bottom line for meetings is (a) make sure that if you call a meeting it is truly necessary and warrants the time of all the attendees, and (b) prepare for the meeting to make sure it is efficient, effective, and accomplishes its purpose.

CHAPTER

23

Ethics

I n this chapter, I'd like to discuss one of the most sensitive, yet potentially most important topics—the subject of ethics.

As we've discussed, the four big risks that every product team needs to consider are:

1. Will the customer buy it, or choose to use it? (*Value risk*)
2. Can the user figure out how to use it? (*Usability risk*)
3. Can we build it? (*Feasibility risk*)
4. Can the stakeholders support this solution? (*Business viability risk*)

Normally, we would consider ethical questions as part of business viability. If a solution is not ethical, it may indeed leave the company in serious trouble.

In practice, however, there are two problems with this:

First, there are already so many different aspects to business viability—sales, marketing, finance, legal, compliance, privacy, and more—that it's easy for ethics to get lost.

Second, unlike the other areas of business viability, there is rarely a stakeholder explicitly responsible for ethics.

The result is that ethics too often does not get the attention it deserves, and we have all seen the damage to the company, to the environment, to our customers, and to society, that can result from ethical lapses.

So, I have been advocating for explicitly considering ethical implications by adding a fifth risk:

5. Should we build it? (*Ethical risk*)

One progressive tech-product company that *does* have a stakeholder specifically responsible for ethics is Airbnb, where my longtime friend Rob Chesnut served until recently as chief ethics officer (he's now an advisor for the company).

Rob trained as a lawyer and began his career as a federal prosecutor, and then joined a young eBay as its legal counsel, which is where I (Marty) first met him. He has gone on to have a terrific career working for and advising a range of leading tech companies, most recently at Airbnb.

Rob has worked in the heart of Silicon Valley for decades and has seen what happens when companies don't pay enough attention to ethics. Rob explains, "Leaders need to recognize that there's a sea change in the world, where companies and their leaders are increasingly going to be held accountable for ethical failures."

There's no question that tech is now big business and is subject to many of the same pressures that have long challenged large, public companies. Rob explains,

In the past, companies had one stakeholder—the shareholder. Do what's good for the bottom line. That's an approach that has led a lot of companies to think about everything in the short term, hitting the quarterly number. And it's also incented a lot of behavior that is increasingly being recognized as unethical and causing more and more people to lose faith in companies. Hit the number, and don't worry about whether what you're building is really good for your customers, or the environment, or your partners, or the world at large.

*It's important for companies to recognize other stakeholders and under-
stand the implications that each product solution will have on those stakeholders. At Airbnb, for example, we not only consider the interests of
our investors, but of other important stakeholders—our employees, our
guests, our hosts, and the communities where we do business. If we consistently make decisions that negatively impact one or more of those stakeholders, we know that we're failing in our mission and, over the long
term, hurting our business.*

How does ethics apply to me in my job?

Ethics applies to every member of the company, but it's also true
that product teams are on the leading edge where new products and
services are conceived, developed, and deployed. So we have a special
responsibility to consider the implications of our work.

As Rob explains:

*Good product teams need to understand the implications of the solutions
they're designing—not just on revenues, but on that broader stakeholder
community. Signals to watch for: Will the product solution be good for
the end-customer? Does it have a negative impact on the environment
in some way, or third parties in the community? Is it something that,
if all of the emails and documents and discussions around the product
were published online, you'd be embarrassed? How would government
regulators react if they knew everything? Will the product be something
that you will be proud of as part of your personal brand?*

As leaders coach their product teams, these are the types of questions we need to be discussing. More generally, it's important for us to
get this topic out on the table. "You want a company where everyone
is comfortable asking the uncomfortable questions—that helps protect
your company against disastrous ethical failures."

So, what do you do if you identify an ethical issue?

One of the toughest situations for a product person is when they
spot a brewing ethical issue, but they're not sure how they should handle the situation. Clearly, this is going to be sensitive and potentially
emotional. Our best answer is to discover a solution that does not have

these ethical concerns, but in some cases, you won't be able to or you may not have the time.

Rob's advice:

> *Speak up in a thoughtful way, raise your concerns, but not in a holier than thou nor accusatory way. Try to explain in a way that makes it clear that you care about protecting the best interests of the company.*

I have found that it's essential to have a deep understanding of how your business works so that you're not perceived as naive or ignorant about the economics. This is also a situation where you may need the help of your manager.

So, what do you do if you are working at a company that you believe is fundamentally not interested in ethics?

I rarely encourage people to leave their company; however, when it comes to those companies that are clearly ignoring the ethical implications of their work, I have and will continue to encourage people to leave.

Rob's response is:

> *If you're not proud of where you work, not proud of how your company is impacting the world, or believe that leadership really doesn't care about integrity, it's probably time to start looking for another job.*

Fortunately, in my experience, the vast majority of tech companies do care about ethics and they are genuinely trying to help improve the world in some meaningful way. But even good intentions can have unintended consequences.

As a product leader, it's become increasingly important to coach your product people on this topic of ethics, starting with getting them to explicitly consider the question of whether we *should* build something.[1]

---

[1] I strongly encourage you to read Rob Chesnut's excellent book, *Intentional Integrity: How Smart Companies Can Lead an Ethical Revolution* (New York: St. Martin's Press, 2020).

24

Happiness

This chapter may seem an odd topic. You may be thinking that it's not the manager's job to be responsible for her team's happiness.

However, pretty much anyone that's worked in tech for any amount of time knows that a manager can easily be responsible for a product person being miserable. That old saying about people joining a company but leaving a manager is unfortunately demonstrated every day.

It's true that I don't usually refer to this topic as "coaching happiness." However, I do emphasize how important it is that the manager focus at least weekly on whether each of her product people feels she is doing meaningful work, progressing in her career, and building the necessary relationships with her team and with the execs that enable her to effectively and successfully lead an empowered product team.

With the big caveat that everyone is different and what's most important is that you as manager get to know your people well enough that you understand what is meaningful to them, and what makes them happy, I have found there are some near-universal truths to coaching happiness.

Meaningful Work

Most people in the product world want their work to be meaningful.

In fact, unless the manager is bad—in which case that dominates—in my experience this is usually the largest factor in happiness, even more than compensation.

But it's not always clear to the product person how or why her work is meaningful, or how her one small team contributes in a meaningful way. So, it's important to very clearly and explicitly discuss this and reinforce this frequently, both publicly and privately.

Personal Relationship

I (Marty) will admit I have always wanted the people who work for me to like me. But I want them to like me for very specific reasons. I want them to believe that I am committed to helping them succeed professionally and personally. I want them to trust me so that I can be honest with them and give them the feedback that's so essential to their growth. I want them to be able to look back on their time working with me as among their favorite in their career.

These professional relationships are built on *personal* relationships. I talk about my family and friends and interests outside of work and invite them to do the same. I have always made it a point to get to know them as *people*.

I have always believed I can be a much better manager and coach if I know what their aspirations are and what motivates them.

Personal Recognition

Lots of people tell me they don't need recognition, but I rarely believe them. What I believe they're telling me is that they might not feel comfortable with certain forms of *public* recognition. But in my experience, pretty much everyone wants to feel valued. Especially by people they respect.

Promotions, compensation, and equity are obvious ways to recognize someone, but beyond that, I'm a big fan of more frequent and more personal forms of recognition, especially once I've come to know their interests:

- A nice bottle of wine
- A book I think she would enjoy
- A ticket to an industry conference or event
- A gift certificate for a nice local restaurant
- A weekend getaway for two

Most of the time, I've had sufficient budget to just cover these things, but there have been a couple of companies I've worked where I had to pay for them myself. But any good manager knows that they are only as good as their people, so helping my people feel valued helps me as well.

Work Habits

It's no secret in the product world that people sometimes work crazy hours. But it's critical here to point out that, when people work long hours, there are two fundamental and very different reasons: working long hours because you *want* to versus because you *have* to. This is a very different situation when it comes to coaching.

In too many companies, people either feel pressured to work crazy hours, or sometimes they are literally forced to. If this is the situation in your company, then you very likely have teams of mercenaries and not missionaries, and this entire topic of worrying about your people's happiness is probably not something you care about.

I'm talking about the other situation. Where you have truly empowered product teams, and the teams believe they are doing especially meaningful and important work. They sometimes get so wrapped up in that work that, by the time they look up from their computers, it's late into the evening. Or, a year flies by and they have taken literally no vacation (not so much a problem in much of the world, but a real issue in the United States and China especially).

A good manager will notice this and discuss at the 1:1. She will explain how easy it is to burn out, how important it is to play the long game, and how the job is essentially creative problem solving, which requires time to recharge. If this is an ongoing issue, then it's very likely something that will need serious and active coaching.

It's also true that occasionally something really big and important will come up and the team will have a big push. So long as the motivation for this is coming from within the team, these situations may turn into people's proudest achievements. It's not always a bad thing.

But again, the manager can help by making sure this isn't the norm.

Modeling Good Behaviors

There are many managers out there that work crazy hours yet try to tell their people they don't need to. It's the "do what I say not what I do" approach to management.

But, of course, many people feel pressured to work at least as hard as their manager, which of course can lead to this silly spiral of getting in early, leaving late, and responding to emails at all hours.

Again, if you truly care about the happiness of your people, you know your actions speak louder than your words.

The manager needs to be sensitive to this, and in fact go out of her way to share how and when she's personally recharging, being conscious about when she's sending emails, and how she's managing her time.

Career Planning

It's also important to point out that sometimes, in order for the product person to be truly happy in her life, it may mean helping her into a different job or even career. If the product person is not able to do the job, then this may be uncomfortable, but it's fairly straightforward. But sometimes this isn't the issue at all.

One of the most personally difficult situations for me was when I (Marty) had an exceptionally strong product manager who was a close to ideal example of the type of person I try hard to recruit and coach. She was so smart and so savvy with people, and she learned so quickly, that I had little doubt she had a terrific career in front of her.

But, eventually, she came to trust me enough to admit to me at one of our 1:1s that, while she knew she was good at the job, and she felt she was making a real impact, she had come to realize that this was not what she wanted with her life. It was hard for me, as I hated to lose such a talent, but I encouraged her to pursue her passion (writing fiction). She did, and was able to beat the odds and make it her career.

More generally, I try to encourage managers to recognize and acknowledge just how important a role they play in the lives of their employees. They have the power to make an employee's life miserable, or to help them achieve their professional and personal goals.

The Greatest Coach

You may have been surprised in the introduction to this book to learn that during the early, formative years of their respective companies, Steve Jobs of Apple, Larry and Sergey of Google, and Jeff Bezos of Amazon were all coached by the same person: Bill Campbell, known as "The Coach of Silicon Valley."

Most people outside of Silicon Valley aren't aware of this, and that's largely because Bill did everything he could to avoid being in the limelight. He wanted the attention to be on the people he was coaching.

In fact, I tried to write about him back in 2007, but he asked me not to publish because he didn't want the attention. It turns out I wasn't the only one he turned down.

To be clear, I was never fortunate enough to be one of the people he coached. I truly wish I was. But I met him several times because I was lucky enough to work for people he did coach.

Bill passed away a few years ago, and I'm still learning of others he coached. Just recently, two of the people he coached—Eric Schmidt, the former CEO of Google, and Jonathan Rosenberg, the former SVP Product of Google—interviewed many of the other people Bill coached, and put together a book of his leadership and coaching principles called *Trillion Dollar Coach*.[1]

It's always hard for me to describe Bill because his personality was such a big part of the impact he made. But I think this book does a good job.

I've shared some of his quotes throughout this book.

I would argue that even though Apple, Amazon, and Google have very different cultures, they all understand the essential role of product, and they all understand that empowering product teams to do great work is the key.

While I loved reading the book on Bill Campbell, it was also personally humbling for me. I've been doing product for so long, it's hard for me to remember what things I learned from others and what things I figured out for myself. But hearing so many of the points I feel most strongly about emphasized in this book, it made me realize that I owe much more to Bill Campbell than I knew. It's clear to me now that these points were drilled into me by those he coached, who then went on to coach me. But I think that fact would make The Coach especially happy.

One last point from *Trillion Dollar Coach* that really resonated with me personally:

> *Bill would say that he had a different way of measuring his impact, his own kind of yardstick. I look at all the people who've worked for me or who I've helped in some way, he would say, and I count up how many are great leaders now. That's how I measure success.*

I'm often asked why I'm still coaching product people after so many years (and make no mistake, I don't consider myself in the same league as Bill Campbell), but I do feel a similar pride when the people I've spent time teaching or coaching go on to create great teams and great products.

---

[1]Eric Schmidt, Jonathan Rosenberg, and Alan Eagle, *Trillion Dollar Coach: The Leadership Playbook of Silicon Valley's Legendary Bill Campbell* (New York: HarperCollins, 2019).

Leader Profile:
Lisa Kavanaugh

Path to Leadership

I first met Lisa in 2010 when she was the VP Engineering at Ask.com.

Lisa studied computer science at UC Santa Barbara, and began a long career in technology, initially as an engineer at HP, but soon she joined a young ask.com (do you remember "Ask Jeeves"?).

Over the next 12 years, Lisa earned her way through the engineering ranks to eventually becoming the CTO of what by then was a very large, global engineering organization.

What has always defined Lisa, however, was her passion for coaching, and for continuously improving both herself and those who worked for her.

For the past several years, she has dedicated her career to coaching others, helping technology leaders to become the leaders their companies need them to be.

Leadership in Action

I asked Lisa how she generally goes about helping technology leaders to become skilled leaders of empowered teams and organizations.

Here's Lisa in her own words:

Different leaders have different motivations for seeking coaching. Some desire a major promotion, some are facing an obstacle standing in the way of their goals, and others want to establish a better working relationship with their team or peers. They all desire an outcome that feels out of reach.

Whatever the case, transforming to a strong, confident, inspiring leader can take effort and personal courage.

These are four key skills that each leader needs to complete that transformation.

Self-Awareness

It begins with being honest with yourself and understanding what behaviors or traits might be getting in your own way, or in your team's way. Ask yourself, what are the behaviors that may have served you well earlier in your career, but now are no longer advantages?

Here's a remarkably common example of that. I often meet technology executives that have built a reputation for absolutely dependable execution. They have consistently put in the effort and delivered what they had promised. In many cases, they have had to move mountains to deliver, but they did. They are known for their reliable execution and that is a large part of their identity.

But now the leader has been promoted to the level where her personal effort can't scale, and her teams feel like they are being micro-managed. The self-awareness that is needed here is to realize that the skills that got her to this level won't get her to the next level.

Courage

When you have built a career and identity out of one set of behaviors and you realize you need to change, especially in ways that now depend on other people, this can take real courage.

It takes courage to make space for teams to learn and make mistakes. It takes courage to give meaningful and honest feedback. It takes courage to take this leap of faith that trusting your team will have better results than just trusting in yourself. It takes courage to leave your tactical skills behind and move into the world of strategy. It takes courage to be vulnerable.

As an example, I had a technology executive that was struggling to truly partner with a particular peer, because an earlier project they had worked on had not gone well. She was convinced that this peer thought poorly of her and her response was to avoid this peer. But she knew she needed this relationship, and she mustered up the courage to reach out and have a truly difficult conversation. She confessed that she had been avoiding him, the reason why, and what she wished for their partnership going forward. It took bravery and vulnerability to put herself out there like this, and it proved to be the turning point in their relationship.

Courageous leadership is going forward despite the discomfort.

Rules of Engagement

For many leaders, learning to trust their teams can take a very big leap of faith. Especially because they know they are still ultimately responsible for successful outcomes.

Rules of engagement are simply an agreement with the teams on what type of visibility the leader needs in order to give the teams the space they need to work. What information does the leader need in order to trust? What context does the team need to understand to be successful? What does the team need to feel safe in surfacing risks and problems early or asking for help?

It's important to emphasize that these rules of engagement typically evolve as the trust and learning is built over time, but establishing some agreement around what information to communicate when, can help both the leader and the teams to work out effective ways for each party to get their needs met.

Disrupting Yourself

Even if the leader is self-aware, has the personal courage to make the necessary changes, and has agreed to rules of engagement, it's no secret that long-held habits can be very hard to break. Especially habits and behaviors that get to the very core of someone's identity and feelings of self-worth.

Effectively, we're asking the leader to disrupt herself. We're asking her to commit to change. We acknowledge that there will be mistakes and regressions, but each time that happens we'll identify the triggers and look at better ways to respond. We acknowledge that the first days and weeks will be the most difficult. But every day that goes by, the leader will be able to access the new behaviors more easily.

Every leader's journey is different, but I have found over the years that if a leader truly wants to improve, and has the courage to take the leap of faith necessary to learn to trust others, that they can indeed disrupt themselves and become the leader their company needs, and that their employees deserve.

PART

Staffing

I n the next series of chapters, I focus on the manager's staffing responsibilities.

I've made a big deal in the chapters so far about how important it is to coach and develop your people, but I have not talked yet about how to *find* these people.

Of course, much has already been written about staffing and hiring by many others.[1]

What I'll be focusing on in these chapters is what is special about staffing when it comes to empowered product teams—especially product managers, product designers, and senior engineers/tech leads.

I'll start with recruiting, and then cover interviewing, hiring, onboarding, annual performance reviews, terminations, and promotions.

This might not seem like such an important or interesting topic to you—I know early on in my own product leadership career it was not—but I hope to change your mind about this, as it's one of the

---

[1] My favorite is Laszlo Bock's *Work Rules!: Insights from Inside Google That Will Transform How You Live and Lead* (New York: Hachette Book Group, 2015).

clear and essential differences between strong product companies and the rest.

There are three higher-order problems I see in companies when it comes to staffing:

The first is that there is often very fundamental confusion about what to look for when hiring strong product people. Too often the company thinks that, if they want to compete with the likes of Google and Amazon, they need to hire exceptional people. This is a dangerous misconception.

Let me be clear on this: the best product companies hire competent people of character, and then coach and develop them into members of extraordinary teams.

This is why staffing and coaching go hand in hand.

The second is that, in far too many companies, the leaders equate staffing with hiring. But it's a much larger problem than just hiring, and in fact, if you focus just on hiring, you will dramatically reduce your chances of building the organization you need.

The third higher-order point is to realize that staffing *is the responsibility of the hiring manager*.

Far too often, I find that the hiring manager believes this is the responsibility of HR, and that while she might review some resumes, and participate on the interview team, she thinks of herself as just a passenger on the journey and not the driver.

While HR can hopefully assist with some of the supporting and administrative tasks (such as posting job descriptions, passing along resumes, and preparing offer letters), effective staffing begins with realizing that a successful outcome requires that *the hiring manager step up and take responsibility for this*.

If nothing else, I hope this series of chapters makes clear why this is the case.

More generally though, staffing is another one of the areas where strong product companies are dramatically better than most companies.

The most important decision at Amazon, has been, and remains, hiring the right talent.

—*Jeff Bezos*

And this is in no small part a direct result of the strong company's reliance on the empowered team model. This is because the empowered team model is truly a people-first model. You are hiring capable people and giving them the space to do remarkable things.

For companies still in the feature team model, the people are mercenaries. They believe they can always hire others, or they might even hire an agency and outsource the work.

But for those companies committed to the empowered team model, everything depends on hiring competent people who share your values and are passionate about pursuing your product vision. And that means that staffing must move from a necessary task to a strategic skill.

Most people coming from a feature team-style company are surprised to see the differences in terms of recruiting, the seriousness of the interview process, how much time they devote to new employee onboarding, and most important, the ongoing effort in coaching and developing their people to reach their potential.

I am not suggesting that there is only one good way to handle staffing, but I am suggesting that these activities deserve much more attention than most companies and hiring managers devote to it.

I'll go further and suggest that skill in staffing is one of the most important and telling leading indicators for a company's success.

26

Competence and Character

When I talk to executives and managers that don't trust the people on their product teams, I find that they often have very antiquated, and I believe harmful, views on what types of people to recruit and hire.

So I ask these leaders to consider a very different approach to staffing.

First, when I say that strong product teams are composed of "ordinary people," I'm not suggesting that you can hire anyone off the street and turn them into members of extraordinary teams. They do need to have the necessary skills to succeed.

However, I am suggesting that rather than obsessing over the university the person attended, or the ambiguous concept of "cultural-fit," or whether the person is a so-called 10X performer, or thinking you need to hire people with a deep knowledge of your domain, focus instead on what I'm about to describe.

To be clear, there is most definitely such a thing as a 10X employee. These are people who have demonstrated their ability to contribute on the order of 10X more than their peers.

However, it's also no secret that having a 10X employee does *not* necessarily translate into having 10X results. That's because results in product companies come from product *teams*, and in fact if that 10X employee brings along toxic behaviors, they will likely cause far more damage to your organization than good.

Let's discuss the characteristics you should consider when recruiting and assembling strong, cross-functional, empowered product teams.

Competence

Stephen Covey explained that:

> *Trust is a function of two things: competence and character. Competence includes your capabilities, your skills, and your track record. Character includes your integrity, your motive, and your intent with people. Both are vital.*

We'll discuss character next, but table stakes for any of your hiring onto an empowered product team is *competence*. The person must have the necessary skills—as an engineer, a product designer, or as a product manager.

This is often where so many organizations plant the seeds of their future struggles.

You've probably heard the old adage that "A's hire A's, but B's hire C's." A manager that is not an accomplished product manager, designer, or engineer herself is ill-equipped to assess a candidate, and it is easy to see how the company can end up hiring someone that is not competent at the job. Moreover, without the necessary experience herself, the hiring manager is not able to coach and develop that person to competence.[1]

Normally, we hire for competence; however, there's nothing wrong with hiring based on *potential*—but if and only if the hiring manager is willing and able to sign up to actively coach that person to competence. And if they fail in that, to find that person a different job. That's a big commitment of time and effort on the hiring manager.

Staffing is one of the three key responsibilities of management, but to be clear, it's absolutely critical to ensure competence. Without competence, the person and the team cannot expect to be trusted by management or leadership. So there is no lasting empowerment without competence.

Character

Once we know the candidate has the required level of competence, most companies focus on what is usually referred to as "cultural fit."

This is probably one of the most damaging concepts for your efforts to build a great organization.

Of the vast pool of people in the world, companies filter out almost everyone except those who are perceived as a cultural fit, which of course is a very ill-defined concept.

For too many organizations, cultural fit is the politically correct term for what essentially translates into: "Hire people who look and think like we do."

In our industry, that usually means hiring males with technical degrees from top-tier universities. In my experience, this is not usually conscious or intentional, but the results are plain to see.

I'd like to try to convince you that cultural fit is the wrong objective here.

Most people don't know that the most successful sports franchise in history is not the New York Yankees, or the Chicago Bulls, or

---

[1] Again, if this is your situation, it's critical that you find someone experienced to provide you with the product leadership coaching you need.

Manchester United. It's New Zealand's All Blacks national rugby team. They have an unmatched record of sustained dominance (more than 100 years).

The All Blacks learned a long time ago that character matters. So, they have a very clear and unambiguous policy in place when evaluating players and coaches for their team: the "No Assholes Rule."[2]

They understand that it doesn't matter how exceptionally skilled a player or coach may be, if he's an asshole, then he will be toxic to the team overall.

So rather than narrowing a very large pool of people to the small subset that are perceived as a cultural fit, I argue to instead keep the pool very large and just filter out the relatively few assholes.

The irony is that we know that competence and character are all-important to establishing the necessary trust, yet so many companies and managers hire either people who are cultural fits but not competent, or they justify hiring an asshole because they believe the person is exceptionally skilled.

One of the unintended and damaging consequences of hiring people like us is that they too often think like us.

It's not that the way we think is bad, it's that what we really need are people that think *differently* from us. This is one of the most tangible and immediate benefits of adding diversity to your team. The chances of solving hard problems goes up substantially if you can approach the problem from several perspectives.

So, rather than looking for people like yourselves, make it an explicit point to look for people that are clearly *not* like yourselves. People who come from different environments. People who were educated differently. People with different types of work experience. People with different life experiences.

I find that when candidates are viewed through this lens, there are many excellent candidates to be found, all over the world. Often, they are hiding in plain sight in your own company. Just make sure they are competent and not assholes.

---

[2] Fans of the All Blacks may know that they actually use a more colorful term than "asshole." But since their term is offensive to some, I took the liberty of substituting the still vivid term "asshole," which I borrow from the excellent book by Stanford professor Bob Sutton: *The No Asshole Rule: Building A Civilized Workplace and Surviving One That Isn't* (New York: Business Plus, 2007).

27

Recruiting

Most people think that staffing begins with sourcing, but as you'll see, in strong product companies staffing begins with active *recruiting*.

In an HR-driven approach to hiring, a hiring manager might provide a job description, but things don't really get going until HR starts providing resumes (known as *sourcing*). In fact, one of the obvious symptoms of this problem is when the hiring manager complains that she's not getting enough high-quality resumes.

Yet for strong managers, it's the opposite. The hiring manager identifies what she wants, and then she goes out and *recruits*.

It's analogous to a college or professional sports team. While a coach might get an occasional "walk-on" (the rough equivalent of someone sending in their resume), mostly the coach actively works to *recruit* the necessary talent: visiting prospects, getting to know them personally, and working to persuade the desired talent to join their team.

It's worth pointing out that *recruiting* rather than *sourcing* is the fastest way I know to improve diversity. Especially when the hiring manager understands that innovation thrives in a team where each person thinks *differently*. We generally don't want or need more of the same. We need people with different educations, different approaches to problem solving, different life experiences, and different strengths.

The truly strong manager knows that, through recruiting, she is crafting *product teams*, and not just a collection of people.

So, where do you find these people?

Building your network of potential recruits is an ongoing activity—not something you start doing once you have an opening. You meet people at industry conferences and professional meetups, at competitors, during visits to partners and customers, via introductions from referrals, and even socially.

Schedule calls or coffees with people when you'd like to further develop the relationship. You have the opportunity to begin a mentoring relationship that can hopefully develop into a coaching relationship when the time is right.

I'm also a fan of hosting talks at your offices with selected industry speakers who can attract candidates, and also help build the reputation of your organization.

Another great technique is a company blog written to demonstrate your dedication to the craft of great product.[1]

If you work at a large company, often the right talent can be found inside your own company. I often find people in random roles who are recognized as exceptionally smart and always find a way to get things done, but who never considered themselves to be product people.

I always encourage hiring managers to cast a wide net when looking for exceptional product talent. I've found them in engineering, finance, marketing, sales, legal, and in a business owner or stakeholder role.

You need to be sensitive to the rest of the organization here as you're not trying to poach people, but rather, you're trying to make sure everyone is in the best position to utilize their talents.

You also need patience when developing this network of potential recruits. I have literally worked on recruiting some people for several years—getting to know them and their career goals and planting seeds by sending them articles on the product role, sharing books, and generally talking with them about their career goals and what steps they can take to reach them.

---

[1]Check out the wonderful *Code as Craft* blog (www.codeascraft.com) for a very effective example of this.

As an example, when recruiting product managers, I seek out entrepreneurial people. Many of the type I'm looking for aspire to start their own company one day. So I explain to them that product management is considered the proving ground for a startup founder or CEO, and I explain why that's the case.

Now, it is true if you establish a reputation as a strong manager who makes a sincere and sustained effort to develop her people, there will be more people who approach you for a job, which is great. But this is not a substitute for ensuring you are recruiting the people and team you *need*. In any case, it can take years to build that personal brand.

It is essential that recruiting be a proactive and consistent activity for every manager. Realize also that, if you genuinely care about developing your people, you will be amazed at how many referrals this can generate.

Also note that, for product talent, the product vision can and should be one of your most effective recruiting tools. And of course, the products you create, if successful, will help people take notice.

If you make recruiting an ongoing and high-priority activity, then soon enough you'll have a healthy network and funnel of strong candidates. As you open new positions, and as people reach good transition points in their careers, you'll be well positioned to bring them in.

Making Recruiting a Priority

I (Chris) experienced the power of real coaching in my first job as a product manager at a startup. My job was predominantly as an individual contributor, with the expectation that I would eventually build out the product management team. The company was growing fast, and my product was gaining momentum and customers. I was impossibly busy, and I was finally given the approval to hire another product manager to help me out.

The demands on me as an individual contributor hadn't changed, so I relied heavily on our small HR team to drive the process. I would check in with them once or twice a week, review resumes, and conduct phone screens, but was otherwise quite passive. I had so much other work, and besides, this was what the HR department was there for, right?

During this time, I had regular 1:1s with my manager. He asked me about how the recruiting was going and I filled him in on the promising resumes and phone screens. I would quickly pivot to discussing the product and the business, and without irony, how completely underwater I was.

After two weeks, I still hadn't found any candidates worthy of bringing in for an interview, and in our 1:1, my manager refused to let me move to a new topic. He told me with no uncertainty that hiring a new product manager was my single most important task right now. This was my day job, not all the other things that were consuming my time. To underscore the importance, he said that until that role was filled, I should expect to spend a minimum of 50 percent of my time on that task. Everything else was secondary.

This was a complete shock to me. I wasn't able to get my current tasks done, so how could I possibly free up that much time? We proceeded to go through everything I was working on and together discussed what could be temporarily deprioritized, what could be shifted to other people in the company, and what could be shifted directly to him.

After we had created space for the hiring work, I was hit with my next realization: I had no idea how to even spend that much time on hiring. My manager then led me through a process where we brainstormed strategies for me to tap and develop my personal network, actively scour resources for candidates, reframe the job description, and generally how to play a much more active role in driving recruiting rather than slotting into an HR-sourcing process.

This single 1:1 was one of the most memorable in my career.

It profoundly expanded my view of my job, it built a new level of trust with my manager, it shined a bright light on where I needed to grow, and it gave me a glimpse of what real leadership looked like. I was newly inspired and plunged into the hiring task.

What had happened was a change in my mental framing. This was not simply learning new tools or skills, though that was a part of it. I glimpsed the mindset of my manager as he coached me, and I realized I would need to adopt that mindset as I transitioned into a first-time manager position.

Outsourcing

Seriously? I certainly hope that anyone who has read this far already knows what I'm about to say about the prospect of outsourcing.

But first some caveats. I'm speaking here about outsourcing as it pertains to the core roles in a tech product organization: product managers, product designers, engineers, data analysts and data scientists, user researchers, and the managers of these people.

Your products are the lifeblood of your company, and these skills must be core competencies.

Your customers depend on these products and services.

Outsourcing these things will almost certainly kill any chance you have of teams of missionaries. Just the opposite, you literally have created teams of mercenaries.

You might say that you don't have people on staff with the necessary skills. Then either hire these people or invest in your existing staff to learn and develop those skills—primarily through coaching and training.

You might say that you think you'll save money by hiring some low-cost, offshore firm. I promise you that you will end up spending much more and getting much less for it. The amount of overhead in terms of time and communication—and even more important, the opportunity cost of losing your ability to innovate—makes this a very poor investment.

Occasionally, we have some large burst of work such as test automation or a large migration and using an outsourcing firm for this is not going to be a problem.

Just remember that a smaller group of missionaries will always outperform a larger group of mercenaries, especially if you consider the need for both discovery *and* delivery.

28

Interviewing

To continue with our series on staffing, in this chapter I discuss the interview process.

As with recruiting, the hiring manager needs to take responsibility for the *interview effectiveness of the interview team*, and the *interview experience for the candidate*.

The hiring manager may have some administrative help and/or some HR help, but the hiring manager needs to own and actively manage this process.

Your overarching goal is to ensure you hire competent people of character, and that every hire—at least for product managers, product designers, and tech leads—should raise the average.

Note that since we have more than one engineer on a product team, it is not a problem to have a range of experience and capability levels in our engineers. However, for product managers, product designers, and tech leads—since there is just one each per team—it's critical to ensure a high standard of competence. Those are not "junior" roles.

The most common problem I see is in determining the interview team. Too often the primary concern is to be inclusive, and make sure everyone who wants to has a say. But this approach will rarely raise the bar, and often leads to a consistent, gradual decline in the average capability level.

So instead, the hiring manager should very carefully select and curate the interview team. Each person should be selected both for her competence and for her character. These should be people that a strong candidate would be proud to work with and would also enjoy getting a beer with.

Ensure that every team member understands specifically what she will be interviewing for—the skills and experience will depend on the specific role you're hiring for—and make sure she has prepared.

Most larger companies have interview guidelines that speak to appropriate and inappropriate questions, but rarely provide any meaningful guidance on the interview content itself.

Your objective during the series of interviews is to ensure that any open questions are resolved by the end of the interview day. This is normally done by each interviewer communicating to the next interviewer any open questions so that the next interviewer can investigate. And the hiring manager, or whoever is the last interview, should extend the time as necessary to resolve any open questions.

Likewise, if the hiring manager receives feedback from the interviewers during the day that indicate that this candidate is clearly not a fit, then it is fine to end the day earlier.

Three points are worth special mention:

First, there is a difference between hiring for competence and hiring for potential. Normally we are looking for people who have demonstrated the competence to perform the necessary role.[1]

However, in some cases, we will hire based on potential—someone that has not yet shown she can succeed at the job, but we are willing to make a bet on her. A university hire would be a common example. In the case of hiring based on potential, it is essential that the hiring manager clearly communicate this to the interview team, and also that the hiring manager personally commit to invest the necessary time and energy to coach that person to competence.

---

[1] An excellent book to help you learn how to identify competence during interviews is Geoff Smart and Randy Street's *Who: The A Method for Hiring* (New York: Ballantine Books, 2008).

This typically involves not just the normal weekly 1:1 but also daily coaching—often for a period of months. And, moreover, if the person is not able to reach competence in a reasonable amount of time, the hiring manager needs to take responsibility for correcting that hiring mistake.

Second, always remind the interview team that we are *not* looking for more of the same. Innovation thrives with people who think *differently*. So, candidates with different education, different life experiences, different cultures, or different approaches to problem solving are highly desired.

Third, many hiring managers make the mistake of hiring primarily for domain knowledge, but for most positions—if you are hiring the right person with the right skills—she will be able to learn the domain much faster than someone with the necessary domain knowledge can learn the necessary product skills. In fact, in many cases, too much domain knowledge is more of a liability (they make the mistake of thinking they are the customer).

My Favorite Interview Question

The question comes late in the interview. The setup goes like this.

Now that I know you a bit, I'd like to give you a list of four broad work attributes. You're a product person, so I already expect that you're strong in each. But I highly doubt that you consider yourself equally competent in all of them. So, I'm going to ask you to stack rank them in order of strongest to weakest.

This setup should be disarming. The candidate must understand that there is no correct answer to the question, hopefully setting up an honest conversation.

Now for the four attributes, in no particular order. I (Chris) usually describe them this way:

1. Execution — how well do you get things done, do the right thing without being asked, and track lots of simultaneous targets?

(continued)

(continued)

2. Creativity — how often are you the person in the room with the most or the best ideas?

3. Strategy — how well do you get up above what you're working on and put it into a broader market or vision context and then make this clear to others?

4. Growth — how good are you at figuring out ways to multiply effort through smart use of process, team management, and so on?

The surface value of this question reveals how a candidate engages in a conversation that is ultimately about their self-assessed weaknesses.

I put a lot of importance on a product person's level of self-awareness and her ability to identify and admit areas of growth. (You can think about this question as a less contrived and more effective version of the old "tell me about your weaknesses.")

I'm skeptical of a candidate who is unwilling or unable to venture into this conversation, or when her self-assessment seems wildly at odds with what I've already observed in other parts of the interview.

If you're the hiring manager, this question serves another purpose: it is a check on your own biases, and it helps ensure that you don't end up hiring a bunch of clones (usually of yourself).

CHAPTER

29

Hiring

After interviewing, hopefully you have found a candidate you believe will be a strong addition to the organization. You need to prepare an offer and close the candidate.

Much of the hiring process will be dictated by HR compliance and compensation, but there are some essential points for the hiring manager.

First, if you have found a truly strong candidate, then it's critical to move quickly. Strive to produce an offer in 24–48 hours. Beyond that, you may lose a good candidate. And even if not, it demonstrates to the candidate that the company has a hard time making decisions, which is not a good look.

Second, take reference checks seriously, and do them personally—*don't delegate this to anyone else*. Be sure to ask if the person would hire the candidate again.

One of the most important goals of a reference check is to try to identify candidates that are going to prove toxic due to their personality. Most such people can hide the problematic parts of their personality during an interview, but their previous employers know.

During a reference check, people are often reticent to share negative information, so be sure to give that person every opportunity to share what they are willing to. Note that an email reference check is rarely useful for this reason. A call or meeting for a coffee is much more likely to yield useful feedback.

But go beyond a reference check. One of the surest ways today to spot toxic personalities is to explore the candidate's behavior on social media. Find their profiles and look at how they interact with others.[1] Do they have thoughtful, respectful interactions or do they assume the worst and respond before thinking?

If the candidate is consistently rude in public on social media, it is very likely they will eventually act the same at work.

The official offer may come from HR or from the hiring manager, but in either case, what is most important is that the hiring manager call the candidate, and explicitly tell the candidate that if she joins and commits to putting in the effort, then you will promise to *personally invest in coaching and developing the candidate to reach her potential*.

If the candidate is especially good, it's very possible that she will receive multiple offers, and this is when I would typically request that the CEO or other key leader reach out and offer to talk. This sends a very valuable message to the candidate and can also help get the relationship off to a good start.

Realize that, while an offer for employment is made on behalf of the company, the hiring of talent is personal—a personal commitment from a manager to the personal and professional growth of an individual, and the personal commitment of the new hire to contribute to the vision and success of the company.

For most candidates, having someone that is committed to being in their corner, and actively working on their behalf to help them grow professionally, is more important than any other factor. And of course, the hiring manager will need to fulfill that pledge.

---

[1] In certain countries, you must first get permission from the candidate.

Span of Control

Span of control refers to how many direct reports a manager has.

Many companies have standard ranges, but if a company is to make a serious investment in coaching and product strategy, this will impact the number of reports a given manager is responsible for.

Every people manager's first responsibility is to coach and develop her people; however, depending on the type of people being managed, the amount of time required for that coaching can vary substantially.

Here are the primary factors to consider.

Level of Operational Responsibility

If your role carries significant operational responsibilities, such as product strategy, design strategy, and architecture/tech debt strategy, that will consume real time.

Level of Experience of Employees

Many companies have little choice but to hire people that are inexperienced in their new roles and to coach them to success. There is often such fierce competition for talent that companies either have to pay extraordinary salaries or hire based more on potential than proven performance.

This can work quite well, but with two very important caveats. First, the hiring manager must be skilled at coaching, and willing and able to provide the necessary time and effort. Second, it requires a smaller span of control—for example, the manager might have four to five direct reports rather than six to eight.

Level of Experience of Manager

Similarly, the experience of the manager plays a significant role in the appropriate span of control. Just as with any skill, coaching skills can

(continued)

(continued)

be developed, and an experienced manager who takes pride in her coaching gets substantially more efficient and effective in developing her staff.

Organizational Complexity

Finally, and this is often counterintuitive, in larger organizations the amount of "connecting the dots" and "managing up and across the organization" goes up considerably.

Some of that is simply a function of the number of dependencies, interactions, and resulting communication, but some is a function of the interpersonal dynamics (aka politics) of large organizations.

Ratios

So, how many people should report to you as a manager?

The smallest span of control (within the broader tech product organization) is typically a group product manager, which is a player-coach role where the GPM is responsible for at most two or three other people.

The largest span of control is typically an engineering manager, where it's not uncommon to have as many as 10 to 15 individual contributor engineers of varying levels.

Most fall in between, somewhere on the order of five to seven direct reports.

Some companies pride themselves on having very flat org structures with a large span of control, but in my experience, those companies are paying a substantial premium for experienced talent—even at the individual contributor level. That or they don't care at all about coaching and developing their people.

CHAPTER

30

Remote Employees

Normally, the question I focus on in my work and in my writing is "How can we leverage the best practices of the very best companies in order to give ourselves the very best chance for continuous innovation?"

While there are many practices that are important and contribute to this, I have long been a champion of the power of the co-located product team.

This Jeff Bezos quote sums up my experiences quite well:

At Amazon, a product team has a clear mission, specific goals, and needs to be cross-functional, dedicated, and co-located. Why? Creativity comes from people's interactions; inspiration comes from intensive concentration. Just like a start-up, the team huddles together in a garage, experimenting, iterating, discussing, debating, trying and retrying, again and again.

I don't think it's an accident that Amazon is the most consistently innovative company in our industry.

All that said, for many companies today the question has changed.

Now I'm being asked, "How can we leverage best practices to give ourselves the best chance at innovation, in the scenario where the product team is distributed and some or all of the team is working remotely?"

Addressing this important question is the subject of this chapter.

There's no need to discuss the well-understood tools and methods that distributed teams have adopted to communicate and manage their work. I will assume you are already familiar with the range of cloud-based collaboration tools, and video-based communication services.

Instead, we'll dive deeper into the nature of cross-functional product teams and discuss where you should focus your attention to continue to make forward progress as a team.

First, there are two major types of activities in every empowered product team: discovery and delivery.

When people talk about the magic of co-location, they are mainly talking about discovery, as in the Bezos quote above.

In delivery, it's more of a trade-off. Communication is, of course, easier when sitting together, but so are unwanted interruptions. Overall, I find teams with remote employees do quite well in delivery, occasionally even better than when the team is co-located.

The real challenge of remote employees is when we consider the discovery work.

The overall methods and mechanics are not really very different when working remotely versus co-located for discovery work.

We still have many product ideas, and we still try them out quickly—usually by creating a prototype and then testing on real users, either qualitatively or quantitatively.

Obviously, our qualitative testing is not likely to be literally face to face, but we can and do make up for that with increased video-based testing.

The important differences impact the dynamics of how the product manager, product designer, and tech lead collaborate to discover a solution worth building.

There are three serious problems that I consistently see, and any of these three can meaningfully damage your ability to innovate.

Artifacts

As soon as you separate the product manager from the product designer from the tech lead, a very common anti-pattern arises.

Instead of the three sitting down together to discuss the question "How do we solve this problem?" there is a nearly gravity-like pull to start producing artifacts for one another.

The product designer asks the product manager to write down some type of "brief" or requirements or constraints.

The tech lead asks the designer when she can provide some wireframes so the engineers can start planning.

The product manager asks the engineers for estimates.

Very soon, the new remote work process has reverted back to waterfall-like passing along of artifacts. And not only will innovation suffer, but the entire discussion will quickly move back to *output* rather than *outcome*.

This is a tendency that you have to continuously fight. It may feel less efficient to discuss these topics in a video call between the three of you, but it's essential that you return to the "How do we solve this problem?" discussion.

During discovery, the main artifact should be prototypes.

Now, it's true that once you do decide to build something in delivery, the engineers that are now remote will likely not be as up to date on the latest prototype. So, you will need to spend some time describing in sufficient detail what the engineers need to build and QA test. But that's only after you believe you have a solution that is valuable, usable, feasible, and viable.

Trust

Discovery in general, and innovation in particular, depends on the concept of *psychological safety*.[1] This essentially means that the members of your product team feel respected and their contributions are welcome and valued.

---

[1] https://rework.withgoogle.com/blog/five-keys-to-a-successful-google-team/.

I've written earlier about how even one asshole on the product team can destroy this dynamic. Fortunately, most people are not assholes—at least not in person. Unfortunately, it's no secret that when people are separated from one another, and you're not speaking directly to someone's face, the normal filters and sensitivity can fade.

More than a few people have shared with me that they are seeing a different side of their colleagues, and it's not always a good look.

This is where coaching is so essential. In my experience, most people don't intend to be cruel or insensitive, they just don't have as many social cues to go on. A good manager can coach the employee on her online interactions with the rest of the team and help her realize where she can improve.

Also, it may seem like it would be more efficient to send an email or Slack message. But if a poorly phrased message breaks the trust and requires hours of damage control, it maybe wasn't so efficient after all.

When working remotely, it's always better to handle anything that might be interpreted as sensitive over video. It's not as good as in-person, but it's still much better for including the facial expressions, tone of voice, and body language that are integral parts of communication and so important to developing and maintaining trust.

Time

Some people have a work-from-home environment that is largely insulated from interruptions, and they find themselves feeling more productive than ever, especially when it comes to quality time to think through hard problems.

However, many others—especially those with family obligations that may include childcare—yearn for the ease of going into the office where they can escape the burdens of home life and get work done again.

The reality is that not all members of your product team will likely have the same amount of contiguous quality time to meaningfully contribute. Getting even an hour a day of uninterrupted time where you are all available might be very difficult.

My main suggestion here is to try to be flexible. Let's suppose your product designer has young children and can only manage a solid hour of uninterrupted time at an early or late hour. If the product manager and tech lead can find a way to accommodate that, it's worth doing.

I realize that none of these three items—artifacts, trust, or time—are easy challenges to deal with. They're not.

But if you find your distributed team is not delivering the results you are used to, this would be where to focus your coaching.

With the members of the product team being aware of the potential for these problems, and with the managers providing coaching on avoiding or dealing with these problems, you can manage to do good product discovery work in a remote employee environment.

CHAPTER
31

Onboarding

C ongratulations, you have now landed a competent person of character who is ready to start contributing as a member of one of your product teams.

Unfortunately for you, your work as a hiring manager is just getting started.

The first three months for a new member of the team are absolutely critical and will very likely set the tone for the new employee's tenure at your company.

Some helpful checkpoints along the way:

- *At the end of her first day.* Has she made at least one hopefully future friend on the team? Does she know what is expected of her?
- *At the end of her first week.* How was her first week? Has she had a chance to get to know personally every member of her product team?
- *After she receives her first paycheck.* It's normal for the new employee to do a subconscious assessment of the choice she made in joining your company.

- *After her first month*. At this point, the new employee has a fairly good idea of the company and her potential in it.
- *After her first 60 days*. Has she scored a public "win" that helps establish her value to the company?

Realize that many first impressions will be made—especially by senior leaders from across the company—and for many executives, there may be few opportunities to correct those first impressions if they are not positive.

No matter how competent the new employee is, there is always a ramp-up. Learning about the customers, the people, and workings of the company, the culture, the technology, and the industry are all critical to coming up to speed.

One of the first things you'll want to establish as the hiring manager is how open the new hire is to being coached. Most people are truly grateful to have a manager that is committed to helping them succeed. But there are some who can feel threatened or confused by this.

Some people have it in their heads that if they need to be coached, there must be something wrong with them, and maybe they are already at risk in their new job. I'm not a psychologist, but it's not hard to recognize when the new employee is behaving defensively or showing signs of insecurity, and to address it up front. I do this by sharing my own journey, and how people helped me all along the way.

One way or another, you need to establish a relationship based on trust. You're trusting that she will put in her best efforts, and she's trusting you will do everything you can to help her succeed.

As a hiring manager, I learned early on that when I invested in the onboarding of my new hires, it saved me countless hours of grief and damage control. In fact, some of my biggest regrets as a manager are the times I did not put in the necessary time and effort.

First, assess the new employee and use that assessment to create a coaching plan. Be sure to provide the time and opportunities to develop the necessary knowledge and skills, and then personally ensure the new employee is competent.

Beyond establishing competence, your focus during this onboarding should be on establishing solid relationships. First with you and with her product team, and very soon, with the company's executives and stakeholders. For product managers, that's primarily around gaining a deep knowledge of the customers and a deep knowledge of your business. Everything is built on this foundation.

For product managers, this typically includes a series of customer visits, with an extensive debrief on the learnings afterward. The debrief covers not only the customers, but the go-to-market mechanisms—especially sales and marketing—and how customer service is handled. The onboarding also includes time with the finance organization learning the critical KPIs—what they mean to the business and how they are calculated.

Whatever onboarding you decide on, I strongly encourage you to have deep exposure to true users and customers at the foundation. This applies to all members of the product team—including your engineers.

Once you believe the new employee has learned what is necessary, then personally introduce her to the key leaders and stakeholders—one at a time. Be sure to highlight the preparation the new person has done, and her desire to serve as a true partner in collaboration.

For at least the next several months, be sure to check in with these leaders and stakeholders to track how their experiences with the new employee are going, and any areas they'd like to see further developed.

Remember that, as a leader, you are only as good as your weakest employee. These people *are* your product.

APM Programs

I find that most of the strong tech product companies out there are always working to find more very strong product managers.

I have written many times in various ways about how critical it is to put very strong people in these roles, and I meet execs every week who tell me they need more.

One company that realized this a long time ago is Google. Their first product manager, Marissa Mayer, set a very high bar, and they have worked hard over the years to recruit and develop a very strong competency of product managers. Most people know that Google has many exceptionally strong engineers, but less known is how hard they have worked to develop a set of product managers and designers that are worthy of these engineers.

Very early on, they realized that strong product managers were in short supply, and one thing they did in response was to establish the APM (associate product manager) program.

Sometimes, this name causes confusion because in many companies outside of Silicon Valley—especially companies using feature teams—the term "associate product manager" refers not to this program, but rather to an *entry-level, junior* product manager. As you'll see, this program is nearly the opposite of that, so please don't let the name confuse you.

Google worked hard to find the absolute best and brightest, from both inside and outside the company. Entry to the APM program gives the lucky aspiring product manager entrance into a two-year coaching program to learn how to become an exceptional product manager and eventual product leader.

The purpose of the program is to take high-performing and/or high-potential individuals with a proven or growing track record in other areas (be that business or education) and coach them into very strong product managers.

Marissa gets most of the credit for this program, and she put countless hours into coaching promising product leaders. The program indeed produced some exceptional talent. Many of these people are behind Google's best products and services, and many have moved on to lead their own companies.

In the same spirit, I'm most proud of the product people I recruited and coached over the years, and I love that they are now all across our industry and leading many of the best product organizations in the world.

I was taught that as people managers and leaders, our most critical job is to develop our people.

So for medium and larger companies, I often encourage the company to set up an APM program for their very high-potential product managers.

Today, many of the top tech companies have APM programs, as the concept has spread far beyond Google to Facebook, Twitter, LinkedIn, Uber, Salesforce.com, Atlassian, and many more. Some

(continued)

(continued)

start the program each year with a new cohort of APMs. Others structure the program around a rotation so the APM can get exposed to multiple types of products. There's no single right way to set up these programs, but there are some principles I'd like to share:

First, you can only do this program if you have very strong and proven product leaders who are both willing and able to spend intense time coaching. Even if the leaders are at the vice president level, and they normally manage other managers, if these leaders are exceptional and believe in developing talent, then enlist them to participate directly in the coaching.

If you don't have these leaders, or they simply do not have the necessary bandwidth to provide the required intensity of coaching, then you can consider engaging with an external, proven product leader who is willing to provide this coaching for you. Give the person at least a year to demonstrate results.

Second, set a very high bar for acceptance into this program. Only accept people who are recognized as among your best minds and highest potential. The type of person that brings value to every conversation. The type of person that is driven to make things happen and get results.

Third, for everyone in this program, do a thorough assessment to identify the necessary areas of skills development. Update this assessment throughout the year.

Fourth, put an individualized, one- to two-year coaching plan in place to help these people reach their potential. They should be meeting 1:1 with a proven leader at least weekly.

Of course, the main way we learn how to create great products is by jumping in and discovering and delivering great products, so be sure to put these people right in the thick of it on a key product team. But again, you only want to do this if you are providing this person with intense and ongoing coaching.

There are dimensions to this program that you will want to set up in a way that is consistent with your company's culture, such as how visible and widely promoted the program is and the expectations you set with the members. I generally prefer to keep things low key. Let the people earn the respect of their peers. Keep this about merit.

I think it's worth mentioning that I have found this program to be a very effective way to improve diversity in the product organization. This is because, unlike most hiring, you're not selecting people into this program based on their *experience*. You're selecting them based on their *potential*.

The key is to realize that every tech product company needs strong product managers, and the leaders of the company must constantly seek them out and work hard to develop their most promising people to reach their full potential.

32

New Employee Bootcamp

S VPG partner Christian Idiodi has built a powerful reputation over the years for developing very strong product teams. In his past companies, he created his own new employee bootcamp that is an excellent example of coaching ordinary people into extraordinary teams. I asked Christian to describe his program here.

Hiring product people is hard—especially product managers, product designers, and tech leads.

The best product people in the world are working for companies that want to keep them. They're working on meaningful problems and creating innovative solutions.

In general, companies prefer to hire people who have had success at previous product companies. The thinking behind it goes something like, "Well if they've done well at that company, they'll do great here. They launched this great product at (fill in the blank with any reputable, big company), so surely they'll give us those same results."

The problem is this: product people don't start at a new company with everything they need to succeed, no matter how successful they've been in the past.

New-hire orientations, while they're great for helping a new employee feel welcomed and integrated into the organization, fall far short in preparing product people on some of the more important aspects of their role. Things like making hard decisions and gaining a high level of trust among peers.

For example, product managers need to be able to contribute a deep knowledge of the customer, the business, the industry, and their product. Their first day on the job, or even their first month, won't give them this type of knowledge unless they're very intentionally brought into the organization.

The onboarding of a product person will therefore set the parameters for her level of contribution and success in her role.

I created a New Employee Bootcamp to fill that gap and set product people up for success.

I started the program 10 years ago when I was a head of product and in charge of hiring and equipping the key product hires. I had seen a series of failed product people within the organization, and I realized that these hires had been completely capable for the job. But there was something missing between their capability and their success in the organization.

Seeing this problem, I considered the biggest problems product people were facing, along with what they needed to be successful:

- How are decisions made? How have they been made in the past?
- What is important to the company now? What are we working toward?
- How can I get people to trust me?
- What's the most important thing to do right now?

With these questions in mind, I created a five-day intensive bootcamp program for product people to participate in during their first week on the job.

Every day starts with a personal-growth component where product people look inward and prepare themselves for the work ahead.

They participate in exercises on communication, personality tests, personal skills, and build a career growth path for themselves. This focus on their own personal growth shows these new employees that we, the company, care about who they are and their growth. It also follows the principle of "put on your own oxygen mask before assisting other passengers." If we train our leaders to be healthy, the people who report to them have a better chance, too.

After personal growth, each day covers a different product training topic. We call this *Strategic Context*.

These are some of the most important topics that product people need to understand within the company.

On day 1, we talk about understanding the customer. And while most product people understand how to "understand the customer," we bring them through our own company history and put everything into context.

We share our vision, financial models, talk through our customer discovery, and who our customers have been in the past—and who we want them to be in the future. The rest of the week we talk through validation, building and prioritizing, learning and measuring, and going to market.

All of these topics are specific to the organization's goals and how they "get things done," with the context that gives the product person the background to really understand where she's coming into the story.

These topics might change based on what's important to your company and the values it holds, but the process of breaking them down—and giving the product person the space to explore—is important and can change the trajectory of her success.

Right after Strategic Context, we bring in a product person from the company who can speak to each topic and tell stories from her own personal experience. This step might seem small, but it's key to start establishing relationships and trust with other product people. These product people can speak directly to what it's like to work on a team, be responsible for customers, collaborate with stakeholders, and navigate an often-complex company environment.

After lunch, we enter the Product Workshop, where participants take what they learned in the morning and apply it practically, as if they were on the job.

We bring in the team members they'll be working with, and they have a safe space to practice with the guidance of the leadership. The learning curve to figuring out how others work is shortened and addressed up front, saving everyone time and confusion.

The Bootcamp reinforces a culture of learning and growth. When the product person leaves the Bootcamp she's not asking, "What do I do today?" She already knows the next, right thing to do. She's equipped to make decisions quickly and the relationships she's already built help her get to results faster.

This is how we empower product people—by providing them with the information they need to succeed and then trusting them to do the right thing.

Remember: we're not hiring smart product people to tell them what to do—we're hiring them to solve hard problems in ways our customers love, yet work for our business.

You have to invest in the product people, more than just a new-hire orientation packet.

Consider implementing a bootcamp to set them up for success and give meaning to the work they'll be doing.

33

Performance Reviews

I f it were up to me, the ritual of annual performance reviews would be entirely dispensed with.

However, we all have to pick our battles, and in most companies around the world, the drill is all about legal compliance and compensation administration. So, I've always just bitten the bullet and done what was necessary.

That said, it is absolutely critical that the hiring manager understand that the annual performance review should *never be the primary feedback tool*. If it is, then in my opinion you have utterly failed as a manager.

The annual review is far too little, far too late. Our primary feedback tool is the weekly 1:1, if not daily interactions. And please remember the primary purpose of the 1:1 is not for the manager, it is for the employee.

As such, there should *never* be any performance-related surprises in the annual review. If there are, you have failed.

The common case is a manager that is conflict-averse and avoids giving the constructive criticism that is so necessary. The manager eventually decides the person is not strong enough, discusses this with HR, and then HR forces the manager to document the issues in a performance review. The employee is then surprised and confused to learn she's not actually meeting expectations.

This is unfair to the employee, and in a great many cases, completely avoidable.

Whenever I have learned of this happening to one of the managers that worked for me, I considered it a serious performance problem of *the manager* and treated it as such. Usually this meant that I wanted to see the preparation notes for the weekly 1:1 going forward, and that I would also be discussing the performance issues with the employee directly (to ensure the feedback is making it to her).

And this situation also makes clear that not everyone is cut out to be a manager. The most basic skill required for a competent manager is the willingness and ability to provide honest, timely, and constructive feedback to employees.

It is also important to remember that some people don't take hints very well, and most of us have seen cases where the manager believes she has given negative feedback, but the employee claims to have not understood the seriousness or significance. To be clear, in this case, the manager should have made the issues *unmistakably* clear. If issues are being discussed weekly, even if the negative feedback was missed the first time, it should not be missed the next.

The bottom line when it comes to performance reviews is to do what is necessary for compliance, but make sure your primary feedback mechanism is your weekly 1:1.

34

Terminating

There's little question that the least fun part of being a people manager is dealing with terminations.

Of course, the best way to avoid terminations is to develop your skills in effective recruiting, interviewing, hiring, onboarding, and especially ongoing coaching. And you absolutely should.

However, there are always occasional situations where it is just not working out.

The first thing to realize is that you should not only consider the problem employee. You need to also consider the rest of the product team that is having to deal with the issues or carry the burden, as well as the message it sends to the product team, the broader product organization, and especially to the leaders and stakeholders by not correcting this problem.

There is a balance between being a compassionate employer and acting responsibly and promptly. This will partly be a function of your company's culture, and partly a function of the employment laws in your country.

Your partners in HR will help you understand and comply with the compliance-related responsibilities.

I have always drawn a distinction in my own mind about how I handle the two main situations when it comes to correcting hiring mistakes.

The first and most common situation is that the employee is simply not able to perform the job at the necessary level of competence, despite serious ongoing coaching. Normally, I will give sincere best efforts for three to six months, but if I can't coach the person to competence in that time, I will admit to myself that it is not working. And to be clear, I have been sharing the lack of progress with increasing urgency and clarity during our weekly 1:1s.

But sometimes it just doesn't work. I have always felt like it was partly my fault because I hired this person and should have been able to judge more accurately her ability to perform the job (or our company's fault if someone else was the hiring manager). In this case, I have always felt a responsibility to help the person find a more suitable position, either at our company or at another.

The second and thankfully less common situation is removing an employee that is toxic. By "toxic" I mean that there are some serious behavioral issues that damage trust in the organization and leave people feeling disrespected or worse.

What's difficult about these situations is that everyone has an occasional bad day or may be dealing with serious problems in their personal life. So you need to determine if this is a temporary situation or a chronic problem, and if the person has the willingness and ability to control her behavior.

But again, three to six months of trying to correct is about normal. If the problem persists, then it's time to move the focus to protecting the psychological safety of the rest of the team and organization.

In this case, I am not willing to try to find the person another job, at our company or at another, but I am honest with the person about their behavior and the impact it has on the trust and culture in the team.

What makes this second situation especially difficult is that often the toxic behavior comes along with some exceptionally strong skills, and the organization may be nervous about losing these skills. And, in truth, there may be a period of difficulty while others come up to speed.

But in every case, I've found that removing the toxic person was the right thing to do, and that others in the organization would rise to the occasion and the broader organization was grateful for the improvement in the workplace atmosphere.

I won't pretend here, dealing with hiring mistakes is never fun—I still remember the feeling in the pit of my stomach when I think back to the times I've had to terminate someone's employment. But it's truly essential if you're serious about creating a strong product organization.

CHAPTER
35

Promoting

While terminations might be my least-favorite aspect of staffing, there's no question that promotions are my favorite.

When I first became a people manager, I was taught that the most visible and tangible sign of success as a manager was when your people were promoted.

Nearly every company has career ladders, where people can progress in their careers from junior to more-senior roles. Most promotions happen within a job class (e.g., from an engineer to a senior engineer to a tech lead to a principal engineer).

But promotions can also cross job classes (e.g., from a senior product designer to a manager of product design).

This, of course, begins with understanding the career aspirations of your employees.

Some people want to continue as an individual contributor yet rise to very senior and well-respected levels of capability and responsibility. Others aspire to leadership positions, or in some cases, to one day start their own companies. And yet others aren't sure, so they want to be exposed to different options.

I have always truly enjoyed these career discussions, and once I know the person—and what she likes doing and what she's good at—I'm not shy about sharing what I think the various different opportunities are for her.

But whatever her career goals, I promise her that if she's willing to put in the effort, I'm willing to do my best to help her reach those goals. And, furthermore, it's my job to do that.

I like to give each person a clear path to her next career goal. I do that by performing an assessment of her current knowledge and skills against what is required for the new role.

That always generates a list of gaps, and then we discuss how she can learn and demonstrate the necessary skills. It can also be useful to have the employee do a self-assessment so that you can compare this with your own assessment.

Once she has demonstrated that she is now qualified for the new role, then I do everything I can to get her that promotion.

I'm always up front with the person that there may be others who have to approve a promotion, and there may not be immediate openings for a specific role, but that we can get her ready to take advantage of the opportunity when it comes.

But I also explain that the more skilled the person is, the more valuable she is to the company, so it's absolutely in all of our best interests for us to get her promoted.

One special case is worth calling out here, and that is when promoting an individual contributor to a people manager position. This is, of course, not just a more-senior position, but a fundamentally different job, with very different skills and talents necessary. And it's critical that the person understand what's required and that she want the role for the right reasons.

The main reason tech product companies have dual-track career ladders is because money is not a good reason to make this career change.

As a leader, there is nothing I am prouder of than when I see people I hired years ago go on to become exceptional leaders themselves.

As Tom Peters said, "Leaders don't create followers, they create more leaders."

Retention

I'll repeat the old saying, "People join a company, but leave their manager."

I (Marty) truly believe that this is true. I have done it myself (left because of a terrible manager) and have seen it happen to others countless times.

Some amount of attrition is normal and even healthy. Someone's spouse gets a major career opportunity elsewhere, or after several years with your company someone leaves to found their own startup, or someone decides to retire.

However, if the people you really don't want to lose are consistently leaving, this is a real sign of a potential problem in management.

I have always made it a point to do an exit interview with people that leave, even if they are several layers in the organization below me. I want to decide for myself why I think they're leaving, and I'm looking for feedback I can give the manager.

But, in my experience, those managers who are genuinely concerned about the careers of their employees, and who are constantly coaching and working to get them the promotions they deserve, rarely have retention issues. On the contrary, these people quickly gain a reputation in the company, and the problem is usually people wanting to transfer so they can work for them.

36

Leader Profile:
April Underwood

Path to Leadership

April studied information systems and business and then began her career as a developer. After a few years writing code, she joined Travelocity as a software engineer, where she was immediately put on the front lines of their partnerships with the internet heavyweights of the time: Yahoo! and AOL.

Through her work as an engineer, April began making connections between technology choices and business strategy, and found that product management was a role in which she could help align the two.

Through persistence in stating her desire to become a product manager, and her proficiency as a translator between engineers and businesspeople—both within Travelocity and with its partners—April landed her first PM role in 2005.

I first met April in 2007, after she had finished her MBA, an internship at Apple, and was broadening her leadership experience at Google in a technical, partner-facing organization.

After Google, April joined Twitter as a Product Manager on the Platform, and over the course of five years, saw the company grow from 150 to 4,000 employees. During that time, April's functional breadth expanded as she led not just PM teams, but also business development and product marketing teams. Her time at Twitter prepared her for more-senior leadership roles as she developed the ability to lead teams beyond her own personal area of functional expertise in product.

In 2015, April joined Slack as Head of Platform and quickly stepped up to run product as VP of Product, and ultimately CPO, over nearly four years of hypergrowth in revenue and employees. She oversaw platform and all aspects of the Slack product, as well as two of the critical functions that made Slack stand out among its enterprise software peers: design and research.

Now April invests in and advises startups with #Angels—the group she co-founded in 2015 with former Twitter colleagues.

Leadership in Action

April's career highlights the fact that there are many paths into product management, and an unlimited number of versions of the role itself.

In her own words:

Early in my career, in the aftermath of the dot-com bubble and geographically removed from Silicon Valley, I had one archetype of the product manager imprinted upon me: the business-minded MBA who is fairly removed from technical choices and engineering execution.

When I first expressed interest in moving into product management, I was told I needed an MBA to do so. Once I got accepted to business school, I also got what I'd wanted at the outset—the opportunity to move into a PM role at my then-employer, Travelocity.

I took the PM role, but also went on to get my MBA anyway. I graduated in 2007 to a vastly different landscape: the market had shifted, and there was an increased emphasis placed on PMs being strongly technical. I expected to be well-prepared given the fact I had been an engineer, but when I joined Google in 2007, I learned I could not become a PM because I lacked a computer science degree (a policy which has evolved since then). The goalposts kept moving on me.

In my last 13 years since then as a product leader, a few patterns have become clear to me:

The archetype of a product manager evolves with the needs of the market.

When the core driver of innovation and opportunity has been technical, then more-technical PMs have been in favor. When mobile emerged as the next frontier, PMs with design sensibility who could build apps which could overcome the low switching costs of an App Store were prized. When the innovation frontier shifted to operations (think transportation, real estate, hospitality, grocery delivery), we came full circle to value the business orientation necessary for a PM-as-a-general manager.

None of the different models for PM is categorically better, but any given one is probably better for a given role.

In my role at Slack, building a PM organization growing 5X over five years, I was intentional about what mattered most for each hire: the "flavor" of functional experience they had as PMs, the subject matter expertise they brought from the other products they'd built, or the company growth stages in which they'd worked. By forcing myself to decide what was most important to get right, I was able to narrow the candidate field and hire the right type of PM for each role.

Functional breadth is a prerequisite for moving beyond product leadership to company leadership.

The best product leaders are not just great at defining and building products—they understand that a product is only as good as a target customer's understanding of why they need it. That a platform is only useful if it's being used in ways which accrue value to the developers building on it as well as their customers. That products must be built within a set of constraints that preserve the health of the business.

These insights—the purviews of marketing, partnerships, finance, and so many other functions—are important inputs to building products.

Throughout my career, I have worn a variety of different functional hats—sometimes by choice, to learn a new skill set, and sometimes because the preferred PM "hat" was out of reach for reasons beyond my control.

Now, after having gained experience as a product executive, I realize that these sidesteps are actually my most valuable asset. They help me understand how to hire and develop leaders to fulfill a variety of roles. They help me build bridges across organizational lines. And they help me bear in mind that the product is always in service of the broader company mission—not the other way around.

Product Vision and Principles

STRATEGIC CONTEXT

COMPANY MISSION / OBJECTIVES / SCORECARD

PRODUCT VISION & PRINCIPLES

TEAM TOPOLOGY

PRODUCT STRATEGY

PRODUCT TEAMS

OBJECTIVES

DISCOVERY
DELIVERY

OBJECTIVES

DISCOVERY
DELIVERY

OBJECTIVES

DISCOVERY
DELIVERY

M ost companies have some sort of mission statement that sum-
marizes the purpose of the business (e.g., "organize the world's
information"), but a mission statement typically says nothing about
how we plan to deliver on this mission.

This is the critical role of the product vision.[1]

An inspiring and compelling product vision serves so many critical
purposes that it is hard to think of a more important or higher-leverage
product artifact:

- A good product vision keeps us *focused on the customer*.

- A good product vision serves as the *North Star* for the product
  organization so that we have a *common understanding* of what we
  are hoping to accomplish together.

- A good product vision *inspires ordinary people to create extraordinary
  products*.

- A good product vision provides us with *meaningful* work. A list of
  features on a roadmap is not meaningful. How you can positively
  impact the lives of users and customers is meaningful.

- A good product vision leverages relevant *industry trends* and technologies that we believe can help us solve problems for our customers in ways that are just now possible.

- A good product vision provides the engineering organization with
  enough clarity about what's coming in the next several years so
  they can ensure they have in place an *architecture* that can serve
  the need.

- The product vision is a primary driver of the *team topology*.

Because of these things, a strong product vision serves as one
of our most powerful *recruiting tools* for strong product people. It
also serves as one of our most powerful *evangelism tools* to enlist
the necessary help and support of colleagues from all across the
company—ranging from senior executives, to investors, to sales and
marketing staff.

---

[1] I discussed product vision in *INSPIRED*, but the perspective was from the point of view of
what a product team needed in order to make good decisions. In *EMPOWERED*, I discuss
product vision from the perspective of the product leaders.

Admittedly, a good product vision is also a bit of an art form, as fundamentally it is a persuasion tool. However, it's also important to not be too detailed or prescriptive, which runs the risk of product teams confusing the vision with a specification.

When done well, the product vision is compelling, inspiring, and empowering—leaving the product teams feeling excited to begin the hard work of making this vision a reality.

37

Creating a Compelling Vision

S o, what makes a strong and compelling product vision?

Customer-Centric

The product vision is one of our primary tools for keeping the organization truly focused on what the customer cares about.

Realize that we already have company objectives—typically describing how we want to grow the business and/or reduce operating costs—a company dashboard that shows us the various indicators of the health of the business, and team objectives that tell each product team what company or customer problems we need to solve.

So we generally know how our work is intended to benefit our company, but we also know that none of this will likely occur if we don't solve problems for the customer.

While we need to understand the impact on our company, we need to never forget that all of the benefits derive from providing real value to our customers.

I can't even begin to count the number of failed products I've seen that would have provided real benefits to the company, if only the product had managed to be valuable to actual customers.

When we tell the story of the product vision, we do so from the perspective of our users and customers. The idea is to demonstrate how their lives will improve in some meaningful way.

When I work with a company on their product vision, one of the very first things I do is find a very strong product designer to collaborate with. She may be a senior product designer, or she may be the leader of the design organization. Or if the product design organization does not yet have someone with sufficient experience, this is one of the rare cases I will encourage the product leader to engage with an experienced product design firm for the purpose of the product vision and creating what's known as a *visiontype* (described below).

Our job as the broader product organization then is to figure out how to deliver on the promise of the vision. This requires an intentional product strategy, and years of continuous discovery and delivery.

North Star

The product vision, done well, serves as the *North Star* for the product organization.

Just as the North Star can guide people to their destination even when they're scattered across the globe, the product vision provides this purpose for all of the product teams, no matter where they are in the organization, or on what piece of the larger product they're working.

As soon as a company has grown to the point where there are multiple product teams—supporting many customers with their constant needs—it is very easy for each product team to get caught up in their own problems and their own work, losing sight of the overarching goal.

The product vision represents the *common goal* and constantly reminds us of the larger purpose. For example, explaining how we'll address global warming by providing the world's first mass-market electric cars.

Your team may be responsible for one component of the product vision, but we need each and every product team to understand the bigger picture:

- Ultimately, what is the endgame?
- How does the work of my team contribute to this larger whole?

Be sure that every member of your product teams understands the answers to these two critical questions.

And just to be explicit, it makes no sense for each product team to have their own product vision. That would totally miss the point. The product vision is meant to be the *common* goal.

Scope and Timeframe

Many companies make the mistake of describing a product vision that is not ambitious or meaningful enough. This is especially true when the product vision reads more like a roadmap of features.

The product vision stands little chance of being perceived as compelling or meaningful if the team thinks it's just a matter of a few features.

The product vision describes *the future you are trying to create*. In what ways will you *improve the lives of your customers*?

You are not trying to explain how you will get there—that is to come from the product strategy and the product discovery work. For now, we are just trying to describe what the end state is and why it is so desirable.

Your roadmap is just a set of features and projects that you believe *might* help you get there.

Normally, the timeframe for the product vision is between 3 and 10 years out. Very complex products and devices are at the longer end of this range.

Leveraging Industry Trends

There are always emerging trends, typically enabled by new technology.

There are also fads that get some hype for a while, then fade away.

As product leaders, you need to decide which are trends and which are fads and, most important, which trends have the opportunity to substantially help you deliver innovative solutions for your customers.

Most of the time, our product vision leverages one or more major industry trends.

Examples of major technology trends as of this writing include mobile, cloud computing, big data, machine learning, augmented reality, internet of things, edge computing, and consumerization of the enterprise.

Note that industry trends are not limited to technology trends. There are other trends that are critically important, such as changing behaviors of groups of users, and changing buying patterns.

I can only guess at what the major trends will be in 5 or 10 years, but I'm certain there will be several additions to this list.

Interestingly, I am also quite confident that most if not all of this list of current trends will still be relevant in 5 or 10 years. The real trends are not fleeting.

Remember that customers don't care about our technology—they care about how well we solve their problems. So, while we may make a bet on specific technologies, we must always keep in mind the purpose of that technology is to solve problems in ways that customers love.

Who Owns the Product Vision?

The head of product is responsible for ensuring the organization has a compelling product vision, as well as the product strategy that can deliver on that product vision.

That said, the reality is more nuanced than that.

(continued)

(continued)

First, in order to come up with a compelling product vision, the head of product will need to work very closely with the head of design and the head of technology.

The product vision is a critical collaboration between the customer experience, the enabling technologies, and the needs of the business. It will likely require the talents and best efforts of all three.

Second, to succeed, the CEO (or GM for a business unit in a very large organization) is going to need to feel a very real sense of ownership of this product vision.

In many startups, the CEO is the effective head of product, so this happens naturally. But in other companies, the head of product needs to involve the CEO enough that she feels a true connection to this vision.

Realize that the CEO will need to "sell" this vision literally thousands of times—to investors, to the press, to other business leaders, and to countless prospective customers—and she is effectively putting her job and reputation on the line each time.

That doesn't mean the CEO needs to create the product vision, but she does need to be included and the product leader needs to ensure her concerns are addressed. Good product leaders are skilled at helping others feel shared ownership.

38

Sharing the Product Vision

A compelling product vision is the gift that keeps on giving.

Communicating the Product Vision

It's worth investing some real time and effort into the best way to communicate the product vision. Remember that the vision's purpose is to inspire. PowerPoint presentations rarely inspire anyone.

The minimum is typically to create a *visiontype*, and we often produce a video of this visiontype. A visiontype is a conceptual prototype—a high-fidelity user prototype (realistic looking, but completely smoke and mirrors—and because of that, it is very easy to create, and most important, not constrained by what we know how to build).

The difference between a high-fidelity user prototype used as a visiontype, and a high-fidelity user prototype used in product discovery, is the scope of what's covered by the prototype.

The visiontype describes the world once the vision is a reality—that may be 3 years or 10 years in the future.

The product discovery prototype describes the new feature or experience for something we will likely build in the coming weeks.

Once you have this visiontype, you can show it (demo it) to anyone you like. But many companies today are taking a little extra time and effort and producing a scripted video designed to show off the vision-type in the best light possible.

This may mean showing how different types of users would experience the product, and leveraging the emotional power of music and a thoughtful script to help increase the impact.

Another effective way to communicate a product vision is with storyboarding, much like what is done to create and share an outline of a movie.

As with a video showing off a visiontype, a storyboard focuses on the emotion and the customer experience and not on the details.

Because this is about communicating a product vision, and because the product vision is meant to be told from the users' perspective, your product designers will need to play a key role—both in crafting the experience and in determining the best way to communicate that experience.

Validating the Product Vision

In *INSPIRED*, I explored in detail about how we can use modern product discovery techniques to quickly validate product ideas—to decide if they are worth building.

A common question I've heard since then is this: Can we use these techniques to validate our *product vision*?

It's a little tricky to explain, but very important to understand.

The answer is both yes and no.

We can validate the *demand* for the vision. In other words, if the vision was available today, do people have the problems we think they have? Are the problems serious enough, and their current options weak enough, that they're open to new solutions?

What we can't validate is the *solution*. That's simply because we don't yet know the solution. Most likely, it will take us years of work to discover the components of the solution.

And, of course, while it's good to know we are working on a worthy problem, that's not enough. People will only buy if they believe we have solved the problem well enough to get them to switch.

This is why we explain that pursuing a product vision is largely a leap of faith. We're betting on ourselves; that we'll be able to discover a solution that delivers on the promise of the vision.

Product Vision as a Recruiting Tool

Strong product people want to work on something meaningful. They want to work on something larger than themselves. They want to be *missionaries* and not *mercenaries*.

So, while you can talk about nice employee benefits and show the candidate the foosball table, the best product people care more about your product vision than anything else.

We discussed in an earlier chapter how critical it is to invest heavily in staffing competent product managers, product designers, and engineers.

As a leader, this is one of your most powerful tools. The vision needs to be compelling, and as a leader responsible for recruiting staff, you need to be persuasive.

Product Vision as an Evangelism Tool

It is not just potential employees that you need to persuade.

Your company's executives, investors, stakeholders, sales and marketing staff, customer service and customer success staff, and key influencers from across the company and beyond—you need all of these people to understand the future you are trying to create.

Why? Because in ways large and small, they will all need to help for your vision to reach its full potential.

One other critical point, especially for product leaders. Evangelism is something that is never finished. You need to plan on delivering the message multiple times, to the same people, and you need to expect that just because someone is convinced one day, this does not mean they will be convinced the next.

Sharing Product Vision vs. Roadmaps

In companies with a direct sales force, which are generally there to sell to larger businesses, it is not unusual for the sales force to be asked to share product roadmaps with current or prospective customers.

It's important to understand where this is coming from. These customers or prospective customers are making a significant bet on your company. They know they are not just buying your offering today—they are buying your offering over time, usually for many years. So it's not in the least unreasonable for them to want to make sure that you are heading in the same direction that they believe they need to go.

So, the standard way of requesting that is to ask to see the product roadmap, because that's usually the only option.

The problem with this, as experienced product people know, is that many if not most of the specific product features that we think will provide value end up not solving the underlying problem and therefore do not provide the necessary value. So spending the time to build and release a feature that does not solve the problem is the waste that we are trying hard to avoid.

Which is why we would much rather share the product vision than a product roadmap.

Though the customers don't generally use this terminology, the product vision is usually what they're hungry for.

From your point of view, we would much rather share a product vision than a product roadmap because it is a near certainty that, based on what you learn, you will want to change your roadmap often. But if a customer has made a purchase decision based on a promised feature or capability in a roadmap, it becomes much harder to change the tactics.

It is true that some companies consider the product vision to be proprietary and don't want to share it, but I much prefer to share the vision rather than a roadmap. It in fact helps us to validate the vision.

It's also true that many companies are not allowed to share a product roadmap because it can and will be interpreted as a forward-looking statement, and if you do not deliver on the promised features, there could be legal ramifications.

There are of course cases where you'll get specific questions, such as: "We use Salesforce.com here, and before we buy, can you tell us if and when your solution will integrate with their platform?" It's not hard to see how that would be a reasonable question. Whether or not you integrate would be a strategic product decision, which you could answer once you understand the nature and purpose of the integration they're looking for, and whether you believe it is important for your general offering and not just a one-off special request. The timing question, if you believe it's required, would be treated as a *high-integrity commitment*, which is described in detail in Part VII.

Remember: stubborn on vision, but flexible on details. Sharing the vision is fine, but sharing a roadmap is very dangerous.

Product Vision and Architecture

So much derives from the product vision.

The engineering organization needs the product vision so that they can ensure that the architectural decisions they make will serve the needs of that product vision.

Note that it's not necessary, or even usually desirable, for the engineers to build out in one major effort the full architecture that is necessary for the product vision. But it is essential that the engineers know what the endgame is so they can make good choices along the way and avoid having to reengineer, possibly even multiple times.

(continued)

(continued)

For example, the product vision may imply that the product eventually needs to be able to make highly accurate predictions about how to personalize a user's experience. Even though machine-learning capabilities may not be an immediate need, simply knowing this is coming will have real implications for how the engineering team architects the product.

Similarly, the team topology (described in Part V) is heavily impacted by the product vision and the architecture, especially for platform teams that encapsulate the underlying services.

A product architecture informed by vision becomes especially critical in organizations suffering from serious technical debt.

Few things frustrate me more than an organization—struggling with serious technical debt—that finally generates the leadership support and funding to pursue a significant re-platforming effort, yet does not have a product vision on which to base the new platform architecture. So the engineering organization is forced to make guesses about what will be needed, or else just build a new platform capable of sustaining what was built over the prior years, rather than what will be needed in the coming years.

39

Product Principles and Ethics

Product principles complement the product vision by stating the values and beliefs that are intended to inform the many product decisions that will need to be made.

When we empower product teams, we are giving them problems to solve, and we are giving them the context required to make good decisions. The product vision is a major part of that context, but there will always be issues that arise during the product discovery and delivery work.

A few of these issues will be major enough that the product team will want to escalate them to a broader group of product leaders and impacted stakeholders. But for the majority of normal product decisions, we can provide the team with the information they need. The product principles play a major role in this.

So many decisions revolve around trade-offs, and the product principles help to illuminate the values we prioritize when we make these trade-offs.

The product team needs to understand these principles and the reasoning behind each one.

As a very common example, in most products, there are often trade-offs between ease of use and security. Clearly both ease of use and security are important benefits for users, and it's also true that these two goals are not always at odds. But when these goals *are* at odds, this is where product principles can help. To continue with the example, this conflict often shows up when focused on rapid growth.

If the company is focused on growth, the teams will likely invest heavily in ease of use and may in fact downgrade the importance of security in order to remove friction.

It is not hard for the product leaders to anticipate that many product teams will face this sort of trade-off decision, and while it's impossible to anticipate every situation, it is not impossible to consider and then state the important principles.

Decisions related to ethics are another good example. While we can't anticipate every situation where ethics may be an issue, we can discuss the principles we believe are important when it comes to ethics.

Suppose a product solution provides real value for one group of users when used as intended, but the team realizes that if the product were to be used maliciously, it could hurt in some way another group of users. What are the team's responsibilities in terms of preventing unintended use?

As the product leaders create the product vision, I encourage them to also prepare a set of product principles to complement the vision, and to think through and provide as much guidance to the product teams regarding ethics as possible.[1]

---

[1] Product principles are discussed in more depth in *INSPIRED: How To Create Products Customers Love*. Product teams often tell me that the product principles are the part of the strategic context that they use most often in their daily discovery work, and these principles and the topic of ethics in particular are increasingly important with the advent of new technologies—especially related to machine learning.

40

Leader Profile:
Audrey Crane

Path to Leadership

I first met Audrey in 1996 at Netscape, where she was, even then, establishing a reputation as someone very smart who knew how to get things done. I remember being struck by her unusual mind, and she shared with me that in college she had studied pure mathematics and theater.

Audrey was working at the nexus of product and design when much of the internet was just emerging.

She was very fortunate to be able to learn from one of the pioneers of modern product design, Hugh Dubberly, when Hugh ran design for Netscape (before that, Hugh ran design for Apple).

After Netscape, Audrey joined Hugh's design firm, getting a front-row seat on many of the industry's most difficult design challenges.

For the past decade, Audrey has been a partner at the Design-Map design firm where she's hired, coached, and worked with several hundred product designers over the years. She has helped in the design of literally hundreds of applications of all types.

Audrey recently published the book *What CEOs Need to Know about Design*.[1]

Leadership in Action

Audrey's leadership style is best explained in her own words:

My earliest experiences managing and being managed were in theater, and much of my management style grew out of that.

Most people can't even start summer jobs until they're 15 or so, but I started acting in plays when I was around 10 years old, and continued through middle school, high school, a bachelor's degree, and several years after graduating—until I found design at Netscape.

Don't get me wrong, it was far from being a career, but I spent many, many hours on stage, in the costume shop, backstage, and even doing some directing. I'm certain it informed my approach to leadership.

The Theater Analogy

Some of the basic tenets of a theater production transfer nicely to the workplace. Of course, there is a team of people working toward a common goal. They're selected for their experience, skill, and potential, as well as their ability to work well with other people on the team.

---

[1] Audrey Crane, *What CEOs Need to Know about Design* (New York: Sense & Respond Press, 2019).

The Vision

Especially because the team has such diverse skills (actors, but also lighting and set and sound and costume designers, dressers, stage managers, and on and on), a director's job is to set a shared goal and a vision for the future.

That goal setting certainly has artistic aspirations, but it's also strategic and even pragmatic: What will an audience respond to? What kinds of costumes and sets can we afford? How many actors? What kind of production will pack the house?

Similarly, I try to set a vision, and to make my goals explicit—collaborating on goals before firming them up for myself and the team.

I love this kind of big-picture puzzle solving, and it's my favorite thing to do with teams—gauge and clarify constraints, weigh goals across an organization and with customers, assess capabilities, and create a vision for how we solve for all these things.

It's Not About You

A director casts an actor for a specific role because she believes that the way that particular person will play the part will be great. There is a very old, very firm rule in directing: *no line readings*. A line reading is when the director says the actor's lines to her in the hopes of getting the actor to mimic them.

This is a *huge* no-no and implies that either the director isn't skilled enough to get the performance she wants out of the actor, or that the best the actor has to offer is her ability to mimic the director. This is a limited example, but imagine if everyone on the cast and crew was limited by the best the director could do. It'd be a pretty weak show.

Along these lines, cast and crew trust the director to see the whole and make it great. If they're willing to go out on a limb to trust the director, then it follows that the director must take responsibility if something goes sideways. At the same time, the director will not be on stage for the curtain call (usually). This take-the-blame, give-the-credit philosophy isn't news in management style, but theater illustrates it nicely.

Bring Their Best

Given that goal, a director's highest responsibility is to *bring to bear the best of what each team member has to offer* in service of the shared goal. Rarely is the director the most highly skilled at any of the jobs that others on her team do. Of course, she must be knowledgeable so that she can appreciate, support, and grow each person on the team, but she isn't the best, and in some ways, that's the point.

Similarly, as a manager, I am certain that every person on my team is better at a great many things than I am. I'm not trying to get them to do what I want them to do, and definitely not to do things exactly the way I'd do them. Rather I'm looking for what they're passionate at, brilliant at, nascently savant at, and then organizing a team's worth of brilliance toward a common, shared goal that supports the larger goals of the business and the business's customers.

The most rewarding experiences of my career have been identifying talent and aptitude in people who weren't aware of it themselves, and then convincing them that they're great at whatever the thing is.

And working with a team—all operating in ways that they are passionate about or excel at—means being part of something so much greater than the strengths of any one individual person. Those teams are transformational, both in terms of how it feels to belong to one, and what they can accomplish.

In that vein, as an employee I have been most inspired by working for managers like Marty and Hugh Dubberly (and thank my lucky stars that I had that opportunity). One of the things they have in common is the way they inspire greatness. They were a little bit terrifying to work for, for the same reason: they both believed in me in specific ways and to a degree that I frankly didn't believe in myself. But I had so much respect, admiration, and love for them that I was going to do everything I could possibly do to live up to their expectations, however misplaced I thought they were at the time!

Critique

In both theater and film, a director will "give notes" regularly. The cadence might be hourly, per scene, or per performance, but giving constructive feedback—whether it's "That was great, do more of it," or,

"Totally confused by your choice there"—is a given in any relationship with a director. Mutual respect and collaboration demand clear, direct feedback.

Celebration

The wonderful thing about theater and film is that celebrations are built in. Whether it's opening night, closing night, or wrap parties, everyone takes a minute to step back and consider what they've accomplished together. I think we don't take enough opportunities to celebrate in business, and I look for ways large and small that individuals and teams can be honored.

As a leader, there's nothing better than assembling a talented cast, providing them a story they can get excited about, coaching them to reach their potential, and watching them create something special together.

Team Topology

STRATEGIC CONTEXT

COMPANY MISSION / OBJECTIVES / SCORECARD

PRODUCT VISION & PRINCIPLES

TEAM TOPOLOGY

PRODUCT STRATEGY

PRODUCT TEAMS

OBJECTIVES

OBJECTIVES

OBJECTIVES

DISCOVERY
DELIVERY

DISCOVERY
DELIVERY

DISCOVERY
DELIVERY

M ost technology products today are large and complicated. Though there are exceptions, it's rare that an entire product will be developed by a single product team. Most products require many teams working together—dozens or even hundreds.

This means that every product organization must deal with the question of how to structure their product teams in order to best divide the work.

I've written about this topic of structuring and scoping product teams before, including in *INSPIRED*.

However, because this topic relates so strongly to the level of empowerment, in this series of chapters I want to go deeper.

I've started referring to this topic of team scoping as *team topology*.[1] I like this term because it captures the idea of an arrangement of constituent parts in a larger system.

A product organization's team topology answers questions such as:

- How many product teams should our organization have?
- What is the scope of responsibility of each team?
- What are the skills required for each team, and how many of each skill?
- What are the dependencies between the teams?

More generally, the topology helps answer the question of *how a company should organize its product people into teams to best enable them to do great work*.

If you are a product leader, establishing an effective team topology is one of your key responsibilities. It's also one of the most complex because there are so many factors to consider. This has always been true, but with the rapid rise of remote employees, there is another layer of complexity impacting the topology.

---

[1] The term was coined by Matthew Skelton and Manuel Pais in their book, *Team Topologies: Organizing Business and Technology Teams for Fast Flow* (Portland, OR: IT Revolution, 2019).

First and foremost, your topology choices should be guided by principles that support team *empowerment*.

These include giving teams real *ownership* of the space of problems they will be responsible for, providing *autonomy* in their ability to deliver the solutions to the problems they're asked to solve, and *alignment* with various aspects of the company's customers, business, and technology.

Alignment itself is complex and requires reconciling the scope of individual teams with the broader context of business goals, types of customers, organizational reporting structure, technology architecture, and product vision.

Another important consideration is the number and nature of the dependencies between product teams. Every topology creates its own set of dependencies between product teams, and leaders must consider the trade-offs.

Finally, even though we work hard to keep teams stable and durable, leaders must consider that the team topology will need to evolve over time as the needs and circumstances change.

One practical point to keep in mind as you consider the points in the chapters that follow: The team topology you choose needs to be a decision made by the leaders of product and design, and the leaders of engineering, working together. The best topology will balance the needs of these key product leaders.

In the next several chapters, we'll explore these considerations and how they relate to empowerment. We'll also describe common patterns for designing team topologies and when to use them.

41

Optimizing for Empowerment

E arly in this book, we introduced the concept of *team topology* to refer to the way we organize our people into teams to best enable them to do great work.

Because team topology defines the boundaries between teams and establishes the scope of problems each team will consider, it's one of the most important decisions faced by product leaders.

Still, many companies don't give this decision the thought it needs.

Too often, team topology happens organically by following the path of least resistance. It may mirror an existing organizational chart or engineering skill set grouping, or it may track with the operational responsibilities of some business owner or stakeholder.

While these factors may sometimes be a good way to set boundaries between particular teams, that decision should be made intentionally after considering a wide range of factors. No topology decision should be made just because it's easy.

In many cases, the team topology was set years earlier, and people are reluctant to change the structure. What started off as a rational grouping is now creating unnecessary dependencies or complications that work against team empowerment. Here, leaders may need to make hard decisions to restructure all or part of their topology.

The bottom line is that, if you are a product leader, the empowerment of your company's product teams is greatly impacted by your topology choices.

Optimizing for empowerment requires balancing three interrelated goals: *ownership, autonomy,* and *alignment.*

Ownership

Ownership is bigger than just the team's objectives. It sets the scope of each team's full responsibilities around functionality, experience, quality, performance, and technical debt. Teams are expected to make the necessary trade-offs to best address the work that fits into their scope of ownership.

Empowerment improves when each product team has something *meaningful* that they are responsible for.

When a team has a very narrow scope of responsibility, its members can find it hard to stay motivated. They don't understand how their work relates to the broader business goals, and they can feel like a small cog in a big wheel.

By contrast, a team that sees itself as responsible for a meaningful problem is inspired by their connection to the larger cause. They have more pride of ownership.

In most cases, a larger scope of ownership is better for empowerment, but empowerment can also suffer when the scope of responsibility is too broad for a team's size and skill set.

For example, consider a team that has ownership of a product experience but also requires technical knowledge of one or more complex systems just to make basic changes. Such a team may struggle to gain the depth of understanding they need to innovate in their area of ownership. This high level of *cognitive load* works against the empowerment of the team.

Empowerment doesn't just depend on the *scope* of ownership—it also requires *clarity* of ownership. When teams are unclear on which work applies to them, their empowerment is undermined. While you should expect that there will always be occasional cases where ownership of work is ambiguous, a good topology should resolve more ownership questions than it raises.

Autonomy

Autonomy is a powerful concept, yet is often misunderstood by leadership and product teams alike.

It does *not* mean that a team should never have dependencies on other product teams. Nor does it mean that a team is allowed to go off and pursue whatever it likes.

Autonomy *does* mean that when we give teams problems to solve, they have enough control so that they can solve the problem in the best possible way that they see fit. A topology that results in too many dependencies can make this difficult.

We expect teams to use the tools of product discovery to explore different options and approaches before committing to a solution. And we trust the decisions they make because we know the team is in the best position to make them.

Every team topology will require some sort of inter-team dependencies, but an empowering team topology is one that minimizes these dependencies.

For example, a topology that divides teams strictly by technology subsystems makes it difficult for any single team to figure out a holistic solution to a real customer problem.

Ultimately, empowering teams is about enabling them to figure out the best way to achieve the necessary business *outcomes*. Team autonomy contributes to this.

Alignment

Alignment refers to how well the boundaries between teams track with other aspects of the strategic context.

When alignment is high, teams generally have fewer dependencies to get things done. They can make faster decisions and are more connected with business-level outcomes.

In short, when alignment is high, empowerment is improved.

Alignment is typically the most complicated aspect of topology because there are so many dimensions to consider. The two most significant of these are the architecture and the business.

Let's first consider alignment with the architecture. Ideally, the architecture is based on the product vision, as the job of the architecture is to *enable* the product vision.

If that's the case, a topology that aligns with technical architecture will also be naturally aligned with the product vision. Teams can own a meaningful scope and can be given autonomy to make significant product decisions.

However, in companies with large amounts of technical debt and/or legacy systems, teams may not be aligned with the architecture. Their work is cluttered with dependencies and complexity. Even simple tasks can take a long time, if they're even feasible at all.

Alignment with the business includes how the product team relates to the organization—for example, to different business units, different go-to-market strategies, different customer types, or different market segments.

We'll explore the alignment topic in more depth in the upcoming chapters.

Keep in mind that there will never be a single "perfect" team topology for your organization.

There are many trade-offs to consider, but the overarching objective is to optimize for empowerment. The best way to do this is through driving ownership, autonomy, and alignment.

CHAPTER

42

Team Types

S VPG has had the opportunity to observe and advise on the team topology of hundreds of tech companies.

While every situation truly is unique when it comes to topology, there are some important best practices that can help you optimize your topology for empowerment.

In this chapter we consider the two fundamental *types* of product teams: *platform teams*, which manage services so they can be easily leveraged by other teams, and *experience teams*, which are responsible for how the product value is exposed to users and customers.

It's important to emphasize that any topology must consider both the underlying technology architecture as well as the broader strategic context (including the business objectives, product vision, strategy, etc.) of the product.

This means that it's essential that product and engineering leadership must determine the topology *together*.

Platform Teams

Platform teams provide leverage because they allow for common services to be implemented once but used in many places. Examples of this include:

- A platform team that is responsible for shared services such as authentication or authorization
- A platform team that is responsible for maintaining a library of reusable interface components
- A platform team that is responsible for providing tools to developers for test and release automation

Platform teams also allow for managing complexity because they can encapsulate particularly difficult or specialized areas of the product. Examples of this include:

- A platform team that creates an abstraction for integration with a legacy system
- A platform team that manages payment processing
- A platform team that manages a highly specialized tax calculation

Your end customers—and even your executives and stakeholders—may not have any direct visibility into the work performed by your platform teams, but don't think these teams aren't important.

In fact, in many of the top product organizations, the best engineers in the company are asked to work on platform teams because of the leverage and importance.

In a small company, the platform may be provided by a single platform team. In many of the large, top tech companies, as many as half of the product teams are *platform* teams.

Moreover, platforms reduce the *cognitive load* for experience teams.

These experience teams are able to use platform services without having to understand how they are implemented. Instead, they can focus their energy on the customer or business problems they are working to solve.

Experience Teams

Experience teams are responsible for how the product is experienced by users in the form of apps, UIs, solutions, or journeys.

Users may be customers who buy your product, or (in the case of B2B products) they may be the employees of those customers. Whatever the case, if a product team is working on the experience for anyone who is part of the company's customers—including consumers—this is called a *customer-facing experience team.*

Users may also be internal to your company itself but are critically important for delivering the necessary customer experience.

Examples of these types of users are customer service agents or in-store associates. If a product team is working on a product experience for these types of internal employees, this is called a *customer-enabling experience team.*

Whether a team is customer-*facing* or customer-*enabling*, a true experience team will have a direct impact on our customers if its product goes down. For example, if an internal agent can't resolve a customer's question or request because their system is down, we know this is a true product experience.

As with platforms, a product experience may be handled by a single team or divided across several teams. For example, experiences may be divided into teams by user type, by market or segment, by the step in a customer's journey, or by any number of other ways (more on this in Chapter 44 on empowering experience teams).

In too many companies, the topology is defined such that each experience team owns only a very small part of the end-to-end experience. In this situation, each team struggles to feel like they can make an impact without coordinating with every other team, even for small changes.

By contrast, experience teams are most empowered when they are given as much *end-to-end responsibility* as possible. Such teams have a meaningful sense of ownership, more autonomy, and it's easier for them to see their impact on solving customer problems and achieving business results.

Many strong companies have found that a rich platform is a powerful tool for enabling a broader (end-to-end) scope of ownership for the experience teams.

Platform teams reduce the load required to use the underlying technology, creating cognitive capacity for experience teams to own more aspects of the customer problems.

CHAPTER

43

Empowering Platform Teams

In the previous chapter, I introduced the two main types of product teams and described how platform teams create leverage and encapsulate complexity for experience teams.

Platform teams raise the level of empowerment for other teams by abstracting away the underlying complexity of the services and the architecture.

The topic of empowerment for platform teams is always a little tricky. That's because, while the purpose of an experience team is to solve problems for users and customers, the purpose of a platform team is really *to enable the experience teams to better solve problems for their customers*. So, the contribution of a platform team is indirect.

To understand how this impacts platform teams, it helps to separate the two types of work that all product teams—platform and experience teams alike—must do.

On the one hand, they are moving the purpose of their team forward. That's their main work, and we'll come back to that in a minute.

However, every product team also has some amount of what we call "keep-the-lights-on" obligations.[1]

This is the daily work necessary to keep the business running. Things like fixing critical bugs, addressing performance issues, and adding critical capabilities for nonnegotiable things that come up, such as compliance issues.

It is true that platform teams tend to have more of these keep-the-lights-on items than the average experience team, and that's because of the nature of the work involved in enabling the teams that depend on them.

This might be 10 percent of the platform team's work, or it might be closer to half of the work.

So, separating out the keep-the-lights-on work, there are two main ways that platform teams are empowered to move the platform forward: shared team objectives and platform-as-a-product objectives.

Shared Team Objectives

The most common way for a strong platform team to pursue major work is through shared team objectives. With shared team objectives, the platform team has the same objective as one or more experience teams.

We will discuss the mechanics of shared team objectives in Chapter 57, Collaboration, but for now it's sufficient to say that the teams work together to discover and develop the solution.

Sometimes the collaboration is very deep, essentially requiring the teams to work together closely, almost as one team.

For example, consider a content management system (CMS) product, and let's suppose you have a platform team that manages backend storage and API access to content, and an experience team that manages the user-facing content workflow. Suppose further that, so far, the CMS system works with image content, but because of a new market expansion strategy, it needs to now support video content.

---

[1] Some companies call this "BAU," for "business as usual," but I have never liked that term because too many companies think that's all a product team does.

Here, our platform team and experience team may have a shared team objective to enable video. The two must work together very closely to determine the appropriate experience as well as how it will be implemented.

In other cases, the collaboration can be more segmented. The platform team and experience team may be able to define an API that represents a form of contract between the platform team and the experience team, and then each team is able to work largely independently to complete their work.

For example, an e-commerce company may be adding a new payment type. A platform team manages all payment complexity and exposes it to experience teams as an API. The product team responsible for the checkout experience creates the user-facing flows, while the platform team implements the integration with the backend payment processes. The two teams come together for testing and delivery.

Whether the collaboration is deep or segmented, the important thing is that the platform team has the same strategic context and goal as the experience team. They are connected as to why the work is important, and what it means for the business.

Platform-as-a-Product Objectives

For some companies, their products *are* platforms. What they sell are APIs that allow their customers and users (usually developers) to build on those capabilities. We call these *external* platforms.

In this case, the platform *is* the product, and it is treated as such. The customers and users may be developers rather than consumers, but it's a true product nevertheless.

On a related note, an emerging trend is that a growing number of companies are working to manage their *internal* platforms more like *external* platform products.

With these platform products, it's normal to find objectives looking much as for experience products—growing the number of customers, getting customers to adopt the capabilities, or better monetize the customers (in the case of external platforms).

Just as with any product team, experience, or platform, if we had a major quality issue or performance issue or developer-experience issue, rather than just consider this part of normal keep-the-lights-on work, we could elevate this to a team objective.

The bottom line is that, when it comes to empowering platform teams, if you separate in your mind the normal keep-the-lights-on work from the major work to move the platform forward, then the team objectives and the level of empowerment are comparable to experience teams.

44

Empowering Experience Teams

A s we described earlier, experience teams are responsible for how the product value is perceived by the actual users or customers.

A key point was that experience teams are most empowered when they are given as much end-to-end responsibility as possible.

This is more likely to happen when the scope of ownership for each team follows other natural patterns of the business such as the sales channel, market segment, or user type.

More often than not, this means *creating a topology that is aligned by customer*.

Here are some examples of alignment by customer:

- By user type or persona (e.g., Riders Team, Drivers Team)
- By a market segment (e.g., Electronics Team, Fashion Team)
- By customer journey (e.g., Onboarding Team, Retention Team)
- By sales channel (e.g., Self-Service Team, Direct Sales Team)

- By business KPI (e.g., New-User Growth Team, Conversion Team)
- By geography (e.g., North America Team, Asia Pacific Team)

This alignment means that experience teams have areas of ownership that match the outcomes that the business needs. There is little required translation between business outcomes and product work, and the teams can be given the autonomy to solve business problems directly.

Aligning by customer means different things for different types of products. What follows are some examples of alignment. This is by no means an exhaustive list, and these are not the only ways to organize the experience team topology for the cases mentioned. All that said, these are some common patterns that have proven effective and might be applicable for your own topology.

Media Product

For magazines, news sites, or video-on-demand services, experience teams can be organized by content section or sub-publication.

All content management and common capabilities are handled by platform teams that provide generalized services to a set of experience teams (these may constitute the majority of the product staff).

Each experience team then covers the end-to-end needs for each media category (e.g., sports, local news, weather) or brand. In some cases, several similar categories may be covered by a single team, and larger or more specialized experiences would have their own teams.

This approach helps ensure that needs of different types of customers are met. It also aligns the experience teams with the different per-category business goals and go-to-market strategies that are usually common in these companies.

E-Commerce Product

E-commerce can follow a similar pattern to media products, especially when the shopping experience differs significantly by category (e.g., auto parts vs. tickets to events vs. jewelry).

Again, the product is built upon a rich platform of common services (catalog management, billing, account management, etc.) Experience teams are then aligned by the category.

Enterprise Product

Enterprise products frequently must be specialized for different segments of customers. Sometimes, there are differences by the customer's vertical market (e.g., manufacturing vs. financial services vs. retail). Sometimes there are very significant differences based on the go-to-market strategy. Sometimes there are differences because of the customer's size (e.g., SMBs are reached through a self-service portal, while larger customers require a sales force and APIs for customization).

Here, it can make sense to organize experience teams by whatever segmentation is most relevant to the company. Once again, the goal is to organize the experience teams in a way that allows them to best serve their specific customer and also align with other parts of the company.

Marketplace Product

Many products have the purpose of connecting different groups of people who have complementary goals: such as buyers and sellers, drivers and riders, hotels and guests. Most marketplaces are two-sided, but they can have more.

In most cases, the needs of the individuals on each side of the marketplace are quite distinct. This is also true of the rest of the business that is trying to support each side.

For both of these reasons, it is often empowering for the topology to organize experience teams by the sides of the marketplace.

Customer-Enabling Product

Customer-enabling product teams create tools and systems that are used by the company's internal employees who are providing some vital part of the customer experience.

This might include systems to enable customer service or in-store workers, to name just a couple.

Here again, a topology can empower experience teams by aligning them with the end-to-end needs of the different types of company internal users.

One final note on this: Your topology need not align all experience teams to a single dimension such as vertical market or customer size. Some topologies use different alignment dimensions in different areas when that makes more sense.

Topology and Design

Most companies understand that a cross-functional product team, at least for an experience team, includes a dedicated product designer. This is an acknowledgement of how critically important product design is to strong products.

Occasionally, however, the company has a design leader who prefers a different model, referred to as the *internal agency model*. In this case, the design leader has a service team of designers, and the product teams need to make requests of this design team to get designs produced for their products.

It's only fair to acknowledge that this approach does have certain advantages—especially in terms of ensuring a holistic view of design.

However, in the words of Lin-Manuel Miranda (via Aaron Burr), it's essential to be "in the room where it happens."

In the internal design agency model, the designer is usually *not* in the room when the key decisions get made, and therefore the designer—and ultimately our users—have to pay the price for that.

Design is far too important to be run as an internal service. It needs to be a first-class member of the product team, just as the product manager and tech lead are.

The design manager can ensure a holistic view of design by establishing design standards, guidelines, and design systems; reviewing the work of the designers; and also by conducting design strategy and review sessions with the broader group of product designers.

Note that for companies using feature teams, this really doesn't matter because the key decisions have already been made by the time the designer is first consulted.

Topology and Reporting Structure

It's very common for an engineering reporting structure to be organized around specific skill sets. For example, groups of data engineers, front-end engineers, and mobile engineers each typically report to separate managers. This ensures any engineering manager is able to provide skill-specific coaching to every engineer on her team.

This is not a problem, but it can be tempting for technology leaders to want to completely align the product teams with such a reporting structure. For example, making a single product team of just front-end engineers.

This approach rarely produces empowered product teams because the problem is that the teams don't align with anything other than technical skill sets. These rarely have any real bearing on the outcomes that the business needs.

For example, a topology that divides the organization into a web team, iOS team, Android team, and backend team will make it very difficult to give any team the ability to own a multichannel customer experience.

The famous computer scientist Melvin Conway coined an adage that is often referred to as *Conway's Law*. It states that any organization that designs a system will produce a design whose structure mirrors the organization's structure.

Another way to say this is to beware of *shipping your org chart*.

One of the biggest benefits of cross-functional teams is that membership can be determined by what is best for the product.

The bottom line is that there is no reason that reporting relationships should dictate team topology.

CHAPTER

45

Topology and Proximity

So far, we've talked about the composition of product teams and how to scope them, but we haven't discussed the dimension of physical location of those teams. When creating the team topology, this is another important and practical factor to consider.

Even before the pandemic, there was a trend around moving to alternative office strategies mainly driven by the shortage of available talent and very high costs of living in major technology hubs.

In many companies, there is simply no practical way to hire enough people with the necessary skills at the same location as the company's headquarters, so they're forced to consider options.

At one end of the spectrum is to fully embrace remote employees. This has several benefits including being able to hire talent from nearly anywhere, and people can choose to live where they prefer.

At the other end of the spectrum, some companies want to keep everyone working in the same office center, but due to lack of available talent and high costs of living, they opt to move their headquarters to a new location.

However, there is also a very effective middle ground, which is remote offices.

Many companies have been opening remote offices in cities around the world—especially in urban centers with a good supply of engineering and design talent—and then working to staff product teams in those remote offices, supplemented as necessary with remote employees.

This model taps into supplies of local talent, while still providing the benefits of offices.

As always, there are trade-offs, and these remote offices can place additional burdens on the organization. It can be especially difficult for the managers who provide coaching and oversight.

But let's dig a little deeper into the various forms of proximity, and the specific trade-offs involved in each.

Proximity to Team Members

This refers to whether the members of the team are *co-located* (they all sit physically together), or *fully distributed* (for example, if each team member works from home), or a mix (for example, if the product manager, product designer, and tech lead sit together, but the rest of the engineers are either working from home or in another office).

Especially for teams that depend on true innovation, team co-location is a significant advantage. The dynamics of product discovery depend on intense collaboration—especially between product management, product design, and engineering—and while this is not impossible when remote, it is harder.

If the engineers are either in a different office or working remotely, then most of the burden of the additional communication falls on the tech lead.

Proximity to Customers

If your team is building services for consumers or businesses in India, there's a real advantage to being based in India. That said, we do have good tools for connecting remotely with users and customers across the globe, especially when we have a person in country to help us with language or cultural issues. So, we are able to overcome the geographical distance with additional effort, mostly on the part of the product manager and product designer.

Proximity to Business Partners

If your product team needs to work closely with a particular part of your business—such as an operations team, or a customer success team—then this is similar to being proximate to customers, and there are advantages to being nearby. But again, we can overcome this disadvantage with additional effort (e.g., travel, phone and video calls, and increased outreach), mainly on the product manager and product designer.

Proximity to Managers

Normally, the managers of product management, product design, and engineering are managing the individuals on the various product teams, and it is usually easier for these managers to review work, observe the behaviors, and provide the necessary coaching when their employees are local.

That said, in many organizations that are medium to larger in size, managers have been forced by necessity to deal with employees in different offices or working from home. The managers can overcome this distance with additional effort (e.g., travel, phone and video calls, and frequent outreach) to solicit feedback and provide the critical ongoing coaching.

Proximity to Other Product Teams

In many cases, product teams depend on one another, and they often need to collaborate to solve large, complex problems. This is easier for teams that are physically close to one another, but we can overcome the distance issues with additional effort, mainly on the engineers and the product managers (increased outreach and communication, travel, and a technique called *swarming*).

Proximity to Senior Executives

Depending on the company's culture and the strengths of the senior executives, the senior executives may feel a real need to be close to the product teams.

When a team is in a remote office or working remotely, the product manager needs to make extra effort to develop and maintain the necessary relationships with the executives and stakeholders. The managers often need to play a larger role in this case.

Optimizing for the Product Team

Hopefully it's clear that there are trade-offs for each of these dimensions of proximity. As a general principle, we try to *optimize for the product team* as opposed to optimizing for the managers, or for access to customers, or for anything else.

Here are two very common situations where this trade-off comes into play.

Let's say the choice is between having the product managers and designers at the headquarters (near their managers, the executives, and stakeholders), or to have the product managers and designers next to their engineers. With the principle of optimizing for the product team, we would prefer to co-locate the product managers with their engineers.

Similarly, if the choice is to have the product managers and designers located near the customers versus near their engineers, we would again try to co-locate with the engineers.

Keep in mind that these are general principles. There may be circumstances where you will choose differently, but at least it's important to know the trade-offs involved, and what you can do to mitigate the disadvantages.

46

Topology Evolution

M ost companies already have some sort of existing topology, but it had to start somewhere.

With startups, it usually happens when the number of engineers grows beyond 15 or so.

This is when the company realizes that the empowerment the employees had in the early days is now starting to suffer under the burden of coordination. They're also finding it more and more difficult to make decisions and to get simple things done. So, they decide to form two to three cross-functional product teams in order to divide and conquer. Their decisions on how to do this establish the topology.

With larger companies that didn't grow up in the product team model, the starting point is usually when they moved to Agile, where they were instructed to organize around small, durable teams. How the company decides to divide up the teams establishes the topology.

Some topologies are established in response to a major change of product vision and/or the product architecture. For whatever reason, if the company makes a drastic change to strategic context of their product, then the topology may need to be revisited.

Regardless of the reason for reviewing your topology, you should optimize for the empowerment of the teams by focusing on the dimensions of ownership, autonomy, and alignment.

Evolving a Topology

No matter how empowering your initial topology is, it will not stay that way by itself. The realities on the ground are always changing, sometimes in ways that require changes to the topology. Here are a just a few examples of situations that might call for a change to topology:

- A product team that needs to double its engineering resources to expand into the next segment of the market
- A new strategy that includes sunsetting a product currently maintained by several product teams
- A new strategy to make some core capabilities from one product team available to other teams through an internal platform
- A new business objective to develop an offering for an expansion market
- A major refactoring of the architecture

Topology Warning Signs

Even if none of the above cause you to proactively revisit the topology, good leaders are always checking in with their teams and people and should be evaluating their topology through the lens of empowerment.

Here are a few warning signs that can indicate your topology could use some attention:

- You are frequently shifting developers between teams
- You must frequently step in to resolve dependency conflicts
- Your developers complain of too many dependencies on other product teams in order to ship simple things

- Teams have very limited scope of ownership
- Developers must deal with too much complexity in too many areas

So, whether they are caused proactively or reactively, there are situations where we need to revisit the team topology.

As much as possible, you should try to keep your existing product teams intact. Your entire organization has made a big investment in establishing relationships to enable good collaboration.

This means that, wherever possible, it is better to give an existing team a new set of responsibilities, rather than break up the product team and redistribute the people into other teams.

With that said, there will still be times where the required topology changes are more significant. Just be careful about changing things too frequently. If you're consistently making major changes to the team topology more than once a year, it is a sign that something is wrong.

Topology determines who people work with on a daily basis, what they are working on, and the nature of your interactions. When it changes, it can be extremely disruptive.

This same sort of care is needed even if you temporarily move someone to another team to deal with an urgent priority. These moves are hard on the person moving as they must adjust to a new team and new work. It's also hard on the team that was left behind as they are often forced to find a way to fill the void.

CHAPTER

47

Leader Profile:
Debby Meredith

Path to Leadership

I first met Debby at Netscape, where she ran the engineering organization responsible for the Netscape Browser. She had joined Netscape through the acquisition of Collabra in 1995.

You may not have heard of Collabra, but they were an extraordinary team with very strong leaders, and their leaders quickly became key to Netscape's unprecedented growth.

Originally from the Midwest, Debby studied mathematics and computer science at the University of Michigan. She then moved out to Silicon Valley, studying computer science at Stanford, becoming a software engineer and soon an engineering leader at progressively larger organizations.

At Netscape, Debby earned her reputation as one of our industry's top engineering leaders, and later, working through a network of venture capitalists and industry friends, she has become known as the person to call if you want to significantly or urgently raise the bar on your engineering organization.

Leadership in Action

Debby specializes in going into companies, mostly startups, that have a promising business opportunity when either their engineering needs to scale to the next level or is, for various reasons, struggling to effectively execute and deliver products to market. She has done this now for more than 50 companies, many of which today are very successful companies.

Often, Debby arrives to find some frustrated leaders and unhappy engineers, with eroding trust on both sides, running with feature teams and roadmaps. She must earn the trust of these talented professionals, engage them, and transform the organization into effective, scalable product teams.

I have seen the before and after, and the change is dramatic.

I asked Debby to discuss how she is able to so consistently transform these engineering organizations.

Here she is in her own words:

Every company is different, and I begin by talking to people from all across the organization, and listening to what they have to say, and what people think I might be able to do to improve the situation. Also, it's important that I observe interactions in organizational meetings as well as the systems and artifacts of those to understand the company's unique people dynamics and process challenges.

After this "intake period," I generally find the same four fundamental and critical things I need to focus on.

The Example Starts at the Top

If a company's engineering organization is struggling to scale or to deliver, there are likely some serious issues coming from the top. It's important that I understand and address those, otherwise it's very possible any changes will be less impactful or only temporary.

Many startup founders or CEOs have never worked with strong engineering organizations, and it's not uncommon to find leaders with fundamental misunderstandings about the role of technology, and the necessary contribution of engineers as a partner to product management and product design.

Further, I find that many founders and CEOs are unaware of the role they play in the challenges and success of the engineering organization. So, education must happen here.

Focus and Strategy

Building and scaling a successful company is really hard, and every company has far more work they want to do, than people to do the work. So focus is essential, and product strategy is what lets us get the most out of the resources and people we have.

Despite best intentions, upon close examination, often organizations that are scaling quickly or currently struggling have no real focus and no real product strategy. Trying to do too many things at once will damage even the best engineering organizations.

In many cases, my arrival is the event the company needs to reestablish what focus really means. I can't usually make the choices for them, but I can insist that the leaders make the hard choices that are necessary.

Establish Trust

People are the heart and soul of any company. And, trust can enable those people, working together effectively, to create and achieve far more than they ever imagined individually. This is the magic of successful companies.

Each organizational function has distinct expertise it brings to the overall company. In the very best product teams, engineering's unique value is consistently innovating with technology to deliver winning products. For whatever reasons, when an engineering organization is not perceived as able to deliver, there will be trust issues. The executives don't trust the engineering organization, and the engineers don't trust the executives.

Lack of trust causes all kinds of bad behaviors and morale issues, on all sides, and usually results in a downward spiral.

So, it's essential to have healthy ongoing trust. Reestablishing and maintaining trust requires work—including focus and strategy—at every level of the organization, starting from the top but also from the engineers. This leads to the next point.

Deliver on Promises

I need to work with the engineers to understand that when they make a promise or commitment, it is important they deliver on that promise.

There are "why," "when," and "how" components here that the overall organization needs to understand and support. This involves coaching the executives to be smart about when they really need a date, and coaching the engineers on how to assess the work and take the obligation to deliver very seriously.

There are two aspects to this:

First, we need to replace any unreliable estimation games they're currently playing to try to predict dates with some rigor—thoroughly assessing what's involved to get something working and delivered. This can be difficult, often requiring new ways of doing things and almost always lots of practice. I'm a big believer in "crawl, walk, run."

That may mean building feasibility prototypes, or it may mean having some engineers take time to learn or flesh something out. Whatever the approach, they need to be able to reasonably predict dates—when those dates are truly needed—with high confidence.

Second, once the engineers have made this commitment, they need to take this commitment very seriously and deliver. This "do what you say you're going to do" mentality is hopefully true for each person and team within a company. Regardless, engineering needs to become known for following through on its commitments.

There's no question that scaling an engineering organization is not a trivial undertaking. However, the good news is that there are many examples today where this forward motion and successful transformation have occurred, and organizations are able to deliver with pride the products their companies and their customers depend on.

VI

Product Strategy

STRATEGIC CONTEXT

COMPANY MISSION / OBJECTIVES / SCORECARD

PRODUCT VISION & PRINCIPLES

TEAM TOPOLOGY

PRODUCT STRATEGY

PRODUCT TEAMS

OBJECTIVES

DISCOVERY
DELIVERY

OBJECTIVES

DISCOVERY
DELIVERY

OBJECTIVES

DISCOVERY
DELIVERY

Ultimately, empowered product teams are all about giving teams hard problems to solve, and then giving them the space to solve them.

But, how do we decide *which* problems they should solve?

Answering that question is what product strategy is all about.

An effective product strategy is absolutely essential to enabling ordinary people to create extraordinary products, because it focuses and leverages their talents.

Remarkably, most product organizations I meet don't even have a product strategy.

They have no shortage of features and projects being worked on, and everything they are building is being built for a reason, but as you'll see, they have no product strategy.

If you've never seen the great South Park clip on the Underpants Business,[1] I'd encourage you to pause for a minute and take a look.

Seriously, this is really what I see in so many of the companies I visit. They have product teams that are more accurately feature teams, and they're slaving away—pounding out features all day—but rarely getting closer to their desired outcomes.

This results in two things:

First, there is a depressing amount of wasted effort (primarily due to their dependence on product roadmaps).

Second, they are not putting enough concentrated brainpower behind the most important problems to achieve the results their company needs.

You may wonder how it is that so many companies don't have a good product strategy—I know I do. Richard Rumelt gives us a hint:

> *Not miscalculation, bad strategy is the active avoidance of the hard work of crafting a good strategy. One common reason for choosing avoidance is the pain or difficulty of choice. When leaders are unwilling or unable to make choices among competing values and parties, bad strategy is the consequence.*[2]

---

[1] https://southpark.cc.com/clips/151040/the-underpants-business.
[2] Richard Rumelt, *Good Strategy/Bad Strategy* (New York: Crown Business, 2011).

So, what even is product strategy, and why is it so important?

"Strategy" as a term is ambiguous as it exists at every level for just about everything—business strategy, go-to-market strategy, growth strategy, sales strategy, discovery strategy, delivery strategy, and so on.

Whatever the goal is, your strategy is *how you're planning to go about accomplishing that goal*.

Strategy doesn't cover the details—those are the *tactics* we'll use to achieve the goal. Strategy is the overall approach and the rationale for that approach.

While there are many forms of strategy, what I care about here is *product strategy*. Which in short means: *How do we make the product vision a reality, while meeting the needs of the company as we go?*

So many of the companies I meet have a *goal* (such as doubling revenue), and they have a product roadmap (the *tactics*), yet no product *strategy* to be found.

In terms of empowered product teams, product *strategy* helps us decide what problems to solve, product *discovery* helps us figure out the tactics that can actually solve the problems, and product *delivery* builds that solution so we can bring it to market.

So why is product strategy so hard?

Because it requires four things that are not easy for most companies:

1. The first is to be willing to make tough *choices* on what's really important.

2. The second involves generating, identifying, and leveraging *insights*.

3. The third involves converting insights into *action*.

4. And the fourth involves active *management* without resorting to micromanagement.

Choices means focus. Deciding what few things you really need to do, and therefore all the things you won't do.

But I can't tell you how many companies I've gone into that have on an office wall or spreadsheet a list of literally 50 major objectives or initiatives they're pursuing.

And each product team complains to me that they really have no time to pursue their own team's product work because they have obligations that cover more than 100 percent of their available time, not to mention all the "keep-the-lights-on" work and dealing with tech debt.

Moreover, many of these 50 major objectives or initiatives are truly hard problems, and just getting a little time slice and no clear ownership from a dozen-or-so different product teams has virtually no chance of making any real impact.

So, focus comes from realizing that not everything we do is equally important or impactful, and we must choose which objectives are truly critical for the business.

While product strategy starts with *focus*, it then depends on *insights*.

And insights come from study and thought.

These insights come from analyzing the data and from learning from our customers. The insights might pertain to the dynamics of our business, our capabilities, new enabling technologies, the competitive landscape, how the market is evolving, or our customers.

Once we have decided what's critically important (*focus*) and studied the landscape to identify the levers and opportunities (the *insights*), then we need to convert those insights into *action*.

In a company that's serious about empowered product teams, this means deciding which objectives should be pursued by which product teams, and then providing those teams with the *strategic context* necessary for them to solve the problems we need them to solve.

But we're not done there because reality is never static or predictable.

As product teams pursue their objectives, some make more progress than others, some need help or encounter major obstacles, some find they need to collaborate with other teams, some realize they're missing key capabilities, or any of a hundred other possible situations.

Properly managing this activity requires smart, engaged leaders practicing servant leadership.

I've been a student of product strategy for most of my career. After decades of practice, I think I'm reasonably good at it. My favorite activity is still solving the hard problems (product discovery), but if I had to choose, I'd say product strategy is the more important skill, and certainly the more difficult.

In the coming chapters, we'll dive deeper into each of these elements of product strategy—focus, insights, actions, and management. But the bottom line is that product strategy requires *choice*, *thinking*, and *effort*.

CHAPTER

48

Focus

The main thing is to keep the main thing, the main thing.
—*Jim Barksdale*

To continue with our series on product strategy, in this chapter I focus on, well, *focus*. The importance of truly picking your battles as an organization.

And I don't just mean deciding what to work on and not work on, but picking the *few* things that can truly make an impact.

This is another one of those topics, like whether a company cares about their customers. In pretty much every company I meet, the leaders already believe they are reasonably good at focus.

But, often, the company's leaders need a reality check on this topic.

The sheer number of things they believe are critically important, and that need to happen this quarter, or this year, are often an order of magnitude too many. I mean that literally. Instead of 2–3 truly important things, they have at least 20–30.

Now, in fairness, I understand why the key leaders believe they are reasonably good at focus.

They have already had countless meetings where they agreed to so many things they really want to do this year, yet won't be able to. So from their perspective, they think they already know what it means to say no and sacrifice.

In large part, this is a reflection of leaders feeling the need to place a lot of bets—versus the best or most impactful bets—the fear of missing out, and the need to respond to every competitor, every lost deal, every customer request. These are all understandable reactions.

But in this case, they need an intervention and a reset on what focus *really* means in a product organization. In my experience, many organizations need this intervention.

Let's talk about what an organization that doesn't know how to focus on what's truly important looks like.

A few years ago, one of the execs of the music service Pandora shared the "Pandora Prioritization Process"—the company's process for deciding what to work on and build.[1]

The process involved letting stakeholders "buy" the features they wanted from the feature teams until their budget ran out.

I had not worked with them, but when I read this, I immediately recognized the complete and utter absence of product strategy and especially focus. Not *bad* product strategy—literally *no* product strategy.

Combined with their dependence on feature teams and their lack of any sign of true product management, it was clear this would lead to many features built, but little in the way of results or innovation, and the company's inevitable decline.

And over the next several years, that's just what we saw. A stock that IPO'd in 2011 at $16 a share kept steadily dwindling until, at about $8 a share, they were finally sold off.[2]

For years, I've been sharing the Pandora example as a clear case study of *how not to do product*.

---

[1] https://firstround.com/review/This-Product-Prioritization-System-Nabbed-Pandora-More-Than-70-Million-Active-Monthly-Users-with-Just-40-Engineers/.

[2] https://www.fool.com/investing/2019/02/05/sirius-xm-finally-ends-pandoras-misery.aspx.

In most companies it's not quite so obvious, but so many companies have some similar sort of stakeholder-driven roadmap process, where they basically are trying to find a way to "fairly" divide up the engineering capacity across the different business stakeholders.

This is very much what I mean by feature teams striving to serve *the business*, versus product teams striving to serve *the customers* in ways that work for the business.

This is an especially clear example of the lack of product strategy, a lack of focus, and more generally, a lack of product leadership.

To be fair, this way of working is rarely desired by the head of product. Rather, it is usually the CEO and stakeholders that want to work this way, and the head of product is forced to serve as the facilitator.

Whatever the reason, this is an example of a company that is *prioritizing but not focusing*.

It is easy to generate work with this approach, but not results. As Stephen Bungay explains:

> *Generating activity is not a problem; in fact it is easy. The fact that it is easy makes the real problem harder to solve. The problem is getting the right things done—the things that matter, the things that will have an impact, the things a company is trying to achieve to ensure success.*[3]

This is one of the most important lessons in leadership, and successful leaders have learned this one way or another.

Even though I (Marty) learned this early in my career, this lesson was etched in my mind and I've found that this principle applies in so many aspects of a technology business.

When I was a new software engineer, working in HP's applied research lab, I was fresh out of college. This meant that I knew something about the *theory*, but very little of the *practice*.

The way we worked at the time was using a practice referred to today as *pair programming*, where I was paired with a much more experienced engineer and we wrote software "together." I use the

---

[3] Stephen Bungay, *The Art of Action, How Leaders Close the Gaps between Plans, Actions and Results* (London: Nicholas Brealey, 2010).

quotes because the truth is that *he* did most of the writing, and I mostly watched and asked questions.

We were working on fairly low-level systems software, for which at the time—and still is the case today with certain types of products—performance is key. Systems and applications were often so slow as to be unusable. So "performance optimization" was one of our ongoing responsibilities.

The good news was that, for pretty much any area of code that we would examine, it was not hard to think of ways to refactor to improve the performance. I kept pointing out areas that we could improve, but he kept saying, "We could, but no."

Finally, he said, "Okay, time to work on performance," and he proceeded to bring up our performance analysis tool, which let us measure the performance of our software. We could very clearly see where the time was actually being spent.

He pointed out that, while pretty much the entire code base could be improved, the vast majority of this effort *would not matter in the least*. In fact, it would not even be enough to be perceived by the user.

However, there were a few spots where almost all the time was going, and if we could improve those few areas, we could make a real impact. So that's where we needed to focus.

He pointed out that in most organizations, they tell everyone that "performance is important," and so every team works a little on performance. But the vast majority of that work makes absolutely no difference. And, in the few places where it *could* make a difference, it gets too little concentrated attention.

This was a very tangible example of the power of focus, but more generally this is the situation I see in so many companies when it comes to focus and product strategy.

By not picking your battles and focusing on the few truly critical problems, most of the work going on does not make an impact. And for the truly critical priorities, there is not enough attention to actually move the needle.

There is also a very practical reason to focus on just a few truly critical problems.

Most tech product people know about the concept of *work in progress (WIP) limits*. It's an especially common concept in product teams using a delivery process such as *Kanban*.

It essentially says that we'll get more work done (throughput) if we limit the number of things our product team is working on at any one time. For most teams, it's a few items. If you don't have these limits, then work piles up at bottlenecks and we end up constantly switching context, and as a result, get fewer things out the door.

Not a difficult concept, and most product teams see this play out on a daily basis.

However, while this concept is definitely useful at the level of a product team, it becomes absolutely critical at the level of the broader product organization.

When an organization has 20, 30, or even 50 "high-priority" objectives, initiatives, or projects all going on at once, we have the same problem, only much worse.

First of all, if you have even 20 high-priority initiatives, that is likely going to overwhelm your organization. Each team will struggle with delivering on those initiatives, versus trying to take care of their customers or otherwise pursuing the purpose of their team.

Second, there is a real cost to an organization, and especially to the leadership, for each high-priority effort or initiative. This cost involves management time, decisions, monitoring and tracking, staffing issues, and more, and the same concept of WIP limits applies here.

The bottom line is that an organization will get more critical work accomplished if it focuses on just a few items at a time.

So we need to pick our battles based on what really matters, and we need to limit the number of major battles we're trying to pursue at once.

Richard Rumelt reminds us that every good product strategy begins with this focus:

> *Good strategy works by focusing energy and resources on one, or a very few, pivotal objectives whose accomplishment will lead to a cascade of favorable outcomes.*[4]

If the leaders are not willing or able to make these choices, then the product strategy is doomed from the start.

In the next chapter, we'll consider how we identify and leverage *insights* on these few critical problems we've decided to focus on.

---

[4]Richard Rumelt in *Good Strategy/Bad Strategy* (London: Profile Books, 2017).

CHAPTER

49

Insights

In this chapter, I'd like to discuss my favorite, yet the most difficult, aspect of product strategy, which is to generate, identify, and leverage the insights that will provide the foundation of the product strategy.

You've probably heard the stories about the insights about customer behavior that drove early Netflix to rapid growth and profitability, or the insights around new-user onboarding that drove early Facebook to explosive growth, or the insights around customer trials that Slack and Salesforce.com leveraged to spread like wildfire across businesses.

In this chapter, we explore where these critical insights come from, and how to make sure you're finding them, as they can hide among the thousands of other data points you're likely collecting.

There are a few things I need to make clear before we get into this:

First, if you're looking for some paint-by-number playbook or framework for coming up with these insights and a solid product strategy, I'll save you some time and tell you right now you're not going to find that here.

As I've tried to emphasize throughout this book, product strategy requires real effort and thought. Says Richard Rumelt:

> *Good strategy … does not pop out of some "strategic management" tool, matrix, chart, triangle, or fill-in-the-blanks scheme. Instead, a talented leader identifies the one or two critical issues in the situation—the pivot points that can multiply the effectiveness of effort—and then focuses and concentrates action and resources on them.*[1]

Second, in every single case I know of, including every instance where I was able to contribute to the product strategy myself, this *never* happens without real preparation.

You might have an epiphany in the shower, but that's only after you've spent hours studying your data, your customers, the enabling technologies, and your industry.

The information that's in the strategic context—the company objectives, the company scorecard/dashboard, and the product vision—is the foundation for any kind of significant insight. So studying this is all part of doing your homework as a product leader.

Third, it's important to realize that these insights can come from anyone or anywhere. You might find inspiration in an industry analysis, a chat with a salesperson, a new enabling technology, a seemingly random comment from a customer, or an academic paper.

But without that preparation, you probably won't recognize the insight—even if it's right in front of you. My main point here is that you never know what might help you connect the dots, so always keep an eye out and an open mind.

All that said, there are four consistently effective and valuable sources of insights, and strong product leaders spend much of their waking hours contemplating these:

Quantitative Insights

For so much of what we do, the big insights that form the foundation of successful product strategies come from an analysis of the product data.

---

[1] Richard Rumelt, *Good Strategy/Bad Strategy* (London: Profile Books, 2017).

Especially related to your business model, your acquisition funnel, your customer retention factors, your sales execution data, and hundreds of other important indicators of the state of your company.

You might have a theory about which customers respond best to your product, so you run an analysis and realize that, in certain situations, your product is a dramatically better fit. You realize you can either find more customers like that, or work to replicate that dynamic with other types of customers.

Often, you will get an idea about the data, and you'll have to construct a test to obtain the specific data you need. This is normal, and the sooner your organization gets good at running these sorts of live-data tests, the better your chance for lasting success.

It's normal today for product teams to be running live-data tests on a near-constant basis. You learn something from every test, but every once in a while, you learn something truly important—a potentially valuable insight.

The key is to know enough to spot this learning, and then leverage this learning into meaningful action.

Qualitative Insights

User research is all about insights, which is why I'm such a fan of having strong user researchers in the organization. Mostly the insights they generate are qualitative and therefore not "statistically significant," but don't let that bother you—qualitative insights are often profound and can literally change the course of your company.

The user research community generally breaks down insights into two types. The first is *evaluative*, which essentially means, what did we learn from testing out this new product idea? Did it work or not, and if not, why not? The second type of insights are *generative*. This means, did we uncover any new opportunities that we aren't pursuing, but maybe we should?

This is actually the source of a very common confusion in product teams. For the most part, in product discovery, our learning is *evaluative*. We already have a problem we've been asked to solve, so we're not actively looking for other problems to solve—we're focused on finding a solution that actually *works*.

We, of course, have lots of product ideas. We test those ideas with prototypes on actual users, and we can quite quickly learn the major reasons why this product idea may or may not work.

But anytime we interact with users and customers, we have a chance to learn more about them, and sometimes we discover even bigger opportunities than the ones we're looking into at the moment. Even if they love the new thing we're testing out, we may realize there is an even bigger opportunity if we're open to it. This is an example of a *generative insight*.

Or even if a product team is not actively trying to do discovery on a particular problem, as part of the team spending time with users and customers every week (you are doing that, right?), we uncover new and potentially important problems to solve or needs not being met.

Too many organizations are either not doing this ongoing learning about their customers, or, even if they are, they are not set up to leverage the insights that are generated (usually because their feature teams are already over-subscribed just trying to serve the business). So, the learnings are all too often ignored.

Technology Insights

The enabling technologies are constantly changing, and occasionally a technology comes along that allows us to solve long-standing problems in new, just-now-possible ways.

If the technology is new, you very likely don't have anyone on the teams who has been trained on this new technology. This fact ends up scaring off many leaders, or they occasionally think they have to partner with a third party that does have the necessary experience. But if the technology is important to you, your company needs to learn that technology. And the sooner the better.

The good news is that this is rarely that difficult. Your best engineers are probably already considering this technology and would love to be able to explore further.

In the best organizations, it is the empowered engineers that often identify these enabling technologies and proactively bring the possibilities to the leaders, usually in the form of a prototype.

Industry Insights

There is always a great deal to learn from the industry at large. I don't just mean your competitive landscape, but major industry trends, insights in other industries that may pertain to your industry, and insights from similar markets in other regions of the world.

There are always some number of analysts covering nearly every space, and you should be following those whom you consider to be among the best.

More than a few CEOs have decided the best way to obtain these industry insights is to outsource this to one of the management consultancies, such as McKinsey, Bain, or BCG.

I admit to mixed feelings about this. The people at these firms are often very strong, but they have two big factors working against them. First, their focus and experience are almost always on *business strategy*, and rarely *product strategy* (and they often won't even know the difference). Second, the typical duration of their engagement is rarely enough time for them to gain the level of depth in your business needed for true product strategy work.

So, the result is that their insights are not usually considered relevant by the product leaders or product teams. Partly they're right—the insights are not relevant—but partly the issue is that it's very easy to discount insights found by a third party.

What I have found helpful is if you are able to find a small firm or individual that is interested in a long-term engagement—where they can establish themselves as a trusted member of your team—that can be a useful relationship. Or if you can recruit one of these management consultants to come join your product organization, they can often be coached into exceptionally strong product managers and product leaders.

Shared Learnings

In a strong product organization, these four types of insights are always the subject of interest and discussion, both at the leadership level and at the product team level.

But half the battle, especially in larger organizations, is getting the relevant insights into the right minds at the right time.

It is often remarkable how much a product team learns, especially as they are working on product discovery for important problems. Yet it is easy for that learning to stay just with that product team.

The insights that are generated need to be shared and communicated. Unfortunately, the most common way that most teams try to share these learnings is by writing them down somewhere—an email, Slack, or a report. Sadly, this is rarely effective.

The product leader or design leader is often the first person to connect the dots between learnings of different teams and see real opportunities.

The key is to make sure these learnings—whether they are coming from the data, customer visits, enabling technology, industry analysis, or any other source—make it to the product leaders.

In many ways, leaders are given the data they *request*, not the data they *need*—especially to make insightful strategic decisions.

This is an important benefit of the weekly 1:1s.

This is also another example of how empowered product teams don't need *less* management, they need *better* management.

These leaders need to take the learnings and pass them along to other teams that may benefit from these insights, and more generally, help to build their understanding of the holistic business.

One practice I have long advocated is that the head of product should aggregate the key learnings and insights from all the different teams in her areas, and at the weekly or bi-weekly all-hands. She should summarize the most important of these learnings and insights, and share them with the broader organization.

This sharing serves a few purposes:

First, it helps the broader organization—including the other product teams, but also stakeholders—get a better understanding of the learning and insights that happen every week in the product organization.

Second, it ensures that the leader is truly grokking all the key insights and not just passing along some status in an email.

Third, it is very hard to anticipate exactly where key insights will have the most impact, so it's very important to share the insights broadly, especially across the other product teams.

One way or another, as a product leader you will need to identify insights that you can leverage to generate the necessary impact.

At this point, we have focused on a small number of truly important problems for the business, and we have identified what we believe are the linchpins (the insights) for moving the needle for those problems. Now we're ready to turn those insights into *actions*.

Vision Pivots

In this book I've laid things out in the ideal and logical order. We start with an inspiring product vision, we craft a product strategy to deliver on that vision, and then the product teams execute on that strategy. And in many cases, that's exactly how I see things play out.

But it's important to acknowledge that it's not always so linear. The most common example of this is when, during our work on the product strategy, or during a product team's product discovery work, we discover an insight that changes everything.

We realize that there's a larger or better opportunity by changing course, and after discussion with the senior leaders and usually the company's board too, the company decides to change the product vision to leverage this insight.

This is called a vision pivot, and these vision pivots have both saved and created countless companies. Slack, YouTube, Facebook, and Netflix are just a few of the companies that experienced this.

Now I'm always a little hesitant to explain this, because a very large problem in our industry has always been, and remains, that product organizations give up too early on their product vision. As Jeff Bezos says, "We need to be stubborn on our product vision," which I very strongly agree with.

Given empowered product teams with the right skills and enough time, we really can deliver on most product visions. The vision pivot is most relevant when our insights lead to a larger opportunity. Not when we realize that the problems are harder than we thought (which is pretty much always true).

CHAPTER

50

Actions

Continuing with the series on product strategy, in this chapter we need to leverage our *insights* into *action*.

At this point, we have *focused* on a very small number of critical problems, and we have done the hard work to identify the key *insights* that will power our product strategy. Now we need to turn these insights into *action*, but there are two ways to do this.

This is the point where there's a fork in the road, and it's where we can tell if a company is serious about empowered product teams or is still addicted to feature teams.

I need to admit here that even if the company chooses to stay with roadmaps and feature teams, they are still far better off if they have a strong product strategy. Certainly, much better than the majority of organizations with feature teams that have no product strategy.

The difference really boils down to whether you give your product teams features to build, or problems to solve.

Most of the time the difference is obvious (e.g., "Add videos to our online help offering" vs. "Improve the new-user onboarding success rate"). But sometimes the difference is more nuanced (e.g., "We need an app" vs. "Our users need to be able to access our services from anywhere").

In the first example, adding videos is just one of probably hundreds of possible improvements to new-user onboarding.

In the second example, adding an app is very likely to be the primary way of providing access from anywhere, so the difference is subtle, but there are still multiple ways to achieve the objective, and we want to give the team as much latitude as possible to come up with the best solution.

If the leaders believe they know the necessary features and projects to execute on the product strategy, then they'll likely put that info on a product roadmap and assign the work to the relevant teams.

However, if the leaders want the product teams to feel ownership of the problem and take responsibility for discovering and delivering a solution that provides the necessary results, then they'll want to give the relevant teams as many degrees of freedom in coming up with an effective solution as possible.

Note that empowering a team does not mean giving the team a blank check. There are always constraints and context—such as ensuring the solution does not violate an existing contract or compliance constraint.

It's worth pointing out that the first approach is what we mean by a *team of mercenaries*, and the second is what we mean by a *team of missionaries*.

Of course, it's no secret that I am all about the empowered team model, as I deeply believe that it generates consistently better results—especially in terms of innovation and delivering the necessary outcomes.

In the empowered team model, our intention is to provide the teams with the set of specific *problems* they each need to solve, and then give them the space to determine the best way to solve those problems.

There are various techniques for managing these problems to solve, but the most popular is the *OKR* system, which stands for *objectives and key results*. The objectives are the customer or business problem we need solved, and the key results are how we measure the progress.

We have already discussed *company objectives* as a key part of the *strategic context*. But to initiate action, we need to provide the *product teams* with their specific objectives, which are known as *team objectives*.

In the upcoming section on team objectives (Part VII), we'll talk in depth about how to effectively use the *OKR technique* in the empowered team model.

But before we talk about the OKR technique, it's important to point out that you really don't need that or any other technique for this.

All that's really required is for a knowledgeable leader to sit down with the relevant product teams, explain the strategic context—including the product strategy—and then tell each team which problems you need them to work on, and what business results they should measure.

If the team has the right knowledge and skills, they'll get to work.

The OKR system is a technique for formalizing these discussions, but it's only a useful technique if you have staffed for empowered product teams, and the leaders have done their job to create an effective product strategy and are ready and willing to entrust their product teams to solve the problems we need them to solve.

In any case, just because you are empowering your teams, this is not to imply that we can just leave the teams alone and hope for the best. There is still considerable *active management* required to succeed on the product strategy, and that's what we'll discuss next.

CHAPTER

51

Management

A t this point, we have *focused* the organization on a small number of truly important problems, we have identified the key *insights* that we will leverage, and we have converted these insights into *actions* in the form of objectives for each product team.

While this is all necessary preparation for the work that needs to be done, I can tell you from experience that, if the leaders stop here, you will be disappointed at the end of the quarter.

This is because no product strategy survives its initial encounter with the real world.

There are any number of issues and obstacles that will emerge, and while each product team will deal with them and make most of their decisions for themselves, there will be many cases where they will need you to remove obstacles and barriers or otherwise provide assistance:

- The product team realizes they missed a dependency during their planning, and now they have a dependency on another team, and that team is consumed with its own objectives.

- During product discovery, the team realizes that they require the use of a technology that they do not have access to, or knowledge of, today, so they may need to quickly acquire and learn it.

- A major customer issue arises, and the organization is scrambling to determine the best way to take care of the customer yet still make progress on the team objectives.

- A senior stakeholder raises a major concern impacting one of the key objectives, and the product team needs a decision made quickly.

Hopefully, you get the idea. None of this is unusual, but unless the leaders are actively engaged in identifying, tracking, and resolving these types of obstacles, little progress will result.

The main source of information for the product leader will be the weekly 1:1 with the product manager. Of course, if something urgent comes up, you want to coach your product managers to reach out to you immediately and not wait until the next 1:1 to discuss.

During this session, you'll hear about issues or obstacles, and you'll coach on the best way to handle them. In some cases, you'll need to help by talking to a key stakeholder, or finding an additional engineer, or talking to another team about their need to help with a problem, or a hundred similar things.

Please don't confuse this with command-and-control management. You are not taking over control and telling the teams what to do—you are responding to their requests for help. It's more accurately described as *servant leadership* and you're being asked to help remove an impediment.

With all the normal urgencies and interruptions of life in a company, it is all too easy to find yourself halfway through the quarter with very little progress on the team's objectives. This is why weekly tracking and coaching is so important. You as the manager are ensuring that the product team is making progress, and also as important learnings or insights are discovered, or major issues are identified, they are shared with you so this knowledge can be aggregated and disseminated to the relevant teams.

The coaching and the management of the strategy are not so much different responsibilities as they are two sides of the same discussions.

Once again, with empowered product teams, you don't need *less* management, you need *better* management.

52

Leader Profile:
Shan-Lyn Ma

Path to Leadership

I first met Shan-Lyn in 2009, when she was the sole product manager for fast-growing Gilt Groupe in New York City. But it was easy to see her potential.

Shan-Lyn originally studied marketing and economics, and after getting her MBA at Stanford, she joined Yahoo for a couple years before she decided to try startup life.

After four years building a product team at Gilt, she was ready to found her own startup, Zola, an online wedding registry and planning company. The business has been growing for seven years now, and provides services that are loved and depended on by engaged couples everywhere.

Moreover, Zola is considered one of New York's most promising growth-stage companies as well as one of the best tech companies to work for.

Leadership in Action

Here's Shan-Lyn in her own words:

There's nothing that I enjoy more than building things that the world has never seen before, but once they see them, they're like, "How did we live without it?" Products that bring genuine joy. That is the thing I want to keep doing forever.

When my co-founder, Nobu Nakaguchi, and I decided to start Zola, we did not just have a vision for helping couples with their weddings, we also had a vision for the kind of company we wanted to work at.

When I was leading product at a prior job, one of the company's leaders gave me the feedback that I was not a good leader because the engineers liked me too much. The leader said that if I was doing my job properly, the engineers should be complaining about the pressure I was putting on them.

For a little while, I tried changing my approach. But I soon realized that this was the path to damaging collaboration, breaking trust, and likely losing the innovation we depended on.

Both Nobu and I believed that innovation comes from empowered teams of strong people working in a trusted environment. We deeply believed that we could provide an environment that valued and respected the people that worked there, and that this would help us provide the type of experience that engaged couples wanted and deserved.

Many founders say things like this, but we were willing to bet the company on this.

We knew that to succeed with Zola, we would not only need to innovate on the product and experience, but also on our business model and in how we built and ran our company.

In our kitchen you'll find a NO ASSHOLES sign.

You'll also find signs emphasizing NO POINTING FINGERS, NO POLITICS, NO GAMES.

We know that innovation thrives in environments where different perspectives are sought out and encouraged, so we made diversity an explicit goal from the beginning, for every open role.

We of course wanted diversity in skills and talents, but also diversity in gender, in orientation, in education, and in approach to problem solving.

Not only would this help us with innovation, but our users—engaged couples—come in every flavor and combination, so we believed this would help us at every level.

We also wanted a culture that valued both collaboration and speed.

While it may seem counterintuitive, we had found that collaboration early yields not just better results, but *faster* results.

So before we make any big decision, we make sure that others across the company have been consulted and their views considered.

We also value getting ideas in front of our customers as fast as possible because we know that's when the real learning happens.

A few years ago, I was in a serious car accident, and the experience made a profound impact on me. I learned to live life more in the present.

Being CEO of a fast-growing company is tough, the demands are high and increasing, but I get to actually do what I love every day, with people I love working alongside, and I'm thankful to be alive to do this another day.

PART

VII

Team Objectives

STRATEGIC CONTEXT

COMPANY MISSION / OBJECTIVES / SCORECARD

PRODUCT VISION & PRINCIPLES

TEAM TOPOLOGY

PRODUCT STRATEGY

PRODUCT TEAMS

OBJECTIVES

DISCOVERY
DELIVERY

OBJECTIVES

DISCOVERY
DELIVERY

OBJECTIVES

DISCOVERY
DELIVERY

'␣ve been a vocal advocate for the OKR (objectives and key results) technique for many years, but it's no secret that, for most companies that have given it a try, the results have been disappointing.

As I see it, there are three fundamental reasons for this.

Feature Teams vs. Product Teams

If the company is still using feature teams, as most unfortunately are, then the OKR technique is going to be a cultural mismatch, and almost certainly prove a waste of time and effort.

The OKR technique came from companies that had empowered product teams in their DNA. OKRs are first and foremost *an empowerment technique.*

The main idea is to give product teams real problems to solve, and then to give the teams the space to solve them.

This goes right to the core of enabling ordinary people to create extraordinary products.

Yet the telltale sign of mismatch out there is that companies think they can "check the empowerment box" by giving the team objectives, yet still continue to tell them the solutions they are supposed to deliver—nearly always in the form of a roadmap of features and projects with expected release dates.

Manager's Objectives vs. Product Team Objectives

The second issue is that the purpose of a cross-functional, empowered product team is to work together to solve hard problems.

Yet, in so many companies, each manager—the manager of engineers, the manager of designers, and the manager of product managers—creates their own *organizational* objectives, which are then cascaded down to their employees.

This may sound reasonable, and not necessarily a problem for other parts of the company. In practice, however, this means that these employees—when working with their cross-functional colleagues in a product team—are all working on *their own* objectives rather than working collaboratively on the *team* objectives.

To make matters even worse, in many companies there's an additional level of complexity and dilution because they also try to implement *individual* objectives. So not only does the engineer inherit the objectives from her manager, but she also has to work on her own personal objectives.

The Role of Leadership

And finally, and really the root of the problem, is that in the vast majority of companies I see that are struggling to get any value out of OKRs, the role of leadership is largely missing in action.

They literally think that the idea is to let teams identify a set of objectives, and then let them pursue those objectives, and we'll see where we are at the end of the quarter.

They think that empowered product teams, and this technique especially, is about *less* management. But as I've tried to emphasize throughout this book, it's really about *better* management.

It is really any wonder why so many companies get so little value from this technique?

It's no secret that most of the leading tech product companies use the OKR technique or one of the variants. And it's also no secret how much success these companies have had.

Yet people are confusing correlation with causation.

Those successful companies aren't successful *because* they use OKRs. They use OKRs because it is designed to leverage the *empowered product team* model.

And as I have tried to make clear in this book, the empowered product team model is a fundamentally different approach to building and running a tech-product organization.

You can't take your old organization based on feature teams, roadmaps, and passive managers, then overlay a technique from a radically different culture and expect that will work or change anything.

So, in terms of actually getting the *benefits* of OKRs, there are three critical prerequisites:

1. Move from the feature team model to the empowered product team model
2. Stop doing manager objectives and individual objectives, and instead focus on *team* objectives
3. Leaders need to step up and do their part to turn product strategy into action

The majority of this book has been about the first topic.

For the second item, this is mainly education, and hopefully these chapters will set people straight on that.

It is the third item that needs much more discussion, so in the upcoming series of chapters on team objectives, we'll discuss the role of leadership in effective team objectives.

First, we'll discuss specifically how we *empower* teams through team objectives. This is the most important benefit of team objectives, and yet it is often the least understood.

Ultimately, the point of team objectives is to execute on our product strategy, and this is where we convert our strategy into action. We need to discuss how work is *assigned* to product teams in ways that are both empowering yet also accountable.

Next, we'll discuss how leaders manage a portfolio of risk by sharing with teams how *ambitious* they would like them to be as they pursue the problems they've been asked to solve.

It's critical to note that sometimes it's not about the level of ambition, but rather, we need to occasionally make what's called a *high-integrity commitment* and we need to discuss how these are made and managed.

One of the common misconceptions about team objectives is that only a single product team should work on a specific problem. On the contrary, much of our best work requires *collaboration* between teams, and there are several important forms of collaboration we'll discuss.

As with any difficult technology-based endeavor, we need to actively *manage* this work, always being mindful to manage by coaching and servant leadership, and not to regress to command-and-control-style management—undermining the benefits of empowerment.

Along with empowerment comes *accountability*, and we need to discuss what this means in practice.

Finally, we'll put all this in perspective with the most important points to getting the real value out of team objectives.

53

Empowerment

N
ow that we know what actions we need each product team to pursue, we need to discuss how we assign this work in such a way as to *empower* the team.

The essential point of team objectives is to *empower* a team by: (a) giving them a *problem to solve* rather than a feature to build, and (b) ensuring they have the necessary *strategic context* to understand the *why* and make good decisions.

The most important point to understand about team objectives is that, first and foremost, they are intended to give the product team the space to come up with solutions to hard and important problems.

This is in stark contrast to a typical product roadmap, which provides the team with a prioritized list of features and projects to build. If those features or projects do not solve the underlying problems, then we fail, even though we may have delivered what we were asked to build.

Assigning Problems to Solve, Rather Than Features to Build

Some people believe that the difference is not such a big deal. If you think you need your team to build an app, then just tell them to build the app rather than providing them the business and strategic context and letting them figure out we need to build an app.

But one of the major lessons our industry has learned is this: *How work is assigned matters*.

There are many reasons why this is preferred, but the most important are:

- The best people to determine the most appropriate solution are those closest to the problem, with the necessary skills—the *product team*.

- We want the team to take responsibility for achieving the desired *outcome*.

- If we tell the team the feature we want them to build, then if that feature doesn't provide the necessary results, we can't hold the team *accountable*.

- If we give the team the problem to solve, and the space to solve it in the best way they see fit, the product team will feel much more *ownership* of the problem.

- If the first solution the team comes up with does not produce the desired outcome, they know they must continue to *iterate* and/or try alternative approaches until they find a solution that does.

So team objectives are comprised of an objective (the problem that needs to be solved) and some measures of progress (the key results). Let's discuss each.

Note that I am presenting these here in OKR format, but what is important is (1) their focus on a small number of meaningful objectives, and (2) they are measuring the results based on business results, not output or activities.

Objectives

The specific objectives will, of course, be a function of the type of product and the responsibilities of the particular product team, but typical examples of *good* objectives are:

- Reduce the frequency of parcels delivered to the wrong address
- Increase the percentage of shipments delivered with next-day delivery
- Reduce the percentage of images flagged as inappropriate
- Reduce the subscriber churn rate
- Demonstrate product/market fit for an existing product in a new market
- Decrease the time it takes a job seeker to find a new job
- Reduce the operational costs of fulfillment
- Reduce the cost to acquire a new customer
- Increase the lifetime value of the customer
- Reduce the percentage of customers that require customer service assistance
- Reduce the average time spent handling a customer service call
- Increase the percentage of new customers that successfully create an account
- Reduce the time for a user to produce their first monthly report
- Reduce the time required to deploy a new or updated service to production
- Improve the site availability

Remember not to get too attached to the specific wording of the objective. Often, once a product team understands the strategic context and has had a chance to investigate the objective, they find that it may make more sense to rephrase, or change the emphasis, or generalize the objective. This back and forth between the leader and the product team is both normal and healthy.

What's most important about all of these examples is that they are *problems to solve* and not *features to build*.

Some are *customer* problems, and some are *business* problems, but in each case, there are any number of potential solutions. The point is that the product team is best suited to determine the most appropriate solution.

Notice also the example objectives are all qualitative. The quantitative dimension will be discussed in the key results.

It's also important to acknowledge here that many of the most important objectives will require the product team to either collaborate with other product teams or, in many cases, to collaborate with different parts of the organization to achieve the goal.

That is not only okay, but very much intended, although in practice this depends on having a product manager on the product team who has a deep understanding of the business.

Key Results

While the objective is the problem to solve, the key results tell us how we define success.

And it's essential that we define success by *business results* (aka outcome) and not simply activity or output.

The second most common reason that teams go wrong with team objectives is that they end up listing activities or deliverables as their key results. Hopefully, at this point it is clear to you that output would miss the point. But, just in case it's not, the reason this is so much of a problem is that it is very easy to ship a deliverable yet not solve the underlying problem. In which case, we're back to the same old problem we have with product roadmaps.

Generally speaking, we want between two and four key results for each objective. The first key result is normally the primary measure. Then we have one or more key results as a measure of quality—sometimes called *guardrail or backstop key results*—to ensure that the primary key result is not inadvertently achieved by hurting something else.

For example, suppose we consider the objective of:

- Reduce the frequency of parcels delivered to the wrong address

Now, the primary key result would likely be the actual percentage of incorrect deliveries. But if we were to achieve that by burdening the ordering and fulfillment process, it's possible to reduce the percentage, but also significantly reduce the absolute number of deliveries, or significantly increase the cost of delivery, neither of which would be a helpful solution. So, potential key results could be measured by:

- Reduce percentage of incorrect deliveries
- While ensuring that total deliveries continue to grow
- While ensuring the cost of delivery does not grow

Notice that, while these key results do imply specific KPIs, we don't yet have the expected values or timeframes because those will need to come *from the team*.

The reason for that is because, if we were to provide to the team explicit measures of success including timeframe, they won't feel that *ownership* over the commitment that we want in an empowered team. So the actual quantitative values need to come from the teams.

It's also important to note that sometimes the most appropriate measure of success or KPI is not yet clear, especially in the case where it's a problem we haven't worked on before. In this case, the team may need some time to better understand the dynamics and the most appropriate measures.

The higher-order point here is that the best team objective will come from a back-and-forth dialog between the leader and the team. As teams investigate and consider, they often find new and better approaches that may suggest different key results, or even a modified objective. Moreover, it's the leader's job to ensure that this back and forth is happening. As a leader, you don't want a passive team—if the team is not actively engaged and debating, be sure to explicitly ask them what they think and why.

A related issue is to be sure the team does not "let the tail wag the dog." What that means is that sometimes a team will be tempted to define their key results by something that is *easy* to measure rather than what's most *meaningful* to measure.

Sharing Strategic Context

If we are to give product teams the space to solve hard problems, we must also provide these teams with the context necessary to make good decisions.

We need to share the strategic context—especially the product vision and product strategy—with the product teams for four main reasons:

First, it's critical that the team have a deep understanding of the ultimate goal and *why* this is an important problem to solve.

Second, we want teams to start thinking through the insights, and considering how they each might be able to contribute to solving the key problems.

Third, we want the teams to start thinking through the implications of the upcoming work. Perhaps there are dependencies that are not immediately visible. Or technologies or skills that we will need to acquire.

Fourth, we love it when teams express a special interest in working on specific problems. We can't always accommodate every team working on the problems they request, but we are certainly motivated to try.

With these principles in mind, we're now ready to assign objectives to specific product teams.

CHAPTER

54

Assignment

Keeping in mind the principles of empowerment that team objectives are designed to encourage, we are ready to have the product teams get to work. So, let's consider the mechanics of assigning objectives to product teams.

Assigning Objectives to Product Teams

To be very clear, and to address head-on another one of the very common misconceptions about team objectives, *it is the responsibility of the leaders to decide which problems should be worked on by which product teams.*

Many companies think that the idea is to let the product teams come up with their own objectives, yet are somehow surprised when the organization complains of lack of direction and little is accomplished. And it's important to point out that this is not the fault of the *teams*—it's the clear fault of *leadership*.

More explicitly, the whole point of assigning objectives to product teams is to execute on a product strategy. The product strategy is all about deciding which problems to work on.

Assigning objectives to product teams is both a top-down and bottom-up process, and it often requires iteration.

These assignments are a function of the product strategy and the team topology (aka team scoping). In other words, the strategy tells us which problems we need to solve, and the topology will imply which teams are best positioned to tackle each problem.

Now, we love it when teams volunteer to pursue an objective, and we try hard to accommodate that desire, but we also are clear with the teams that we can't always accommodate them because we have to ensure that, *in aggregate, the organization is covering as much of the overall organizational objectives as possible.*

So, even though a team may wish to pursue a specific objective, it is up to the leaders to decide this.

Hopefully this is understood, but this is not a power thing or a control thing—this is just about the managers doing their job. Someone has to look holistically at all the teams and the full set of objectives.

Determining Key Results

Once a team is asked to pursue an objective, the first thing they need to do is consider what the appropriate key results should be, and what they believe they can accomplish.

If the team has worked in this area before, they probably already have a reasonable sense.

However, if it's the first time they have worked on this problem, then they will likely need some time to learn the space, start collecting some data to establish a baseline, and get a sense of what the possibilities are. In this case, encourage the team to jump in and not get stuck in paralysis by analysis, and acknowledge with them that they will learn much more as they progress, and that the confidence level will, of course, be low in this first quarter because they are still learning what they don't know.

The team will also need guidance from leadership on how *ambitious* or conservative they should be in pursuing solutions. More on this topic in the next chapter, but for now, let's just say that it's important that the leaders provide the team with some guidance on how aggressive they would like the team to be in pursuing solutions.

But suppose the team is asked to pursue two objectives, and management considers the results they propose to achieve to be insufficient to achieve the necessary business results over the year. What then?

In this case, the leaders might ask the team to instead pursue just a single objective rather than two, or they might ask another team to collaborate with them on one of the problems.

What's most important is that if the leaders want the product team to feel ownership of the results, then the key results *must come from the team*.

Alignment

Once the leaders have worked with the product teams to decide which product teams will pursue which problems, they then need to ensure that the product teams and the broader organization are *aligned*.

For example, let's say we're working to bring to market a significant new offering to meet the needs of a new type of customer.

We need to ensure that any necessary platform team efforts are aligned to do the work necessary to support the experience product teams.

Similarly, we need to ensure the sales and marketing efforts are appropriately aligned.

If the sales and marketing teams were pursuing a different market, or not preparing for the new market, that would be an example of not being in alignment.

Keep-the-Lights-On Work

It's important for everyone—leaders and product teams alike—to keep in mind that the team objectives are not the *only* work that a product team is responsible for. It may be the most important work, but there is always what we call "keep-the-lights-on" work involving fixing critical problems, responding to customer issues, providing assistance to other teams, technical debt work, and more.

Over time, teams get a better understanding of what this ongoing cost is. In some cases, this ongoing work can reach the point that it consumes the team, in which case the leaders will need to potentially grow the team, or else not expect anything beyond this overhead work, or they can look into ways of reducing this overhead burden.

In the next chapter, we'll discuss one of the most important dimensions to a team objective, which is how *ambitious* the team should be in pursuing solutions.

Longer-Term Objectives

It's important to realize and acknowledge that, if you have a strong product strategy—based on focus and insights—and the product teams are working on important customer and business problems, where the work is hard but would cause meaningful impact, then in many cases the objectives will span multiple quarters.

Yet this often causes confusion.

First, it's important to distinguish long-term objectives from long-term key results.

Having an *objective* that lasts for multiple quarters is not the least bit unusual or problematic.

Good examples might be re-platforming work—which is usually on the order of one to three years of work—or major product challenges such as reducing customer churn or establishing product/market fit.

Where things get harder is with the *key results*. Now, it would be easy to just list some *activities* as our key results (an example of an activity would be to say we'll be "code complete by the end of the quarter"). But that's not what we want because that is output, not outcomes. The point is to show *results*.

The normal and preferred way we handle this is to break up the work into intermediate *product results*.

Here's an example: Let's say the goal is to get six referenceable customers on the path to product/market fit. That's a very powerful business result, and it's one of our best leading indicators of future sales.

(continued)

(continued)

The problem is that it may take two or three quarters of time to get the product deployed and in use by the customers and get them to the point where they're referenceable.

So how do we know in just the first quarter that we're making meaningful progress?

One possibility is that we might have the goal of just getting to two references this quarter.

If even that is not achievable, we can find a leading indicator for this. For example, a good key result would be getting eight prospective customers to sign a *non-binding letter of intent to buy*.[1]

That's clearly not as good as having actually bought the product, but it's a strong leading indicator and it has real business meaning.

---

[1] This technique is described in *INSPIRED*.

55

Ambition

We have now assigned each product team one or more specific problems to solve, but we're not quite done providing the necessary context.

When leaders ask a team to work on solving a problem, it's important to be clear with the team about the level of *ambition* they should strive for in their discovery work.

Should the team focus on low-risk but low-reward "sure things," or should they strive for more substantial and dramatic improvements?

One useful way to think about team objectives is that the leaders are placing a series of bets. Some are low risk, some are high risk, and some are in between.

They're making bets primarily on the people, but also on new enabling technologies, changing market conditions and customer behaviors, and the strength of the insights behind the product strategy.

As you'll see, if something is important enough, the leaders might choose to have several teams each attack a problem in their own way—some going for low-risk, quick wins, and others maybe going for much more ambitious but higher-risk approaches.

It's important not to confuse the level of ambition with the level of effort or sense of urgency.

Work ethic and sense of urgency are more a function of the culture—and also very likely your company's cash situation—and not what we are addressing here.

Teams that pursue low-risk/low-reward solutions will test product ideas that are much different from teams pursuing high-risk/high-reward solutions. The nature of the product discovery work will be different, and the techniques they use will likely be different as well.

It's also important not to confuse the level of ambition with a *high-integrity commitment* (which we'll discuss next). In this case, they are related, but a commitment is a special and critically important concept in its own right.

This is really all about risk management. If you have a very difficult and critically important problem—such as a churn rate that is too high to sustain a business—then experienced leaders will want to attack that problem from different angles and different levels of risk. They may have a couple of teams pursuing low-lying fruit, but they're worried that won't be enough. So they'll also have a couple teams pursuing much more ambitious approaches to the problem.

Some people like to refer to level of ambition as either a *roof shot* or a *moon shot*.

A *roof shot* refers to a team being asked to be conservative and pursue lower-risk, but also highly likely, tangible results. Optimization work fits well here.

On the other hand, a *moon shot* is when the team is asked to be very ambitious, such as going for a 10X improvement. It is expected that this is high risk, but we also believe that it's not impossible and the team is well-positioned to make a serious attempt. Yes, it's high risk, but it's also potentially high reward.

The point of a moon shot is to encourage the team to think beyond the small and safe optimizations, and revisit how the problem is solved today in the hopes of breaking through.

And still other companies prefer to attach a degree of confidence to the objective, such as 80 percent likely to achieve a roof shot versus 20 percent likely to achieve a moon shot.

These techniques are useful for communicating the desired level of ambition to the teams. But realize that, in terms of managing a portfolio of risk, there can and should be any level of ambition in between.

Imagine a professional poker player in Las Vegas being told she could only place bets of $1 or $10,000. That would seriously hinder her ability to work because she would rather be able to place a range of bets in various amounts based on the circumstances.

The point is that the leaders are essentially managing a portfolio of potential risk and reward. They may have certain teams that are more ambitious than others, even for the same objective.

Whatever the level of ambition associated with your key results, be sure to clearly communicate this across the organization. You especially don't want anyone to assume that something is a very-high-confidence result when it's not.

56

Commitments

While most objectives are meant to be aspirational, where we aren't sure which will succeed and to what degree, and we can vary the degree of ambition the team strives for, there are always certain cases where we need the team to make what is called a *high-integrity commitment*.

High-Integrity Commitments

Few people like what I'm about to say, but if you haven't learned this yet about the commercial product world, it's time you do:

In all businesses there are occasional situations where something important must be delivered by a specific deadline date.

The deadline might be a major industry trade show–driven date, or it might be a partner-driven date due to a contract, or a calendar-driven date due to tax days or the holiday period, or a marketing-driven date due to a purchased advertising campaign.

Realize that one of the main reasons leaders gravitate toward the command-and-control model of management—especially with old-style roadmaps of features and projects delivered on dates—is precisely because of this need to know when important things are going to happen.

So a key condition to moving to empowered teams is that the teams be able to provide dates and deliverables when necessary—not just the low-integrity dates of the roadmap era (because we really had very little understanding of what was being committed to), but *dates the leaders can count on.*

If you're used to conventional-style Agile processes, you probably know that coming up with a high-confidence date is very difficult if not impossible. However, if you're used to the model of doing product discovery in parallel with product delivery, then you know that coming up with a high-confidence date is not hard, so long as the company is willing to wait until the necessary product discovery work has been done before the date is provided (usually a few days).

Now, if a company has too many of these date-driven commitments, it is usually a sign of more serious issues, but I always try to explain to product teams that some amount of high-integrity commitments is necessary when trying to run a business.

Even if you don't have these external commitments, there will be cases where you depend on other product teams. An example is when you depend on a new capability from a platform team.

Now, most of the minor dependencies on changes from a platform team will be considered "keep-the-lights-on" work, but occasionally something more significant is required, and we'll treat that as a high-integrity commitment.

Remember that, just as a product team does not need all of their work to be an OKR, not all dependencies need to be a high-integrity commitment. The vast major of dependencies are not.

High-integrity commitments are intended for situations where you have an important external commitment or a very important and substantial internal commitment.

Deliverables

In these cases, we need to know with very high confidence if a team can deliver on this promise.

In the event your product team is asked to make a high-integrity commitment, you will need to investigate the commitment. This typically involves doing sufficient product discovery on the item so that your product team (especially the product manager, product designer, and tech lead) can determine whether the solution will be *valuable*, *usable*, *feasible*, and *viable*.

This often involves creating a quick prototype, such as a feasibility prototype, to ensure the engineers understand the scope of the necessary work to produce the necessary deliverable.

Once the product team believes they understand the solution sufficiently, they can estimate with high confidence how long it will take for them to deliver on this commitment (feasibility), and also whether that solution will work for the customer (value and usability) and work for your company (viability).

In the case of an experience team depending on a commitment from a platform team—where that platform team may need to provide an API or a new service that the experience team will build upon—the platform team can inherit from the experience team their objective and key results.

Most important, for high-integrity commitments, the actual deliverable that is the commitment needs to be noted and tracked independently of the key results.

Tracking High-Integrity Commitments

High-integrity commitments are given special treatment. We do not talk in terms of how ambitious the team needs to be. These are binary. The team either delivers what they promised or not. And a team that makes a high-integrity commitment is absolutely expected to deliver, or at the first sign of trouble, they need to raise the flag early and ask for help.

Further, we normally track these high-integrity commitments explicitly. In some companies, the CTO must personally agree to each high-integrity commitment because it is her reputation on the line.

As I've said many times in this book, empowered product teams are predicated on trust, and high-integrity commitments are one of the important ways that product teams build trust with leadership. So when you are asked to come up with a high-integrity commitment date, it is essential that you and your team be sure you can and will deliver on this commitment.

One final note of warning: high-integrity commitments and deliverables should be the exception and not the rule. Otherwise, it is a slippery slope and pretty soon your objectives become nothing more than a list of deliverables and dates, which is little more than a reformatted roadmap.

57

Collaboration

There are several forms of collaboration that are essential, yet often confusing to product organizations as they work to optimize for team autonomy and empowerment. Let's consider two specific kinds of collaboration: shared team objectives and common objectives.

Shared Team Objectives

The first and most basic form of collaboration is the concept of a *shared team objective*—when multiple teams share the same team objective. For an important objective, this is not at all unusual.

This is especially common in the case of large, company initiatives, which are essentially problems large enough that they require help from many product teams.

The most straightforward example of this is when both an experience product team and a platform team have the same objective because the platform team is expected to need to provide one or more new services to enable the experience product team.

In this case, the teams will normally collaborate to establish a simple form of contract with each other in the form of an API, and then both proceed to figure out their sides, and then they will again collaborate on testing and delivery.

Another form of shared team objective is when multiple teams temporarily combine their talents to solve a particularly hard problem. Especially on problems that benefit from a range of different skills brought to bear, bringing the teams together can often provide the knowledge and synergy required to quickly come up with an effective solution.

In certain situations, the teams will co-locate for a few days or a week in what is sometimes called a "swarm," which is an intense, highly collaborative technique to dive deep together on either or both discovery and delivery work for a particularly challenging problem.

Common Objectives

Another form of collaboration is a *common objective*—when multiple teams are asked to pursue the same problem, but each in their own way.

The reason for this is really risk management. We have a solid product strategy built on focus and insights, but we still need to execute on this strategy, and sometimes that involves solving some very hard problems.

If the problem is especially difficult, then we know that it can be hard to know which approach, if any, will produce the necessary results.

In this case, we may ask multiple teams to pursue the same problem and hope that at least one of those teams will be able to generate the necessary impact. It would be even better, of course, if all of them made a significant impact, but we know that's highly unlikely.

A good example of this might be when one of the focus areas is subscriber churn, where too many of our customers are leaving the service. There are, of course, many ways this problem can be addressed, and having multiple teams address this from multiple angles is often a good way to mitigate the risk.[1]

---

[1] I often encourage teams to pursue multiple approaches to difficult and critically important problems. "Opportunity Solution Trees," invented by discovery coach Teresa Torres, is a

In this case, the teams will need to communicate to ensure there are no conflicts between the work, but normally, each team tackles the problem based on the unique perspective and angle of their team and the code and technology they own. So, these approaches are usually largely independent and cumulative.

One of the questions that often comes up with common objectives is how to attribute progress to a specific team when multiple teams are making changes in parallel. This is referred to as the *product attribution problem*, and there are two common approaches to this which will be discussed in Chapter 59, Accountability.

The higher-order point is that it is normal and often wise to have multiple teams pursue the same objectives simultaneously.

Companies that avoid shared or common objectives in the name of autonomy or communication often limit their ability to solve the toughest and most important problems.

---

helpful technique for identifying and evaluating multiple approaches to solving an important problem.

58

Management

Continuing our series on team objectives, once product teams have their team objectives for the quarter and are pursuing them, active management will still be needed.

Much as the product strategy requires ongoing tracking and managing by the product leaders, the team objectives require ongoing tracking and managing by the product team.

Keep-the-Lights-On Work

Remember that the team objectives are not the only work that a product team is responsible for. We also have the "keep-the-lights-on" work we discussed earlier. We do need to keep an eye on this ongoing work because, if it spikes, the team won't be able to make much progress on their team objectives.

Weekly Tracking

The key is to make sure the product teams are actively managing progress on the team objectives, otherwise it is all too possible that weeks and then months will fly by with little progress.

At a minimum, product teams stay on top of progress by discussing at weekly check-ins where they are, what is upcoming, and where they might need help. These weekly team objective check-ins are the key mechanism that teams use to track and manage their own progress.

This check-in might happen in its own meeting, or it might get included with a standup once a week.

Occasionally, the teams will raise an issue that requires the leaders to coordinate to resolve conflicts or issues.

Staying on Track

In terms of handling issues that arise, there are two key points:

First, the product manager specifically needs to communicate any important issues with her manager, so that the manager can have the chance to provide assistance where possible.

Second, it's critical that each member of the product team get the ongoing coaching she needs to develop. And some of that coaching will pertain to the team objective-related issues she faces.

For product teams that are not yet experienced, the managers will need to be more proactive in their questions and coaching to ensure that the teams are making progress on their team objectives.

If the team needs the assistance of management, then the sooner this need is raised the better chance management has of helping in a timely and effective manner.

It's also an important obligation to alert management as early as possible in the event that there is a question as to the team's ability to deliver on a high-integrity commitment.

Similarly, if there is a dependency—such as on another product team—this dependency will need to be managed and tracked carefully. If they are a dependency for another team—whether this is a high-integrity commitment the team made, or just normal keep-the-lights-on work—then they will need to keep this in mind and ensure this work is completed in time for the team that depends on them.

Helping Our Colleagues

While so much of empowered product teams is about optimizing for the product teams, it's also important to recognize that we will often need to help out our colleagues on other product teams, and we very likely have situations where we will depend on them helping us out as well.

The best product teams know that, when it comes to tech companies, we either *all* succeed, or *none* of us succeed. And it's not unusual to find yourself in the situation where you believe you must do something that's not in the best interest of your product team, but you see that it is in the best interest of the customer and of the broader organization.

CHAPTER

59

Accountability

The companion to empowerment is *accountability*.

Product teams are given the space and time to come up with the solutions to the problems they are assigned, but with that empowerment comes responsibility and accountability.

So, what happens when a team fails to deliver on one or more of their team objectives?

The first thing to keep in mind is that accountability is directly related to ambition. If the team was asked to be very ambitious (e.g., a moon shot) and the attempts failed to generate the desired results, then that is largely expected.

However, if the team was asked to be conservative (e.g., a roof shot), or even more important, if they were asked to make a *high-integrity commitment* and they failed to deliver in this situation, then this is where accountability comes into play.

Each product team, as well as the organization as a whole, needs to continue to grow and improve. These cases can provide excellent learning opportunities.

If a team fails substantially on their team objectives, then I encourage the team to treat this in much the same way we treat an outage.

Get the product team together with a set of their peers—especially peers from any product teams that were impacted by their failure—and have the team discuss what they believe was the root cause of their failure. Ask them to explore what they believe they could—and should—have done differently.

Perhaps if they had shared with management at the first signs of a problem, they could have received help? Or perhaps the product team that was depending on them could have made other arrangements, or even helped themselves?

Note that these lessons learned also apply to the team's managers. Were there signs that were missed? Was there coaching that could have been provided earlier? Were there questions that should have been asked by management that weren't?

These *team objective postmortems* are not fun for the team, but they are typically very constructive and helpful. Is there some embarrassment at admitting your failures to your peers? Sometimes. But that's part of the feedback we all need to continue to learn and grow.

Attribution of Key Results

It is not in the least unusual to have multiple teams working on the same problems to solve (objectives), and/or sharing one or more measures of success (key results). In fact, that can be a very powerful strategy.

But you may be wondering in this case, how would we hold teams accountable to results if many things are changing every day, and we don't know which changes by which teams are helping, which are hurting, and which make no difference?

This is known as the *product attribution problem*, and in general, there are two common ways of answering this.

The first, which depends on strong levels of traffic, is with an A/B test. This isolates the contribution of just one team's changes from everything else going on in other teams or from elsewhere across the company (e.g., marketing programs).

(continued)

(continued)

The second, which involves dividing up the various contributions to the relevant key result by channel or source, is referred to as *slicing*.[1]

For example, suppose we have three different product teams in a job marketplace company—all working to increase the number of job applications. We could slice the number of job applications between the different channels:

- Mobile team: Applications from mobile notifications
- Search team: Applications from search results
- Recommendations team: Applications from recommendations

Slicing is simpler conceptually than running A/B tests, and teams often like the feeling of control over a more narrowly defined target that is more directly within their influence, although it is not usually as rigorous or predictive. For example, the same user often interacts with more than one channel.

Slicing is not always possible, as sometimes there are several contributing factors at play (for example, many factors influence subscriber churn).

On the other hand, A/B tests depend on sufficient traffic to yield dependable results in a reasonable amount of time.

---

[1] This term was coined by my friend and OKR coach, Felipe Castro.

60

Objectives in Perspective

We need some way to manage and assign work to product teams, and we want to do this in a way that is empowering and executes on our product strategy. This is the purpose of team objectives.

Assuming you have embraced the empowered product team model, and you have capable leaders (admittedly, these are two big assumptions), it is fairly straightforward.

Here are the 10 most important keys to effective team objectives:

1. The most important thing is to empower teams by assigning them *problems to solve* and then give the teams the space to solve them. For them to make good decisions, they will also need you to share the strategic context, especially the product strategy.

2. We love it when product teams volunteer to work on specific objectives, and we try to accommodate this when possible to

leverage their motivation and enthusiasm for the problem. But we can't always do so because we need to make sure we cover everything we need to.

3. Selecting the objectives to be worked on, and ultimately deciding which team or teams works on each objective, is *the explicit responsibility of product leadership*. However—and this is critically important for empowerment—*the key results need to come from the team*.

4. It's normal that there's a back and forth—not that the leaders doubt or question what the teams propose as their key results, but rather judging which investments are worth the effort and associated risk. For example, suppose a team believes that, with their other objectives, they can only make a very minimal improvement to a specific, important KPI. The leaders might consider having that team focus exclusively on the one objective or decide to ask a different team to pursue it or help in some way.

5. There is nothing wrong with assigning the same objective to multiple teams—each team tackling the problem from its own perspective and skills. In fact, for difficult product problems, this is often a very effective technique. On hard problems, we expect that not all teams will make the same level of progress, and we can't anticipate in advance what the teams will learn when they each get deep into their product discovery work.

6. Similarly, there is nothing wrong with asking multiple teams to *collaborate* on the same team objective. It's not unusual to ask multiple teams to work together—especially when the problem requires different sets of skills. A common situation is asking a platform team and an experience team to collaborate on a difficult problem.

7. For product teams to come up with key results, it's essential that they understand the level of *ambition* you want from them. We need to be clear with teams when we want them to be very ambitious (aka *moon shot*), when we want them to be conservative (aka *roof shot*), and when we need them to make a *high-integrity commitment*.

8. Product teams can only be accountable to the results if they are empowered to figure out a solution that works and if they are the ones to come up with the key results.

9. The product leaders have to realize that while team objectives are critically important, they are not the only things that the product team is working on. Every team has some level of on-going "keep-the-lights-on" activities. This includes such things as fixing critical bugs, handling customer situations, and so forth.

10. Normally, these team objectives are created or updated every quarter. That gives teams enough time to make real progress, yet not too much time that the business can't adjust to changes. There may be occasional situations where team objectives need to change *during* the quarter, but these should be the exception rather than the rule.

To keep all this in perspective, remember that the essence of this is simply having a knowledgeable leader sit down with the product team and explain the strategic context. Then, explain the problem you need the team to solve, and how success is measured.

Whether you use a formal technique like OKRs to do this is much less important. The key is to have this conversation, and for leaders to provide the necessary coaching, and give the product teams the space to solve the problems in the best way they see fit.

Leader Profile:
Christina Wodtke

Path to Leadership

I first met Christina in 2003, when she was running a design team at early Yahoo. Christina had studied photography in art school and learned product design working with several early internet teams.

I then watched her career as she spent time in both product and design leadership roles at LinkedIn, MySpace, and Zynga.

But no matter where she worked, she was known for her commitment to coaching and developing the people fortunate enough to work for her.

Which is why I felt she found her true calling joining the faculty at Stanford, where she teaches human–computer interaction and product design.

Christina has also published several books, mostly around the theme of strong, empowered product teams—including a popular book on OKRs and another on leadership and team empowerment.[1]

This is why I've always considered her a kindred spirit.

Leadership in Action

Christina was very fortunate to learn product and design directly from some exceptional leaders. They showed her the real power of an empowered team.

Here's her story in her own words:

I joined Yahoo in 2002, when the internet was still very young, and Yahoo was at the time a very fast-growing and influential tech company.

I was the first designer for the search team and was lucky enough to work for Irene Au.

Irene had been a product designer for Netscape, and she went on to build the design team at Yahoo and later Google.

Irene believed I had potential, and even though I didn't have management experience in tech (I had been a restaurant manager back in my starving artist days) Irene mentored me and gave me my first direct reports.

Her real teaching, though, was watching her empower and grow everyone who worked for her. She gave me the role model I needed: someone who was strong yet always kind. She taught me that you don't have to choose between empathy and authority.

---

[1] Christina Wodtke, *Radical Focus* (San Francisco: Cucina Media LLC, 2015) and *The Team That Managed Itself* (San Francisco: Cucina Media LLC, 2019) are good examples.

Soon, another very influential person played a significant role in my career.

Jeff Weiner ran the search business at Yahoo, and he later went on to join LinkedIn (coincidentally, when I worked there as a product manager) and has been their CEO for nearly 12 years.

Jeff was the person who first encouraged me to move into a leadership role, running the Search design team, which meant at least 20 people. Overnight, I managed way more people than I had ever done before.

I definitely had my doubts. I had been getting more comfortable with managing the two folks who reported to me, but this position was likely to develop into a serious leadership role, and I wasn't at all sure I would be able to do the job.

I'll never forget the moment. We were sitting in the cafeteria, and I told Jeff he should try to find someone better. He said, "I know you can do this job." He believed in me so hard I *had* to believe in myself.

During this period of rapid growth for Yahoo, and especially search, I soon found myself not just a manager, but a manager of managers for a fairly large-sized group. A total of 80 people reported into 9 managers who reported to me.

I realized I needed to stop designing *products* in order to start designing *a place where good design could happen*. I had to design teams that could manage themselves.

With such a large group covering such a range of design skills, it was clear to me that there was no way I could be an expert in all of these areas. And even if I was, I didn't have *time* to do everything. I realized then that, if I ever wanted to sleep again, the only way I would succeed was if I could trust and depend on my team.

When I sat down for the first meeting with the managers who reported to me, one asked me a question about how to handle a problem. I don't recall what it was, but I do recall that I asked him what he thought we should do. He made a suggestion, and I said, "Great. Let's do that." That was the moment when the power shifted from me to *we*. From then on, those meetings were a place where anyone could bring any problem and we'd all work on it as a team.

I've been making teams out of groups of individuals ever since. Teams can make miracles happen when no individual can.

Finally, I'd be remiss if I didn't mention one other person who changed how I saw teams at Yahoo. Ken Norton also worked for Jeff, and Ken ran product management for Yahoo Shopping. Ken went on to a long and very successful career in product at Google, and then Google Ventures.

Until I met Ken, I thought product managers were essentially project managers I had to chase away from my designers so they could get work done.

It was the first time I had seen real product management up close, and Ken set the bar for me on what good product teams need and deserve from their product managers. Ken taught me that product and design should always be partners, and this begins with respect for each other and each other's disciplines. We are better together.

I know so many designers that have never met a strong product manager, but once you have, you don't want to go back.

I am truly grateful for the leadership skills I learned from Irene, Jeff, and Ken, and these lessons have served me well in my career since Yahoo. Most important, I have always tried to pay it forward by investing in the lives and careers of others.

VIII

Case Study

This case study is necessarily quite detailed. To get a true understanding of why a company and product organization make the decisions they do, you need considerable context.

If you believe you already have a solid grasp of the concepts in this book, especially in terms of team topology, product strategy, and team objectives, then feel free to skim this part.

However, my hope is that you will consider the effort to understand the details of this example worthwhile, as you will see how these important, but difficult, concepts play out in practice—in a real organization struggling with rapid growth, scale, and tech-debt challenges.

You will also be able to see a detailed example of how a company staffed with ordinary people was able to achieve extraordinary results.

This case study is based on my experience with an actual jobs marketplace company.

I chose this company because I think this is a good, representative example of a growth-stage company dealing with challenges of scale.

The company also has elements of an enterprise business and elements of an early-stage startup. So, I think this case study applies to most companies.

I also like using a jobs marketplace company because they sell to businesses on one side (employers) and consumers on the other side (job seekers), and they have an internal platform supporting both.

However, there are two important caveats:

First, this example represents the company at a specific point in time (from a few years ago). There is obviously relevant history that impacted the situation I encountered, but in this case study, we take their situation as a given.

Second, while this is based on an actual example, I did take the liberty of layering on a couple additional complexities that did not occur during this particular quarter, but do occur frequently enough—and did in fact did occur at this company at a later point in time. I feel it's helpful to illustrate how these situations were handled in practice. So, in this case study, I portray that all of these things happened in the same quarter.

I do not share in this case study the actual company name or identifying information. That's because, for a case study to be truly useful, I need to share with you the good, the bad, and the ugly. Most companies are understandably not eager to share anything other than the good, even if things managed to turn out well, as was the case here.

One of the benefits to choosing a jobs marketplace is that there are many of them around the world, and I've had the chance to work with quite a few of them. I've found that, while every situation truly is unique, most of the important dynamics are not so different between them. That helps me have confidence that I can be candid here and not worry about embarrassing anyone personally.

You'll see that there's a lot going on here, and it can appear messy, which is simply a reflection of reality in this, and indeed most companies—even ones that do very well.

Finally, please don't confuse a case study with any sort of ideal situation. There are many things that could have been done differently, and arguably better, but the point of a case study is to show what was actually done and why.

Hopefully, this example will give you a good sense for the types of considerations you will want to keep in mind as you face these and similar questions yourselves, and the type of leadership you will need to provide.

62

Company Backgrounder

To understand this case study, it's important to have at least a high-level understanding of this company's business. It's a typical, two-sided marketplace with employers on one side and job seekers on the other.

On the employer side, the company sells job postings to businesses, ranging from individual hiring managers at small businesses, up to medium-sized businesses. They were starting to see interest from larger enterprises with dedicated HR departments, but the product at this point in time was not yet designed or suitable for this market.

On the job-seeker side, the focus is on people actively looking for new employment—in their case, mainly for professional (aka white-collar) jobs. Specifically, these are not hourly or temporary workers.[1]

---

[1]In terms of the business dynamics, I am simplifying here. Especially because, in a jobs marketplace, there are both active job seekers (need a job now) and passive job seekers (if something better comes along I'll check it out). They have different needs, and there is real value in understanding and identifying each—both for the seeker as well as for the employer.

At the time of this case study, the company is currently five years old, with annual revenues of approximately $45MM and growing at roughly 30% per year. They are close to profitability but are trying to focus on growth.

There are approximately 230 people in the company—95 in product/engineering, 45 in sales, 17 in marketing, 33 in customer success, 10 in IT, and 30 in G&A.

In terms of the executive team, there was a CEO, CFO, head of sales (CRO), and head of marketing (CMO). Then, of course, there was a head of product (CPO) and a head of technology (CTO) and you'll read about both of them below.

It's worth pointing out that in large enterprises, this is also about the size of a typical business unit.

63

Company Objectives

E ach year, the company's board of directors sets annual company objectives. This involves a substantial amount of consideration and debate among the executive team and the members of the board about business strategy, competitive landscape, and potential levels of investment.

The board has the option of raising additional capital, or using other forms of financing, or deciding the company should focus instead on becoming cash flow positive—potentially at the expense of growth—or anything in between.

The overall guidance this year was to continue to grow and improve the core business—not taking the eye off the ball in terms of helping employers fill jobs, helping seekers find jobs, and continuing to grow the business with strong growth rates.

This year, however, the company has decided there is a promising expansion opportunity in pursuing large enterprises,[1] and they want to look into broadening the company's products and go-to-market capability to better serve this market.

They have decided to increase the investment level by funding an additional product team (6 additional people), as well as additional enterprise-specific sales, marketing, and customer-success staff (11 additional people).

The board explained that, if this initial foray into enterprise goes well, they expect to make a more sizable investment the following year.

As a reminder, these company objectives are coming from the senior executive team, with the support and approval of the board of directors. These are presented here in OKR format, but what is important is (1) their focus on a small number of meaningful objectives, and (2) they are measuring the results based on business results.

Objective 1: Continue to grow core business.

- Key Result 1: Grow core business revenue by at least 25%.
- Key Result 2: Reduce annual employer churn from 6% down to 5% or lower.
- Key Result 3: Increase seeker success rate from 23% to at least 27%.

---

[1]The company had been getting multiple inquiries from enterprises for at least two years. These were primarily coming from HR people who had used the jobs marketplace at former companies and believed it would be a better solution than what they found at their new company.

Objective 2: Establish company as a proven provider for enterprise-class companies.

- Key Result 1: Demonstrate product/market fit by developing no fewer than six enterprise-class reference employers.

Product Vision and Principles

The company has a strong and compelling product vision and principles, but I will not share it here as it would make obvious the actual company being profiled.

However, I can say that the company was founded on the desire to help people find the best job possible given their capabilities, and to help employers find strong candidates for their open positions.

While that's easy to say, this company depends on repeat business from employers, and when faced with decisions that trade off short-term benefits for their company versus the long-term benefit for their customers, I saw them consistently deciding in favor of their customers.

I saw those values and principles play out multiple times, so at least I was personally convinced that they weren't just empty words.

Most important, the leaders of product management, engineering, and design—and the members of the product teams—had the product vision, product principles, and especially the product strategy in mind as they decided on, and then pursued, their team objectives.

CHAPTER
65

Team Topology

At the beginning of the quarter, the company had 16 product teams comprised of 60 engineers, 12 product managers,[1] 10 product designers, 2 user researchers, and 3 data analysts.

There are 2 directors of product management (one for employer and one for seeker) and 1 director of user experience design (all three reporting to the CPO), along with 3 directors of engineering (one each for employer, seeker, and platform—all reporting to the CTO).

---

[1] You'll note that they only have 12 product managers but 16 product teams. This will be explained below.

Team Topology Overview

They have two types of experience teams—those focused on employers and those focused on job seekers—designed to align with the two main types of customers. They also have about a third of their resources devoted to an internal platform that the experience teams are all built upon.

EMPLOYER TEAMS		JOB SEEKER TEAMS	
Employer Home	Employer Communications	Seeker Home	Job Applications
Recruiter Tools	Enterprise Tools	Job Search	Seeker Communications
Premium Services		Job Recommendations	Mobile Apps

PLATFORM TEAMS		
Shared Services	Data and Reporting	Tools
Payments and Billing	Infrastructure	

Employer Teams

- Employer Home
- Recruiter Tools
- Premium Services
- Employer Communications
- Enterprise Tools (new team)

Job Seekers Teams

- Seeker Home/Personalization
- Job Search
- Job Recommendations
- Job Applications
- Seeker Communications
- Mobile Apps

Platform Teams

- Shared Services
- Payments and Billing
- Data and Reporting
- Infrastructure
- Tools

Employer Organization

The Employer organization is there to serve the needs of the hiring managers and HR departments. They currently offer a freemium service where the first job posting is free, but to get additional postings—or premium services including featured jobs—there are listing and promotional fees.

These are the actual product teams and what each is responsible for:[2]

Employer Home—This team is responsible for the dashboard for employers showing current job postings and applications in various states of review. This team also provides the ability to post a job, and to ensure that job is visible in organic search results (SEO).

Recruiter Tools—For employers that have HR departments, there are advanced capabilities for loading and managing large numbers of open jobs and managing the flow of applications, interviews, and decisions. This team also provides ways to search the marketplace for seekers with specific attributes, and then allowing the recruiter to reach out to these job seekers rather than wait for them to apply.

Premium Services—Employers have several optional services that are all designed to help them fill their open positions more quickly or generate an increased flow of applications. These premium services include having the jobs included in emails, featured jobs, and so on.

---

[2]Just to be clear, the "product" is the jobs marketplace, and each of these 16 product teams is responsible for a subset of this larger product.

Employer Communications—This team manages the several forms of ongoing communications with employers, especially having to do with the status of their open jobs, including emails, text, and notifications. This is both transactional (information about a specific job) and marketing (encouraging the employer to post additional jobs). This team is also responsible for online recruiting of new employer customers looking to post jobs (SEO and SEM).

Enterprise Tools (newly formed team)—As the company moves toward helping large enterprises with their recruiting, they believe they need several enterprise-specific capabilities, such as integration with large-scale applicant-tracking systems (ATS). This team is focused on identifying what is necessary to satisfy enterprise employers and delivering those capabilities.[3]

Job Seeker Organization

The Job Seeker organization is focused on helping people who are looking for a job to find a job.

Seeker Home—This team provides the core experience for the job seeker on both the web and native mobile apps. This includes a dashboard of jobs the seeker is currently tracking, the status of applications, and recommendations for other jobs that may be a fit.

Job Search—This team provides the services that allow a job seeker to search the marketplace based on job attributes.

Job Recommendations—This team utilizes the data that has been collected in terms of searches and the seeker profile, and generates recommended jobs.

---

[3] This team ended up embedding a product marketing person full-time on the team because there was so much critical work to be done in terms of developing the reference customers, the go-to-market considerations, and starting to understand and prepare the sales-enablement materials. This turned out to be very important and is a great practice for any product where messaging more specifically to a target segment or a new business is important. The book *LOVED* goes into more depth on scenarios where product marketing is particularly important in unpacking what's necessary for go-to-market success for a product in situations like these.

Job Applications—This team allows a seeker to apply for a specific job—collecting the information that has already been provided and combining it with any job-specific information that may be needed for that particular job.

Seeker Communications—This team handles the various forms of communication with job seekers including email, text, and notifications. This is both transactional (status of a job application) as well as marketing (encouraging the seeker to return and apply for additional jobs). This team is also responsible for online recruiting of new job seekers (SEM and SEO).

Mobile Apps—This team provides job seekers with a native mobile experience for both iOS and Android devices. This team works very closely with the Seeker Home team as they try to keep the web experience and the mobile experiences comparable.[4]

Platform Organization

The Platform organization exists to help the Employer and Job Seeker teams be more efficient in serving their respective customers. By providing a reliable platform, the experience teams can focus on innovating in terms of value for their users and customers and not have to worry about the lower-level services.

Shared Services—Whenever teams realize that there are potentially duplicate efforts going on across different teams, the Shared Services team works to provide a single solution that meets the needs of the various teams. This includes services such as authentication, preference management, and dozens of other similar capabilities. The Shared Services team is there to help make the Employer and Job Seeker teams more productive.

Payments and Billing—This team handles all financial transactions including recurring payments, discounts, promotions, and the

---

[4]When this work was going on, many companies had a special, dedicated "native mobile apps" team because so few engineers had at that point been trained on iOS and Android native app development. Within a year or so, this work moved into the other seeker teams—especially the Seeker Home team—which is, in general, a much better solution.

various payment methods. There is a significant amount of complexity managed by this small, but very experienced team, but the benefit is that the other teams don't have to understand this complexity in order to use the services.

Data and Reporting—Many parts of the company depend on reporting of the marketplace activity, starting with the product teams, but also including finance, marketing, sales, and company leadership. This team provides the reporting infrastructure that is fed to the employer and seeker dashboards, as well as enabling self-service reporting by the rest of the company.

Infrastructure—The Infrastructure team is responsible for ensuring that the technology infrastructure is able to meet the needs of the business. As such, they have taken the lead on major technical debt issues as well as assisting the engineers in the product teams with overcoming scale and performance challenges.

Tools—The Tools team is there to help all the product teams— Employer, Job Seeker, and Platform—with tools and services to help them be more productive and generate more-reliable systems. This includes site-monitoring services, test-and-release automation (DevOps) tools, and miscellaneous productivity and team collaboration tools.

66

Product Strategy

N ow that the company objectives are clear and the product vision and principles are in place, the leaders of the product organization (in this case, the CPO, the CTO, and their managers) need to update their product strategy to deliver on the company objectives.

COMPANY MISSION / OBJECTIVES / SCORECARD
PRODUCT VISION & PRINCIPLES
TEAM TOPOLOGY
PRODUCT STRATEGY

STRATEGIC CONTEXT

OBJECTIVES   OBJECTIVES   OBJECTIVES

PRODUCT TEAMS

DISCOVERY   DISCOVERY   DISCOVERY
DELIVERY   DELIVERY   DELIVERY

Note that there is no guarantee that they will be able to come up with a way to do everything the board is hoping for in the year.

If the product leaders determine this is just not plausible, then the leaders will need to raise this back up to the CEO to either consider increasing funding or reducing some of the expectations, or possibly a blend of the two. But before that can be known, they will need to work closely with the product teams to determine what they believe they *can* do.

It's also important to note that, while the company objectives are annual, the product team objectives are quarterly. So, the product leaders and product teams have the ability to adjust course based on progress, obstacles encountered, new learnings and new insights, and new opportunities uncovered.

As a reminder of the big picture regarding product strategy:

Recall that a product strategy begins with *focus* on a small number of truly important objectives.

Then we will search for *insights* that can be leveraged to make a real impact on these company objectives.

Next, we will map the insights into *action*, which means identifying a set of one or more objectives for each product team to work on.

Finally, the managers will need to actively *track progress* on the objectives and be prepared to remove obstacles and make adjustments in support of the product teams.

Focus

The leaders of the company have identified two company objectives for the year. One is around continuing to grow the core business, and the other is around exploring a new expansion product.

In this situation, the senior leaders of the company have helped considerably with focus by narrowing down the company objectives to just two key objectives. If the leaders had a much larger list, then the product strategy likely would have needed to begin with narrowing that list down.

In every company, there are many opportunities that could be pursued. In this case, they were seriously debating geographic expansion, as well as offering additional services to employers (e.g., verification services and drug testing services), but none of these made the cut for this year.

Note that the context also included guidance that pursuing the new business opportunity should not come at the expense of the work on the core business.

Insights

Growing Core Business Objective

The first company objective pertains to growing the core business.

The business result the company hopes for is 25% growth, and of course, there are any number of strategies for achieving this growth. But the leaders realize it's unlikely that just optimizing the current product will yield more than 5–10% growth.

There is organic growth still occurring in this space, but there are also several new competitors now, so they do not want to count on organic growth.

They believe they must do a better job than ever in taking care of their current customers—both employers and seekers—and, in addition, they must go out and win new customers.

A key part of the product strategy work involves a review and discussion of the key marketplace health KPIs and user research learnings.

In particular, they know that employers want to fill jobs quickly, but they want to make sure they are providing their hiring managers with a choice of *qualified candidates.*

Employers are obviously disappointed when they receive no applications, and they are frustrated and slow to decide when they have only a very small number of applications. That much was well known.

However, what was not well known—and was a consequence of doing some user research motivated by an observation from the data—is that, if there are *too many* applications for a given job, it creates its own set of problems. This is because it takes too long for employers to sift through and make a hiring decision. Further, on the jobs where too many people apply, this also leaves a disproportionate number of disappointed job seekers.

Their analysis of the data shows that positions are filled the fastest, and hiring managers are happiest, when they receive a minimum of *8* but *no more than 25 qualified applications.*

Based on these numbers, they know that 28% of employer job postings receive too few applications and 7% receive too many. While this doesn't sound so bad, it's worse than it looks because the most-appealing jobs are getting way too many applicants, and disappointing far too many job seekers. Once a job posting has enough qualified applicants, maybe the algorithms could direct those candidates to more promising jobs?

They believe this correlates directly with employer churn, especially for those receiving too few applications.

They also believe this correlates directly with seeker satisfaction, especially for the many people who apply for a job they're excited about but never hear back.

So, as a strategic focus for the next quarter or two (depending on progress), they want employer teams to figure out ways of helping a higher percentage of jobs to get at least 8 qualified applications, and they also want to reduce the number of jobs that get more than 25 applications. They believe this will reduce employer churn, generating more job postings per employer while also generating more successful responses for job seekers.

From the job-seeker perspective, they know job seekers need to find a job. The clock is ticking. They are looking for a good fit, and they would like to have a choice of jobs, but it is primarily about quickly finding a match.

They know from the data that, if a job seeker does not submit at least one application in her first 48 hours using the marketplace, then she is very unlikely to return. They also know that only 27% of seekers who register actually submit at least one application.

They also know from the data that there is a substantial difference in seeker success for those job seekers that download the native mobile app to help them in their job search (32%), versus those that don't (15%).

While the first insight was not a surprise (you only have a 48-hour window to get a seeker engaged), the second insight *was* a surprise. Registering is such a large percentage of the work involved in submitting an application, and they struggled to understand why so many people would successfully complete the registration process, yet not apply for at least one job.

So, as the second strategic focus for the next quarter, they want seeker teams to figure out ways of helping more job seekers find a match and submit at least one application in that first 48-hour window—especially for the people who have registered.

Enterprise Employer Objective

The second company objective is fairly straightforward. Not easy, but clear. They will have a new-product team, and that team will have a clear assignment based on the company objective.

They know that many of the assumptions around the core business may not hold true for this new product, as selling to enterprises is substantially different from selling directly to hiring managers. Therefore, they want to approach this objective by starting with identifying product/market fit. Further, they don't want the team distracted with anything else as they pursue product/market fit. It is all too easy for a team to get ahead of themselves with a new product.

While the work for the new team is straightforward, they are expecting that some of the work the new team needs to do will impact several of the other teams.

Demonstrating product/market fit in the enterprise will likely be an initiative that spans most of the year and will require changes and support from several other teams—probably most, if not all, of the Employer organization teams, and at least the Job Seeker organization Job Application team, and most, if not all, of the Platform organization teams.

Therefore, they will need to ensure that those teams have support for this work as an objective.

Re-platforming Objective

While the two company objectives will drive much of the product work, there is another objective that comes not from the company executives or board, but rather from the product leaders.

The organization had been struggling with some very substantial technical debt due to the rapid growth of the business during the preceding several years. The previous year, the engineering organization proposed a two-year plan to move the organization to a more modern, AWS-based, microservices-based implementation.

The plan enumerated 20 major system components and proposed to tackle several of these components each quarter—in a specific, intentional order—over what they estimated would take roughly two years.

Note that the engineering team believed they could accomplish this re-platforming work in a shorter timeframe if they were willing to pause or suspend other work. However, this would have caused major disruption in the ability to add ongoing capabilities for the business.

This was therefore considered too risky to the business, so they instead decided on an incremental plan to strategically rebuild the infrastructure over a two-year period. This quarter represents the third quarter of work on this plan.

Much of this work, but by no means all, was expected to fall on the platform product teams.

Action

The leaders are now ready to turn these insights into action, which means to get teams working on solving the problems they need to solve.

They know they could simply assign problems to each product team, but they also know that this would miss some important information.

While they understand the problems and the insights, what they know they can't know is the enabling technology available to each team, and their own ideas and enthusiasm about the various problems.

Therefore, their next step is to open up this quarterly team objectives discussion to the broader product organization. The leaders want to get the product teams thinking about how best to tackle these topics.

So, the product leaders ask for the members of the product teams to meet with them to discuss the product strategy.[1]

---

[1] In this company, they encouraged all members of the product teams to attend this strategy briefing. In some companies, they only push for the product manager, product designer, and tech leads, while in other companies, it is just the product managers. This is partly cultural and partly a function of the size of the organization and whether they are all in the same

During this session, the head of product starts by updating everyone on the company objectives, then moving into the product strategy work and sharing the relevant data—and especially the insights.

The leaders explain that, in the coming days, they will approach each product team with one or two important problems to solve in support of these three objectives. But, in the meantime, they'd like the teams to consider the problems and the ideas and technology they believe can help.[2]

They explain to the teams that, if everyone wanted to work on the same thing, this would of course not work because they have to do their best to cover all three objectives.

However, they also explain that, if a product team is especially optimistic about a problem they believe they can help on, they are motivated to try to accommodate those desires wherever possible.

Note that this process is necessarily a combination of top down and bottom up. The teams have all been provided the company objectives and product strategy (top down), and they are all asked to consider what they may be able to do to contribute (bottom up). This begins a back and forth with the leadership to ensure that as much of the company objectives can be completed as possible. However, the key results always come from the bottom up.

Management

In the next chapter, we'll share where the team objectives actually ended up for each of the product teams. However, it would be misleading to share these results without describing the many obstacles and challenges that had to be dealt with to get to where they landed.

---

office. The reason this company pushed for most if not all engineers to attend is that they were big believers in the role engineers play in innovation.

[2]Just to be clear, we don't expect every team to contribute to every objective, as different objectives are more relevant to different teams. However, we do want each team to consider what they might be able to do to help with the specific team objectives and the more-general company objectives, and to make it known when they identify promising opportunities.

Therefore, here are the major obstacles that emerged, along with how those obstacles were dealt with:

- Too much work landed on one particular team—in this case, the Employer Home team. The two solutions the leaders came up with were to either pass some of the work to other teams or add one or more engineers to this team. They ended up doing some of both.

- The most common obstacle was when one team identified a dependency on another team and needed to know whether or not they could count on getting what they need during the quarter. This happened both while planning for the quarter, and in multiple cases during the quarter, when the teams were deeper into the work. The dependency was mostly on a platform team, but sometimes, for example, a change to an employer team required a change from a job seeker team. In each case, it required the managers to talk directly to the parties involved to see if and when the dependency could be accommodated. In most cases, a little "horse trading" was able to satisfy both parties.[3]

- The Employer Home team identified that they needed some significant SEO help from product marketing to be able to deliver on their objectives. The managers ended up embedding an SEO person into this team for the quarter. They believed from their data analysis of the new-seeker funnel that, if they could do a better job on SEO, they could attract more-qualified job seekers and as a result improve the success rate.

- The Infrastructure team had shared the technical debt re-platforming plan, as they had the prior quarters, but one of the teams (Enterprise Tools) realized that the timing was not going to be good for a critical area they needed to work on. The Infrastructure team ended up changing the specific modules planned for the quarter to avoid wasted work.

---

[3] However, there were some cases where the platform team could not commit to providing what was needed early enough for the experience team to use in time to finish in the quarter. In this case, the experience team was not able to deliver their solutions until the following quarter.

- The Shared Services team ended up with a very long list of work that they needed to do in order to support the various experience teams, and they needed help prioritizing all the different requests coming in from all the different teams. This was addressed in part by providing guidance on priorities. However, in certain cases, it worked best to allow the experience team to write the necessary software and then contribute that code to the platform (pending approval by the Shared Services team).

67

Product Team Objectives

W hat follows below is the result of the negotiation between the product leaders and the product teams, and also the negotiation between the teams themselves when one identified a dependency on another.

COMPANY MISSION / OBJECTIVES / SCORECARD
PRODUCT VISION & PRINCIPLES
TEAM TOPOLOGY
PRODUCT STRATEGY

STRATEGIC CONTEXT

PRODUCT TEAMS

OBJECTIVES OBJECTIVES OBJECTIVES
DISCOVERY DISCOVERY DISCOVERY
DELIVERY DELIVERY DELIVERY

In some cases, the objectives that were initially suggested by the team worked out fine, but in other cases there was substantial back and forth so as to maximize the likelihood that as much of the company's annual objectives as possible could be achieved.[1] Much of this was reflected in the discussion on the desired level of ambition for each objective.

---

[1] It's important to emphasize that this back and forth is normal. It is a reflection of the fact that some things come from the leaders and other things come from the teams.

Please keep in mind that the team objectives are not meant to cover everything a product team works on—they all have other work, especially "keep-the-lights-on" work and other issues that will inevitably arise. The team objectives are intended to cover the critical work in support of the company objectives.

Remember that these objectives are *problems to solve*—they are not solutions. The teams are expected to try out potential solutions in discovery and pursue solutions where they have evidence they will work. This is what is meant by an *empowered team*.

You'll also note that several of the teams have been assigned the same problem to solve. In most cases, these were *common objectives* because these were the most important problems that needed to be solved, and so multiple teams were asked to tackle them as they pertained to their area. This is fine, and is a consequence of their product strategy, and I would argue appropriate in their particular case. But it's important to note that it's not necessary either.[2]

With these common objectives, the teams will need to communicate and coordinate closely, and also management will need to help connect the dots where necessary, which mainly occurs during the ongoing coaching.

Company Dashboard

What follows is a subset of the company's dashboard, containing the KPIs related to the product strategy.

Employers: Improve success rate for employers
(% of jobs that successfully fill during 60-day posting cycle)

- Current employer success rate: 37%
- % postings with fewer than 8 qualified apps: 39%
- % postings with more than 25 qualified apps: 7%
- % postings with between 8 and 25 apps: 54%
- Average number of postings per account: 5.9
- Employer churn rate (annualized): 6%

---

[2]Unless otherwise noted, all the key results are aspirational. The specific level of ambition is discussed in sidebar "Level of Ambition."

Job Seekers: Improve success rate for seekers
(% of seekers that successfully find job in 60-day job search period)

- Current seeker success rate: 23% (average)
- % registered seekers that submit ≥1 application in first 48 hours: 27%
- % seeker success rate for app users: 32%
- % seeker success rate for non-app users: 15%
- Average number of applications per job search: 3.2

Employer Organization

Employer Home—The Employer Home team believed they now had enough historical posting and seeker data to make intelligent recommendations to the hiring manager during the creation of the job posting, which would significantly increase the likelihood of a successful posting.

Objective: Improve success rate for employers via recommendations.

- Key result: Increase employer success rate from 37% to 39%.
- Key result: Increase postings with more than 8 qualified applications and less than 25 from 54% to 58%.

Recruiter Tools—The Recruiter Tools team expected to be significantly impacted by the enterprise objective, so they proposed to essentially work alongside the new Enterprise Tools team as they pursued this new market. They would do whatever they needed to in order to improve the recruiter tools to meet the needs of enterprises. Note that this is a *shared team objective* with the Enterprise Tools team.[3]

---

[3] Note that this is an example of a shared team objective. The Employer Tools team will be working closely with the Recruiter Tools team, as well as two of the platform teams, in order to collaborate to solve the shared team objective.

Objective (shared with the Enterprise Tools team)

- KR (shared with the Enterprise Tools team)

Premium Services—The Premium Services team had a risky, but potentially significant, theory where they believed that certain of their services should be made available to *all* employer postings. They believed this because they had evidence that these features generate more successful postings, hence less churn, and that overall, total revenue would rise. They proposed to pursue this theory by running a series of targeted tests. They expect that the reduction in churn rate will take time to show up, but that employer success rate increase should be predictive.

Objective: Improve success rate for employers via premium services.

- KR: Improve employer success rate (for test cohort) from 37% to 40%.
- KR: Listings revenue impact neutral or positive (for test cohort).

Employer Communications—The Employer Communications team believed they could leverage new CRM best practices to improve the efficiency of the interaction with recruiters and hiring managers to enable the hiring manager to more quickly close the loop with candidates.

Objective: Improve success rate for employers via communications.

- KR: Improve employer success rate from 37% to 40%.
- KR: Increase % postings with >8 applications and <25 from 54% to 56%.[4]

---

[4]See sidebar "Attribution of Key Results" to understand how teams were able to know which changes caused which impacts.

Enterprise Tools (new team)—This new team took the lead on the enterprise objective initiative and worked with the other teams as needed. Their intention was to immediately begin a customer discovery program with eight prospective enterprise customers that had already been identified by the sales organization. Their intention is to use these early prospective customers to discover and deliver product/market fit for this new market.

Objective: Demonstrate product/market fit for enterprise.

- KR: Get at least 8 customer discovery program customers to sign letter of intent to buy.[5]

Job Seeker Organization

Seeker Home—The Seeker Home team believed they could leverage historical data to introduce intelligent personalization to the seeker's home dashboard to guide job seekers to more-suitable jobs. Note that this is a *shared team objective* with the Job Recommendations team.

Objective: Improve success rate for seekers via recommendations.

- KR: Increase seeker success from 23% to 25%.
- KR: Increase first application in first 48 hours from 27% to 30%.

Job Search—The Job Search team believed they could expand the search paradigm so that, once a seeker has described their desired positions, the search capability can continuously scan new postings and ensure the seeker is notified immediately upon a new match.

---

[5] Ultimately, the measure of success for this Enterprise Tools team is to develop at least six reference customers for the initial enterprise product offering. However, the leaders and the team expected that it would likely take more than a single quarter (but hopefully less than two quarters), so then the question was what would be a good proxy KPI for real progress towards this business result. The decision was made to use active participation in this customer development program, with the belief that if at least eight customers sign the (non-binding) letter of intent to buy, then it's reasonable to expect that some number of them will actually buy when the product is ready. This is very much dependent on the team delivering on the promise of the product.

Objective: Improve success rate for seekers via search.

- KR: Increase seeker success from 23% to 25%.
- KR: Increase percentage of applications from search results from 0% to 3%.

Job Recommendations—The Job Recommendations team believed they could improve the quality of their recommendations and help seekers find the jobs they didn't realize they were qualified for. Note that this is a *shared team objective* with the Seeker Home team.

Objective: Improve success rate for seekers via recommendations.

- KR: Increase seeker success from 23% to 25%.
- KR: Increase % of applications from recommendations from 3% to 5%.

Job Applications—The Job Applications team signed up to make the application process significantly more intelligent. Once a seeker has applied to one job, it would be significantly faster and easier to apply to others, from any device, any time.

Objective: Improve success rate for seekers via applications.

- KR: Increase seeker success from 23% to 25%.
- KR: Increase average number of applications submitted from 3.2 to 4.

Seeker Communications—The Seeker Communications team embraced the concept of "first 48 hours" as a theme and planned a series of experiments with a richer and more timely experience during this period—at least until the first application has been submitted.

Objective: Improve success rate for seekers via communications.

- KR: Increase seeker success from 23% to 25%.
- KR: Increase first app in first 48 hours from 27% to 30%.

Mobile Apps—The Mobile Apps team proposed to focus on real-time notifications as a way to encourage more engagement—both during the first 48 hours, but also ongoing as new potential job matches were discovered.

Objective: Improve success rate for seekers via app.

- KR: Increase seeker success of app users from 32% to 35%.
- KR: Increase percentage of first-time seekers that install and use the app from 17% to 20%.
- KR: Increase last 30-day rating in the app store from 3.0 to 3.5.

Platform Organization

Note that as the platform teams exist primarily to help the employer and seeker experience teams meet their objectives, most of the platform teams' objectives for the quarter will necessarily be in support of other teams' objectives.

Shared Services—As several teams believed they needed to pursue notifications, the Shared Services team committed to provide the necessary services support.

Objective: Provide the technology necessary to support the experience teams.

- High-Integrity Commitment: Deliver 1.0 version of notification system.[6]

Payments and Billing—The Enterprise Tools team asked the Payments and Billing team to provide the support necessary for establishing monthly billing accounts on corporate terms rather than handling

---

[6]You may be wondering why this is a high-integrity commitment rather than just a normal "keep-the-lights-on" dependency, or if not that, a shared team objective? We only do high-integrity commitments for the major deliverables, not minor dependencies (of which there are always many). As to why not a shared team objective, the difference is that the teams had already discussed and determined they needed a notification service, so the question was really *when* they could be able to start using it?

transaction-only payments. Note that this is a *shared team objective* with the Enterprise Tools team.

Objective: Demonstrate product/market fit for enterprise.

- KR (inherit key results of Enterprise Tools team).

Data and Reporting—The Enterprise Tools team asked the Data and Reporting team to enable enterprise-wide reporting, and to help aggregate reporting for companies that had multiple users (hiring managers), each with their own accounts. Note that this is a *shared team objective* with the Enterprise Tools team.

Objective: Demonstrate product/market fit for enterprise.

- KR (inherit key results of Enterprise Tools team).

Infrastructure—The Infrastructure team was in the midst of a two-year re-platforming effort to address the substantial tech-debt issues. The emergence of the enterprise effort caused the team to propose adjusting the sequencing of work to ensure the ATS integration work could happen on the new foundation, which should be both substantially faster and also save having to reimplement this later.

Objective: Continue major tech debt re-platforming effort.[7]

- High-Integrity Commitment: Complete migration of four more major system components to the new architecture, while ensuring all teams can continue forward progress during re-platforming.

Tools—The Tools team was asked to focus on more-flexible, real-time monitoring to handle the enterprise integration needs.

---

[7]This is an example of an objective that spans quarters as the tech-debt plan is a two-year plan, so this illustrates an ongoing, multiyear objective, but with meaningful progress no less than every quarter.

[8]This could have been key results rather than a high-integrity commitment, but it is a very difficult problem in software to quantify the improvements in velocity, reliability, scalability, performance, and fault-tolerance from moving to a more modern platform. This is why it's so difficult to do a high-integrity business case for tech-debt work, and I don't recommend even trying. I tell the leaders to just make sure you do the work if you want to stay in business (and keep all your jobs).

Objective: Demonstrate product/market fit for enterprise.

- KR (inherit key results of Enterprise Tools team).

Level of Ambition

With aspirational key results, it's important to have a clear understanding of how ambitious the team is being with their key results for the quarter.

This is often a place where company culture shows through. Some companies encourage their teams to be very ambitious (moon shots), and others want the teams to be very conservative (roof shots). Some ask their teams to project some level of confidence in the key results (e.g., "Your key results should be with 70% confidence.").

In this company, the leaders used subjective terms to describe to the teams the level of ambition they were hoping for. In general, they wanted the teams to be relatively ambitious because they did not believe that roof shots would achieve the results they felt they needed.

68

Business Results

For those wondering how all this actually played out, I have included here quarterly results and also some observations from about a year later.

This concentration of effort around getting more jobs to have between 8 and 25 applications did indeed pay off. This was mostly the result of spreading around the applications that were being wasted by going to jobs that already had enough. At the end of the quarter, the company had raised the "successful posting" KPI from 37% to 41%, but the best news was that this continued to grow and ended the year at nearly 45%. This resulted in substantially decreasing employer churn—from 6% down to 5.1%.

As you have seen, the company attacked these problems from many different angles, in the hopes that some would succeed. The approach that had the most significant impact was the Job Recommendations team, which was all about showing job seekers jobs the system believed they were qualified for, but the job seeker didn't realize they were. Not only did this have an immediate impact, but it continued to improve for at least two more years.

On the job seeker side, they ended up making fairly fundamental changes to the workflow of first registering and then providing the first application. They were able to significantly improve the percentage of job seekers that submitted an application in the first 48 hours (from 27% to 42%), primarily by making the first application submission much easier and more integrated with the registration process.

The native mobile app investment also proved valuable, and in following quarters they better aligned the product marketing efforts to encourage more job seekers to install the app.

In terms of the objective for achieving product/market fit for selling to enterprises, this ended up taking two full quarters to get their six reference customers, but that did result in the company building out a direct sales channel. However, the company found that moving from selling online directly to hiring managers, to selling through a direct sales force to HR organizations, required much larger changes than they had anticipated. It took the better part of a year to get the necessary foundation to the level they needed it, including security and access control, data and reporting, and payment and billing.

If you were to ask the product teams themselves, they would probably say their favorite result was the progress on the re-platforming, which ended up taking the full two years, but resulted in their ability to move significantly faster and much better aligned with their efforts.

Most of the platform teams had the platform product manager role covered by the tech lead. For some of the teams, this was really not a problem (Infrastructure, Tools, and even Shared Services). However, for other teams (Payments and Billing, Data and Reporting), the business complexities and constraints overwhelmed the tech leads, and the company added platform product managers to these teams later in the year.

Overall, while some product teams had more success than others, the employees, leaders, and investors in this company were more than satisfied with the progress, and the level of innovation required was both acknowledged and celebrated. They still had much work to do in the years ahead as they continued to grow, but they had made real progress.

Because the leaders had been very open and transparent with the executives and stakeholders in the company, several of those leaders shared with me that they had a much better appreciation for how technology products get made, especially the level of experimentation required to solve the particularly difficult problems.

69

Key Takeaways

I f you have persisted in working your way through this case study, I'm hoping that you have a clearer picture in your mind about how strong product organizations work in practice.

Here are what I consider the 10 most important points I hope you take away from this snapshot of a real company in the midst of dealing with the challenges and stresses of rapid growth:

1. The critical role that the product leaders need to play—from the topology, to the product strategy, to the team objectives, to actively managing the issues and obstacles that came up during the quarter.

2. The importance of a true product strategy based on focus and insights. The product strategy is what tells us which problems we need each product team to solve. These leaders crafted a strategy around a few high-impact insights and then asked most of the organization to tackle these problems. The results will only be as good as the strategy.

3. The importance of active management of team objectives—both by the product teams themselves, but also from the product leaders. If the teams do not stay on top of their objectives, life intervenes, and pretty soon much of the quarter is gone and not enough has been done.

4. The value of empowering teams and teams of missionaries. The real innovations that occurred were all a direct result of having empowered teams excited to work on a hard problem that can make a real difference for the customers and for the company.

5. The limitations of what you can know and what you can't know. These leaders knew that there was no way to anticipate which ideas would really bear fruit and which would not. They planned for that reality.

6. The risk management element of placing a series of bets, knowing that only some will pay off. These leaders were placing bets based on how strong the data insights were, how much confidence they had in the specific people and teams, and how confident the teams were in their ability to make an impact.

7. The impact that the team topology has on converting the insights into action. A different topology would have resulted in different assignments and likely very different results. Maybe better, maybe worse, but definitely different. This topology has some clear virtues but also some real limitations.

8. The necessary give and take between the leaders and the product teams—partly top down, partly bottom up. The leaders did not abdicate their responsibility by inviting the teams to volunteer for areas they felt strongly about, but their willingness to try to accommodate went a long way toward motivating the teams.

9. The importance of sharing the broader strategic context with all of the product teams. For product teams to make good decisions, they need to have the big picture, and they need to understand the product vision and product strategy—and especially the insights behind the product strategy.

10. Uncertainty is messy, and there are never guarantees. But smart leaders usually find a way to make it work because they trust their teams, accept the uncertainty, and manage the risks appropriately.

Realize that every company is in a unique situation, with different market position, different talent on the teams, different enabling technologies, and different company cultures. Just because something may have worked well for this job marketplace company does not mean it will work for you. But hopefully this example gives you a good sense for the types of considerations you will want to keep in mind, and the type of leadership you will need to provide.

70

Leader Profile:
Judy Gibbons

Path to Leadership

Judy studied at London Business School and began her professional career at the same company (Hewlett Packard), and at the same timeframe, as I did.

　　She joined HP back during the PC era, where she learned product management and product marketing. Judy was based in the UK, and I was based in Silicon Valley, but we met and became friends, and I've watched her career, and witnessed her leadership, ever since.

She went from HP to Apple, where she spent 7 years in product development, product management, and technology evangelism, and then she moved to Microsoft, where she spent 10 years building and leading Microsoft's global consumer internet business (MSN).

After Microsoft, Judy began advising and investing in startups and serving as a board member and chairman for several companies that realized they needed to transform, starting at the very top.

Her career has given Judy experience with nearly every aspect of a technology-powered business, as well as lessons learned from leading several very rapidly growing businesses.

Leadership in Action

Here's Judy in her own words:

Early in my career I was fortunate to work at Hewlett Packard—both in the UK and in Silicon Valley—first as a systems engineer then a product manager.

Bill Hewlett and Dave Packard created a very strong values-based culture and operating principles which were enshrined in *The HP Way*.

These included "The company believes the best results come when you get the right people, trust them, give them freedom to find the best path to achieve objectives, and let them share in the rewards their work makes possible."

This translated into other practices such as "always hire people smarter than yourself," "employee empowerment," and "it's all about the customer."

HP was also a pioneer in the adoption of *management by objectives*, the foundation for today's objectives and key results. My seven years there provided a formidable education which has stayed with me throughout my career.

Whenever I see organizations that don't have strong values along with a culture of collaboration and empowerment, I know they are going to struggle to deliver great customer experiences and therefore business value.

Technology makes many things possible, but if it doesn't deliver on the needs of the customer, it will not deliver on the needs of the business.

After HP, I joined Apple, where Steve Jobs so effectively demonstrated the importance and power of articulating a compelling vision of what can be achieved with technology and at the same time being obsessed about the customer experience.

Product teams at Apple were more diverse and included product design as well as product managers and developers who were able to combine their skills effectively to innovate in extraordinary ways.

I next joined Microsoft to launch MSN, its consumer internet service. This was a product on a new platform—the web—and with constantly updated content. And, of course, new business models. As a result, the product teams diversified further to include news journalists, producers, and advertising professionals.

But the need was still the same: a clear vision, creativity about what's possible, learning from the customer, and constant iteration.

Diversity is talked about a lot these days, but nowhere is it more important than in product teams. Great things can happen when you give creative, passionate people the freedom to explore ideas.

Creativity is needed to come up with original ideas, which need to be critiqued, evaluated, and elaborated. Many different possibilities need to be explored before focusing on those that have the most potential value. And it is product teams that are able to combine these different behaviors—and switch between them in flexible ways—that are best suited to succeed in the world in which we now find ourselves.

When I left Microsoft, I joined Accel Partners, a leading VC firm which invests in technology startups. I listened to hundreds of pitches from would-be entrepreneurs and was astonished how many didn't have technology or product leaders on their founding teams. Many said they planned to outsource product development, which clearly demonstrated a profound failure in their understanding of how great, technology-powered products and businesses are built.

I have spent the last 10 years on the boards of a wide variety of organizations, many of them on journeys of "digital transformation."

The outcome of this endeavor has to be the delivery of compelling digital experiences for customers, and this requires empowered product teams.

To create the conditions for this, leaders need to establish and communicate a clear and compelling purpose and vision—what the organization is trying to achieve and why. There needs to be obsession with the customer from the top—who they are, what they want, and how they behave.

And to develop the solution, there need to be highly-focused and effective cross-functional teams led by a capable product manager, empowered to deliver on the product vision. And this means clear objectives, accountability, constant interaction, and continuous learning.

Leaders need to set the expectations, establish the governance that acknowledges necessary boundaries—but removes barriers to progress—and support the teams with the necessary tools and resources. And then they need to get out of the way. Senior leadership support for the adoption of these working methods, values, and behaviors is key.

Marty asked me why I thought so many companies still prefer command-and-control-style leadership versus empowerment.

I don't know if it's a preference or even conscious; in many cases it seems to be the only model the leaders know. I do know that changing it is very hard, and it only works with strong leadership and a sustained, committed effort to create the right culture and values. The leaders must establish new ways of working which break down silos and enable and support effective cross-functional collaboration.

As a board member, I try to impress upon the senior leaders these principles and values, and emphasize that the product teams need to be empowered. Without this, there will be little progression, and a great deal of frustration, which inevitably means that the necessary digital talent—which has been brought into the organization with great effort and cost—will walk out the door in search of a more worthwhile place to work.

PART

Business Collaboration

aving strong product leaders and empowered product teams is necessary, but it's usually not sufficient.

That's because product work happens in the context of the broader company. Your CEO matters, as do the rest of your key executives and the various stakeholders representing other key areas of your business.

However, establishing the necessary working relationships with the rest of your business is a different level of hard. It requires a lot more sensitivity and nuance.

Realize that your company is currently used to *feature teams* that exist very clearly *to serve the business*, and now you're trying to replace them with empowered product teams that exist *to serve our customers, in ways that work for the business*.

What this really means in practice is that you need to move your product organization from a *subservient* model to a *collaborative* model.

At a very human level, you're asking very senior executives to think differently about teams comprised of ordinary people—individual contributors—who have been coached into extraordinary teams.

This is a very significant change, especially as it impacts the rest of your business. We need to discuss the implications of this change and how you, as a product leader, can guide your company through this change in mindset and responsibilities.

CHAPTER

71

The Role of Product Leaders

Moving the product teams from the *subservient* feature team model to the *collaborative* empowered product team model begins with *trust*—especially between the product organization and the rest of the leaders of the business. And the keys to that trust are the *product leaders*, especially the head of product.

Without a strong head of product who inspires confidence and is trusted by the CEO and the other key executives, it will be a long and very difficult road.

Note that there is a big assumption here, which may not be true in your organization: We assume that the product leaders are generally at the same peer level with the other key executives and stakeholders in the organization.

Normally, in a tech-powered product company, they are. However, in some older, pre-internet companies, the product leaders are buried under someone like a CIO, CTO, or inside of individual businesses (all clear signs of the subservient feature team model).

In this case, it is politically much more difficult to get the senior vice president of sales or the chief marketing officer or the chief financial officer to have a collaborative relationship with the head of product.

Why is this important? Because it's much easier to get an executive to put their trust in a peer rather than in a much lower-level subordinate they don't know, and don't believe has the necessary experience or knowledge.

In any case, the product leaders must establish a direct relationship with the CEO (or general manager in a very large company) and the other key executives. That's usually the heads of sales, marketing, service, finance, legal, and business development. But this list varies at each company.

The basis of this relationship is that the executives need to believe the product leaders have a deep understanding of the business and are committed to ensuring that the solutions provided will work for the various aspects of the business.

This is table stakes for the product leaders. Beyond that, there are three aspects the product leaders will be judged on:

1. Business results
2. Product strategy
3. Product teams

Business Results

Ultimately, the only thing that will truly motivate a company to change to the empowered team model is results—*business results*.

The reason the company even began on this journey is very likely because the old way was not delivering the necessary results. So it's important that the product organization deliver the results. And to do that, it's important that the organization have an intentional and focused product strategy, and that the product teams are empowered and accountable to the results.

Product Strategy

Remember that, with feature teams, there really wasn't a product strategy other than trying to meet the needs of the different parts of the business.

Now, the company has a product strategy, and it's important that this strategy be shared with the executives because that will communicate the reason for the focus, and for the decisions on what to work on.

Note that it's common that one or more of the most important insights were first discovered by one of the key executives or stakeholders, and in such cases, it's important to be generous in crediting the source of that insight. You want to build a culture that encourages the constant seeking and leveraging of these insights.

Product Teams

Companies in the empowered product team model quickly learn that the real work occurs in these product teams, and their ability to solve hard problems for the business depends very much on the people on the team, especially the product manager. So be aware that they will be judging the product managers and, indirectly, the product leaders.

I like to tell product leaders that they are only as strong as their weakest product manager, and this is why.

This is also why it's so important during new-employee onboarding that the manager make sure that the new employee (this mostly pertains to new product managers) has done her homework and truly understands the customers and the business before she interacts with the key executive or stakeholder. Without this deep knowledge of customers, there will be no trust.

Then, the product leader should personally introduce the new employee to the key executive. Realize that when you do this, you are personally vouching for their knowledge and ability, so you are acknowledging that your reputation is also on the line.

As you can see, everything rides on having strong product leaders. Please don't make the mistake of putting someone who's not equipped into this key role. And if you feel you must, please be sure to get that person executive coaching from a proven product leader.

72

Stakeholder Management vs. Collaboration

You might have noticed that we have not talked much about the topic of "stakeholder management" in this book. That's because this term represents a mindset that is more often a trait of feature teams and less so for empowered product teams.

Now, don't misunderstand this. I'm not saying that empowered product teams don't have to pay attention to stakeholders. I'm saying that it's a different relationship.

Recall that in feature teams, they are there to *serve the business*, and usually "the business" is represented by one or more stakeholders that must be "managed" so that the team does not get overwhelmed with demands and requests.

For most feature teams, the most dreaded aspect of the product manager role is dealing with the stakeholders. The product managers of feature teams feel like they can never make all the various stakeholders happy. There simply is not enough time, or enough people, and sometimes the requests from the stakeholders don't even make sense.

Again, I'm not suggesting that empowered product teams can or should ignore these stakeholders, but they do have a fundamentally different relationship—one that I find is much more constructive and conducive to innovation.

In an empowered product team, the team is there to *serve customers, with products that customers love, yet work for the business*. The stakeholders are partners we need to collaborate with to come up with solutions that work (specifically, that means the solutions are valuable, usable, feasible, and viable). In particular, the stakeholders help us with *viability*.

For example, we may need to sit down with a company lawyer to discuss legal constraints and the various ways we might be able to address them. We know that, no matter how much the customer might love a solution, if it's not legal, it's a nonstarter.

Rather than the stakeholder being "the client" that tells us what to build, and as such needs to "be managed," now we have a partner that we need to help understand the constraints so we can discover a solution that works.

The Agency Model

An agency—whether a design agency or a development agency—is there to provide you with design services or development services, respectively.

You may not have thought about things this way, but a feature team is really very similar to the agency model. The main difference is that a feature team is insourced, and the agency model is outsourced.

These agencies generally don't have people with the title "product manager," but they do have "engagement managers" that are there to "manage the relationship with the client" (in most cases, the very same stakeholders that a feature team is there to serve).

And it should be no surprise that companies that use agencies for design and development have much the same problems as they have with feature teams.

In this case, the people at the agency don't just *feel* like mercenaries, they literally *are* mercenaries.

(continued)

(continued)

As with feature teams, in my experience, the people at the agencies are capable of so much more, and they don't usually like the model any more than the people in feature teams do. But the reality for them is that, if they don't want to build the feature "the client" tells them to, then the client will simply go to another agency that will.

There are a few agencies that are trying to provide the services of true empowered product teams to their clients, and I applaud that trend. But, unfortunately, this depends on the client having an unusually high level of trust in that agency.

One other observation: You can often find exceptionally good people to hire from design and development agencies because the people have been exposed to so many types of products.

However, realize that moving to an empowered product team will be a major cultural change. In many cases, the people from agencies bring with them the same problems that cause feature teams to fail. More than a few have told me excitedly, "Now I get to be the client!" I try to point out to them that this would very much miss the point.

73

Shared Insights and Learning

In empowered product teams working on solving hard problems, the discovery techniques that we use generate insights very frequently.

We are meeting with users and customers, normally weekly, and testing our product ideas. We're digging deeper into their context and their needs.

We are analyzing the data from our product's usage, and from the live-data testing of our ideas.

We are constantly investigating new enabling technologies to see if any can help us solve the problems we are facing in new and better ways.

We are tracking industry data and learnings to see if there are relevant trends.

We are also constantly seeking these insights from others across the company—product marketing, sales, finance, customer success.

As we learn important or potentially relevant insights, we want to share these learnings with our colleagues from across the business. There are several reasons for this:

First, the insight may help them as well.

Second, they may have additional insights while viewing the data through their lens.

Third, they may be able to help us explain the dynamics in order to better leverage the insights.

Fourth, it is important that the company learn the difference between a prototype getting a bad response during discovery, and a product failing in the market.

"Failing" in discovery is not really failing—it is very fast and inexpensive learning. "Failing" in the market truly is failing, as these mistakes are typically very slow and very expensive. We want the broader company to understand this difference. We still can't completely avoid market failures, but we can dramatically reduce their frequency.

More generally, the type of relationship you want is one where you are sharing openly and generously. By sharing insights and learnings, you are bringing your business partners on the journey with you.

I love to invite key business leaders to some of our user or customer testing.

I am a big advocate of sharing key learnings broadly across the organization, as well as sharing the ideas that work—along with the ones that don't.

And be generous with the credit when an insight that comes from one of your key leaders or executives turns out to be critical to some innovation or substantial progress. At one company, I even made up and handed out DEPUTY PRODUCT MANAGER badges when I called out the contributions of others at all-hands meetings.

Just make sure that the insights are acknowledged and shared in both directions.

74

Keeping the Lights On

M ost of this book is about how strong teams solve hard problems in ways that our customers love, yet work for the business.

However, it's also true that every team must do some amount of "keep-the-lights-on" work.

When you're trying to run a business, you will always have certain work that is nonnegotiable if you wish to stay in business. Common examples include:

- Fixing critical bugs
- Addressing compliance issues (such as a new law relating to privacy)
- Incorporating minor changes to handle changing reporting needs
- Adding instrumentation for collecting usage analytics

None of these are glamorous, but usually they are relatively minor.

You might address these items for your own purposes (e.g., fixing critical bugs or analytics instrumentation), or you might address requests from someone like your legal officer (e.g., new compliance issue) or your finance partner (e.g., a reporting need).

The product manager is typically the person responsible for understanding these keep-the-lights-on items, collecting whatever data is necessary and putting the work on the backlog. As a general rule, we don't need to do product discovery on any of these items. If we do, then we would consider it more-normal product work.

So, how does this relate to business collaboration?

The source of these keep-the-lights-on items is often one or more of our business partners. They might not know the best way to satisfy the need, but they are usually acutely aware of the need and can provide any necessary context. If a product team can't handle these issues, then the business partner is really in a bind and things can get tense.

Obviously, if the level of keep-the-lights-on items becomes too high, and it impedes the work on the team objectives, the company has a serious issue that will need to be escalated to product leadership.

More generally, it's normal for business owners and key stakeholders to spot new opportunities—new ways to monetize, new services, new capabilities. And if you have a good relationship, they will bring these opportunities to you.

This is where it's critical to be able to constantly remind your business partners about (and evangelize, which is discussed below) the product strategy and the importance of focus. In most cases, they are not bad opportunities, but they would quickly dilute the ability to make the difference on the most important items.

The other thing to keep an eye out for is that sometimes the business leader will try and get the product team to work on pet features by positioning them as keep-the-lights-on work. But, of course, if this happens too much, we are not able to pursue the critical product work and we are back to feature teams managed by stakeholders.

75

Evangelism

One of the critical roles of strong product leaders—especially in medium- to large-sized companies—is *evangelism*.

Evangelism in this context means marketing to your own organization (e.g., product marketing, marketing, and sales).

In this case, you're not trying to get people to buy. You are instead trying to persuade them that this is going to be very important and something they should care about and contribute to making a reality.

There are many techniques to help communicate the value of what you're proposing to your product teams, executives, key stakeholders, and investors. Here are my top-10 techniques:

1. Use prototypes. For so many people, PowerPoint presentations just don't cut it. Show them a prototype. It will probably need to be a high-fidelity prototype, which means that it would look realistic, even though it's just a mirage. This is probably the single most effective technique for persuasion of a product idea.

2. Share the pain. Show the customer pain you are addressing. You can share quotes or even put together a video montage. This is also why I love to bring developers or executives along to user testing. For so many people, they just have to hear the customer's words and witness their pain themselves to get it.

3. Share the vision. People don't just want to know what you're doing today—they want to know where you are heading. The product vision shows where you hope to be in 3–10 years.

4. Share the learnings. As discussed earlier, when your teams are doing product discovery work every week, you will have significant learnings and insights from the data and from users and customers, on a fairly frequent basis. Share these learnings—not just the things that went well but share the problems too. Give your audience the information they need to help come up with the solution.

5. Share credit generously. Make sure the team, the executives, and the key stakeholders view the product as their product, not just your product. On the other hand, when things don't go well, step forward and take responsibility for the miss, and show the people you're learning from the mistakes as well. They'll respect you for it.

6. Learn how to give a great demo. Especially for your executives and your stakeholders, we're not trying to teach them how to operate the product, and we're not trying to test whether they could use the product. We're trying to show them the value. A demo is not training, and it's not a test—it's a form of sales. Get good at it.

7. Do your homework. Your team, your executives, and your stakeholders will all be much more likely to follow you if they believe you know what you're talking about. Be an expert on your users and customers, your data, your business, and your market.

8. Be genuinely excited. If you're not excited about your products, you should probably fix that either by changing what you work on or changing your role.

9. Learn to show some enthusiasm. Assuming you're genuinely excited, it's amazing to me how many product leaders are so bad and/or so uncomfortable at showing enthusiasm. This matters. Absolutely be sincere but let people see you're genuinely excited. Enthusiasm really is contagious.

10. Spend time with the product teams. If you're not spending face time with every product manager, product designer, and developer on your team, then they can't see the enthusiasm in your eyes. Spending a few minutes with every last person on the product teams pays off big in their level of motivation. It's worth your time.

Note that evangelism can never really stop. As soon as you do, things will start to go sideways. Executives will get cold feet. Your engineers will start claiming they don't know why they're working on something. It's remarkable how quickly this happens if you think people have already heard this stuff and it's no longer needed.

Experienced product leaders know that you can never evangelize too much. You can change up the technique, vary the customers you cite as examples, and keep updating the prototype, but evangelism needs to be a constant.

76

Leader Profile:
Avid Larizadeh Duggan

Path to Leadership

I first met Avid back in 2001, when I was running product at eBay. I received a call from a friend I had worked with at Netscape, and he told me just to trust him and hire this person because he was sure she would become an exceptional product person. I did trust him, and he was right.

Avid studied engineering but wanted to learn product. After rising through the product organization at eBay, she decided to get her MBA at Harvard. Afterward, she went back and forth between the venture capital world—mostly at Google Ventures—and leading tech product companies, most recently at Kobalt Music.

Along the way, she's invested and advised several strong product companies, and has been a leader for Code.org (the organization helping women and minorities learn to code).

Because of her contributions to technology and beyond, she was recently awarded the Order of the British Empire (OBE).

Leadership in Action

Avid's own words follow.

My leadership philosophy in an innovation-driven context can be simplified into three main components: (1) trust and safety (2) freedom and autonomy, and (3) culture and purpose.

Trust and Safety

A leader is not supposed to have all the answers, but is supposed to ask the right questions, and more important, create an environment where the right questions are surfaced.

To do so, a leader needs to make her team feel safe. In this environment, no one is smarter than everyone else, trust is established, collaboration is natural, and conflicting ideas are frequent and comfortable because it is safe to be candid.

Teams must feel safe disagreeing with their peers and with their leaders. It is an environment where people don't fear failure because it is part of the process of iteration. That's how good ideas become great ideas.

It is an environment which celebrates a growth mindset rather than success at a point in time, encourages continuous learning, and rejects the know-it-alls. By bringing out the best in your teammates, you find the best in yourself.

Freedom and Autonomy

In a digital world where innovation is key, where data is flowing freely both inside and outside the company, and where change is constant, work has become increasingly complex, changeable, and informal in nature.

As a result, an organization needs to get rid of its traditional hierarchy—which mainly promotes people having interactions with others in their own department—in favor of a system which encourages input and collaboration from people with different skill sets across functions internally and externally with partners and customers.

Therefore, leaders need to focus on bringing strong people together and giving them greater freedom to generate ideas and execute them through collaboration.

A leader should articulate what needs to be done and why, and then let the team decide how to do it.

She will set things in motion, guide her team, and clear the obstacles when the team is in trouble.

This has similarities with the role of a product manager. She will have to work cross-functionally with teammates and stakeholders, lead, influence, motivate, and trust them—without ever ordering them to do anything.

She will ensure they are motivated and know what their purpose is. She will coach them and help them develop in a safe environment. She will connect the dots internally and externally to empower her team with additional information, better tools, and efficiency.

She will ensure that they have the data they need to experiment and iterate quickly, as well as the autonomy to make informed decisions based on their learning. She will clarify the chaos in a world where change is a constant.

Culture and Purpose

Good leaders focus on culture and purpose because culture drives innovation and performance. The greatest capital of an organization is its *people*.

To innovate, people need autonomy and meaning. It is crucial that a leader define what the purpose is to make sure that everyone inside and outside the organization—including customers and partners—knows what they are doing to promote it.

This purpose needs to be clear and consistently communicated in the way it is messaged, as well as consistently reflected in every aspect of the day-to-day running of the company—from the types of hires made, to the processes used, and even to the way the office space is designed.

Innovation in Established Companies. I have applied these principles in startups and established companies. The latter are much more challenging because they often are no longer the innovators.

They struggle with legacy technology and complex processes, while often complacent in the belief that their leading market position is secure because they have been in that position for a long time. They overestimate the speed at which they are able to innovate.

This is where the role of leaders becomes extremely important to the survival of the company.

Unless the senior leaders understand the true nature and urgency of the threat, they will not be willing to put the organization through the stress of change, despite its necessity—especially if that would cause a short-term impact to profitability.

This is because consistent innovation in established companies requires radical changes in the way teams work, the technologies used, the skill sets required, the culture of the company, and as a result, the mindset of the leaders.

They need to put the principles described above in practice, starting with trust. Once the teams trust their leaders, they will be more willing to make change, as they won't fear the repercussions of not getting it right the first time.

This trust needs to go both ways, and leaders need to empower their teams to be autonomous, as most innovation comes from those on the frontline and not from the executives or the board.

And, critically, the teams need to understand why they are going through the upheaval of change and to what end and purpose. They need to be motivated by something larger than themselves.

Once an established company comes to realize that its future depends on significant and ongoing innovation, and it does not believe it has the muscles for this today, then there are really two options: the company can either innovate through acquisition, or it can learn to innovate through its own people.

To innovate through its own people requires the change to skills, culture, methods, and leadership that we've been talking about. And, yes, this is hard, takes time, significant investment, and focused commitment.

So for many established companies—especially legacy companies—they often believe it is easier to innovate through acquisition.

The challenge is that, in order to realize the benefits of these acquisitions, this often requires integrating the acquisitions deeply into the workings of the parent company. And if that parent company does not make most of the same changes to their leadership, culture, skills, and empowerment, they would need to innovate through their own people, the acquired teams that were behind the innovation leave, the innovative products decline, the happy customers are no longer so happy, and the company is back to where it started.

This is why I spend so much of my time and efforts helping leaders of companies to realize their role in leading the necessary changes.

Inspired,
Empowered,
and Transformed

Great teams are made up of ordinary people who are inspired and empowered.

They are *inspired* with ideas and techniques for quickly evaluating those ideas to discover solutions that work—that are valuable, usable, feasible, and viable.

They are *empowered* to solve hard problems in ways their customers love, yet work for their business.

Empowered teams that produce extraordinary results don't require exceptional hires.

They do require people who are competent and of character so they can establish the necessary trust with their teammates and with the rest of the company.

Truly empowered teams also need the strategic context that comes from the product leadership—especially the product vision and the product strategy—and the active support of their management, primarily with ongoing coaching.

There are never guarantees for innovation, but we can substantially improve our odds.

77

Meaningful Transformation

I nevitably, once you realize the scope and scale of what is necessary to work the way the best companies work, it raises the question of how to change from the way you're working today to the way you believe you need to work tomorrow. And this is essentially a question of transformation.

What does it *really* mean to transform to empowered product teams?

The prerequisite for this transformation is getting your senior leaders—typically starting with the CEO—to understand the necessary *role of technology* as the key enabler of the business, and not just a necessary cost of doing business. Without this understanding, your chances of success are low.

But assuming your senior leadership understands why this is essential, and is willing to take the actions required, then we can get to work.

At the highest level, there are three major steps. And as a general rule, they need to happen in the following order.

First, you'll need to ensure you have *strong product leaders* in place. Without this, you won't be able to recruit and coach the necessary staff for the product teams, you won't have a solid product strategy, and you won't earn the trust of the leaders and the stakeholders. So this is really the first and most critical step, which is why it has been the main topic of this book.

Second, you'll need to give those strong product leaders the ability to recruit and develop the staff required for *empowered product teams*. This almost always means raising the bar on the product managers, but it may go well beyond that. Note that you don't need to up-level all teams at once. You just need to be sure that, before you empower a given product team, you have ensured that the team is staffed with people who are up to the task.

Third, for the product teams that are ready to operate in the empowered product team model, you will need to *redefine the relationship with the business*. Recall that, in the feature team model, the stakeholders were largely in control, and the feature teams were set up to be *subservient* to the business. Now, with the empowered product team model, the idea is to be *true partners* with the business—collaborating to come up with solutions that customers love, yet also work for the business.

Please remember that this change represents a bit of a give and take with the leaders in the organization. Realize you're asking them to take a pretty big leap of faith. What's in it for them is that the old way of working has never been very effective, so most are willing to at least give it a try.

Especially for larger organizations, there's of course much more to be said about how this transformation impacts finance, HR, sales, marketing, and nearly every other aspect of the business, but that's a subject for another book.

The Cost of Transformation

One of the great ironies of this entire topic of empowered product teams vs. feature teams is that, in general, it costs significantly less to staff and fund empowered product teams than it does to fund feature teams.

In fact, I have never seen more waste than I find in large companies that are running feature teams. This is especially the case when that company has outsourced significant parts of their engineering to one of the big firms.

It is not unusual to find these large, old companies with literally thousands of outsourced engineers funded by annual contracts in the tens of millions of dollars. This is the literal definition of *mercenary teams*.

The company often thinks they're saving money because they look at the loaded cost of an engineer, not realizing that they need many more engineers, as well as the many people to manage these large numbers of engineers.

Yet a much smaller team of true missionaries will typically dramatically outperform this much larger and much more expensive approach.

Even beyond the cost savings, innovation almost never happens in the outsourced model, and your company's future depends on innovation.

It is true that we will typically pay more per person for the higher level of talent that we require in an empowered product team, but the number of people will be substantially less and the overhead of managing them will be dramatically less.

I have met more than a few CFOs that are skeptical of this argument, so I simply suggest that they run a test. I suggest they pick an area of the business, and for the next several quarters compare the costs and the business results of the empowered product team model against their current model.

78

Transformation in Action

*N*ow that we've discussed what's involved in meaningful transformation, you might be wondering what a strong product organization looks like that has undergone this transformation.

To answer that, I am sharing below a story from SVPG partner Jon Moore, which is based on his experiences at the Guardian *in London, which was one of the most impressive transformations I have witnessed.*

In June 2007, the world of technology changed forever. Steve Jobs stood on stage and unveiled the iPhone—a device that was limited in functionality but rich in intuition. It was a time of revolutionary change for all businesses, and none more so than the UK's *Guardian* newspaper. Under the stewardship of then-editor-in-chief Alan Rusbridger, it was arguably the most digitally ambitious newspaper in the world.

But it was also in crisis. For the first time in nearly 200 years, the *Guardian*'s future was anything but guaranteed. Advertising was in freefall, and virtually all other revenue streams were in the process of being replaced by newer, better, digital-first rivals.

As newspapers all over the world began the task of moving to online subscription models, the *Guardian* chose an alternative, ambitious but potentially perilous strategy: to remain free online. "Nothing good ever comes of putting up a wall" was the message delivered across the organization.

The decision was founded on a belief that the *Guardian's* progressive editorial content would wither and die behind a paywall—even if it meant considerably shortening our runway, as paying newspaper customers switched to free online content. It was a decision of some consequence and one I backed wholeheartedly, believing that a progressive but small echo chamber was never going to change the world. Reach first, revenue later.

It was into this environment that I joined one of the most impressive product and technology organizations anywhere in traditional media. Many of my new colleagues had chosen to leave ambitious startups, Google, or Microsoft, and like me, had also experienced success at scaling other well-known media organizations. All shared a deep desire to ensure the longevity of one of the most exciting and important media brands in the world.

But this rapid influx of smart technologists also created cultural chaos.

The *Guardian's* long-standing identity as a newspaper was under threat, and like many organizations in rapid transition, the working environment was at best confused and often fractious.

Many long-serving journalists and editorial staff were understandably uncertain of their new colleagues. Our ways of working were alien, our desire to create change was threatening, and although it was not always publicly acknowledged, our motivations were frequently questioned.

I had been tasked with creating and executing an immediate mobile strategy. It was a superb challenge at an exciting time. Our then-digital director, Mike Bracken (who went on to substantially advance product management within UK government circles) had created a team of significant talent.

On entry, I had spearheaded the organization's first iPhone app, liaising closely with Apple. Our small team worked hard to ensure we made the most of the then-revolutionary touchscreens and, because of that, I paid special attention to photography from the outset.

Our innovative iPhone-based technology immediately down-loaded the most important and popular content without request on app opening. I wanted our app to always be useful, even when signal strength was poor or absent (as it frequently was in 2007). This feature alone proved a revelation to many.

From the moment we hit the App Store, it was a success. We received hundreds of thousands of downloads over the next few weeks, and in time, many millions more. A significant proportion were from new international customers, fueled by the global reach of Apple's new ecosystem. Our application quality, combined with the *Guardian*'s world-class journalism, shone through in customer feedback. And because of that, Apple was happy to showcase us in multiple, consistent marketing campaigns—both local and global—many above the fold.

While most of the competition had launched apps that were at heart essentially advanced RSS readers, we had worked hard to embrace the myriad new possibilities of the touchscreen form. For Apple, it's never been enough to just get involved. What they really look for are partners who appreciate their tools sufficiently to push the actual cus-tomer experience forward.

In parallel to operational delivery, as the lead PM, it was clear to me that to be truly successful, I was going to need to bridge a growing divide between the editorial and technology teams.

Evangelizing is never more important than when your integrity and motivation are in question. But virtually anything worth doing in technology will usually strongly challenge the status quo, and this was no different.

In countless meetings and showcases with senior editorial managers, over many months, I communicated my strong belief that, if successful, my role would essentially create "more eyeballs for your amazing content, and more eyeballs for us to monetize." My job was to gain maximum reach from the emerging new distribution channels.

To do that, I believed I needed to build a world-class product within which to showcase the unquestionable world-class content.

Having established some success early in my tenure, it was then that the technology world shifted again. Toward the end of January 2010, Steve Jobs confirmed one of the worst-kept secrets in tech by formally announcing Apple's new tablet: the iPad.

The next day, I received a phone call from Cupertino. "Steve loved what you guys did with the iPhone," I was told. "We'd like you to replicate it for the iPad. And by the way, he's planning to showcase his favorite apps on stage at the public launch."

Clearly that was great news, but then came the curveball: "We need the app submitted by the last week in March." That gave us a little over seven weeks to submit our app for final review.

This was a major problem. We had added significantly more functionality than most and designed our product bottom up. And not all of it was portable, even to an iPad.

From the get-go, our biggest risk was feasibility. After a day or two of intensive discovery work, it was clear that achieving the same level of excellence was going to be impossible. We just didn't have sufficient time. With quality sacrosanct, we needed another product—and fast.

I knew exactly where to look. I'd previously made the decision to put photography front and center in our iPhone launch. It was immediately apparent these new touchscreen devices were also the world's most impressive (and expensive) digital frames. The qualitative and quantitative data proved that decision to be a good one.

Our photography content was consistently among the most popular, helped to drive strong frequency, and resulted in consistently positive customer feedback.

There was no more time to collect further evidence. Our new product would focus specifically on news photography, and given timelines, I would "thin slice" the scope. We had a small, empowered product team (five people: product, design, and three engineers).

I had to ensure we were focused on what could be built as quickly as possible. We would then rely on rapid iteration to make it as good as possible.

The concept moved from whiteboard to customer prototype in days. We would deliver a single, curated photo per day that communicated an important world event. We'd include a few other details, but only a few—highlighting the story behind the photo and how it was shot.

The inclusion of the latter allowed us to gain an impressive sponsorship, proving early that we were capable of achieving revenue gains. The photos would build, over time, into a stunning library of the world's most arresting photographs. If we got it right, I figured we could create the world's first and best digital "coffee table" app.

I needed to befriend the *Guardian*'s photography team, then led by a fabulous craftsman, Roger Tooth. He was incredibly patient and very willing to devote time and resources to a project that had a limited chance of success.

With so little time, things moved quickly. While my designer and I focused on iterating our prototype, our three-person engineering team got to work figuring out the base details of how we would create the systems and services to ensure consistent content delivery.

One other key challenge was the fact we didn't have any hardware. We'd seen an iPad, but there was no hands-on opportunity (that would come a little later in Cupertino, but for that to be successful we needed to be relatively code complete). As a result, we had some fun proto-typing both the hardware and software in unison with some creative use of cardboard and laptop screens. It was basic but allowed us to iterate incredibly quickly.

With value, feasibility, and usability starting to work their way down my list of risks, there was one area remaining that worried me significantly: business viability.

Up to that point, very few of the senior stakeholders had had much (or any) visibility of the work. It was a decision I'd taken deliberately, though not lightly, early on. I'd secured agreement with my technology director and with Alan, that in order to take advantage of this oppor-tunity, I would need to move unusually quickly. I would have to seek apology later.

With a product now in late build that I was increasingly confident of, the time to make those apologies had arrived. In truth, although Alan was almost certainly concerned that I had failed to involve more senior editorial figures, he didn't waver in his support once he'd seen the prototype.

I also had very strong advocates in the photography team. I had been so impressed with how passionately and knowledgeably Roger talked about his art. I'd even baked a short video of him into the app.

Alan, a longstanding believer in the power of technology, felt it was time to expose the work fully at the highest level, and invited me to present to the Group's board. In the room were the great and the good of both British media and technology, but there was one particularly friendly face: former Apple and Microsoft exec, Judy Gibbons.

I'd previously worked for Judy at a venture-funded startup, and she was then (and remains) a fabulous external mentor for me. With my showcase over, she immediately responded with words that set the tone for approval: "Truly excellent, it looks amazing and how did you manage to move so fast?" With those words out on the table, the rest of the meeting went smoothly. We submitted the app for approval the next day.

As expected, I heard nothing back from Apple (a conversation with them can often feel like shouting into a dark alley). But when Steve took the stage two weeks later, he rapidly got to his favorite iPad apps. He skipped over many well-known U.S. brands.

"We've got a lot of news apps" he said, "the *New York Times*, *Time* magazine, the *Wall Street Journal*, *USA Today*." But then he paused, took a step back, and turned to look at the huge image of Guardian Eyewitness that had appeared on stage. "This is a cool app," he continued, "Guardian Eyewitness. Rather than text, this gives you the day in pictures. And it's *really* nice."

Virtually anyone who cared about technology was watching that broadcast, which was a pretty big audience. The resulting usage followed a similar path to the iPhone launch, and although smaller due to fewer base hardware sales, in many ways it was improved.

Due to the nature of the content (stunning, family-friendly photographs), we had also unwittingly created arguably the perfect app to showcase the iPad's then-revolutionary screen technology. As a result, Apple was even more industrious in their use of our app in virtually all early iPad marketing campaigns. And for the best part of a year, we tracked close to a 1:1 relationship between unique iPad sales and unique Eyewitness usage.

We had proven that quality photojournalism—combined with an innovative and immersive digital experience—resulted in millions of new *Guardian* consumers. But perhaps more important, we had demonstrated that the *Guardian* could lead the world, not just editorially but digitally. The *Guardian* is now close to being consistently revenue positive, a significant step forward and one that will guarantee a strong global, progressive voice for multiple generations. Long may it continue.

79

TRANSFORMED

S VPG Partner Lea Hickman is publishing another book in the SVPG series, TRANSFORMED, *and her book tackles the very difficult but critically important topic of transformation. Below, Lea explains her motivation for writing the book and the topics she addresses in it.*

There are many books on digital transformations, and even more organizations that have tried and failed to meaningfully transform.

Why is this book any different, and why should you expect to be any more successful after reading it?

From working with many companies, and from experiencing first-hand at Adobe one of the most noted and financially successful transformations in technology history, I can tell you that not all companies are fully vested in their transformations. In fact, most aren't willing to make the changes that are necessary.

Most organizations focus their transformation narrowly on how they develop products, rather than broadly on how they produce and deliver value to their customers. They think they can silo off some "digital transformation" group or have their developers adopt Agile methods.

Let me give you an example. When I joined the Silicon Valley Product Group after building products for more than 25 years, it was very eye-opening to work with multiple product organizations around the world and see the different patterns of behavior.

In some cases, I would be working with world-class product leaders who understood how to get the product organization operating in a way that would yield real results. Their leaders were able to lead, manage, and coach the product organization, and to partner effectively with their colleagues across the company.

However, in other organizations, the product leaders—while they perhaps knew the mechanics of product—didn't have the ability to build the teams they needed to deliver the necessary results, and to influence the rest of the organization. They were viewed mainly as the technology team, and thought of as a necessary (or, sometimes, not-so-necessary) expense.

The most difficult part of these engagements is that I could predict what was likely to happen. Yes, they would improve incrementally, but the full potential wouldn't be realized. For these organizations, they needed more fundamental changes.

If a company wants to raise the bar for the product organization, they need to think differently about product.

Instead of looking at product as just a part of the technology organization (or worse, the IT organization), they need to think about product as *the organization*. I am not talking about power structure or even org structure. I am talking about how product needs to be the value driver of the organization as opposed to just a feature factory for the rest of the organization.

As I engage with these types of organizations, another lesson I've learned is that, if the executive team isn't on board with this product operating model, the chances of successful transformation are slim.

I've found that it is critically important for the executive team to understand, and have the language to engage with, the product organization.

There are also key characteristics of the executive leaders that I have observed. Certain executives have the skills and personality to drive the necessary change, and others don't. The leader's behaviors can make or break the ability of an organization to transform to a true product culture.

One of the things I am most proud of, when I think of Silicon Valley Product Group, is the fact that we operate in the real world. What we talk about isn't academic, and it isn't theory. We focus on what we *know* works. We have all built products for decades. We have all had successes and failures. We have all operated as both individual contributors and senior leaders in organizations. We have all been through the major transformations that I will be talking about.

This book is intended to help you navigate your way through the many challenges and pitfalls of effective transformation.

This book is straightforward and frank. As I say to all of my clients, you may not like what I will tell you, but I will be honest and tell you what I believe you need to hear. Marty Cagan taught me that very early in my career. He also gave me some hard-to-hear feedback when we were going through the transformation at Adobe that was foundational in terms of making the changes we needed to make to transform the entire company.

80

The Most Important Thing

Empowered engineers are the single most important thing that you can have in a company.

—Bill Campbell

In your journey to empowered teams, if I had to pick just one concept from this entire book that I hope you would take to heart, it would be the idea of an *empowered engineer*.

Certainly, I'm not saying that's all that's required, as *extraordinary products come from product teams*. But I am suggesting I believe this is the single most important ingredient.

I could have framed most of this book around the concept of an empowered engineer.

I have explained that the best single source for innovation is your engineers (because they're working with the enabling technology every day, so they're in the best position to see what's just now possible).

The product vision is intended to attract and inspire these engineers.

The product strategy is intended to ensure these engineers are working on the most important problems.

The team objectives give the engineers clear statements of the problem to solve, and the outcomes to strive for.

The product manager and product designer provide critical constraints regarding business viability and customer experience, respectively.

User research and data science provide the engineers with key insights.

And to be very clear, just letting your engineers decide *how to code* a solution is not what is meant by empowerment. Of course, they need to decide *how to implement* the solution.

Letting your engineers *determine the architecture* is also not what is meant by empowerment. Of course, they also need to be able to *decide the architecture*.

Empowerment of an engineer means that you provide the engineers with *the problem to solve* and *the strategic context*, and they are able to leverage technology to figure out *the best solution to the problem*.

An easy way to tell whether or not you have empowered engineers is if the first time your engineers see a product idea is at sprint planning, you are clearly a feature team and your engineers are not empowered in any meaningful sense.

If you're just using your engineers to code, you're only getting about half their value.

Hopefully, this is obvious at this point in the book, but a strong tech-powered product company would no sooner outsource their engineers than they would outsource their CEO.

The best tech companies understand this. They all have dual-track career ladders for a reason. Their top engineers are generally compensated at the level of a vice president.

The engineers are the easiest way to tell if the company has teams of missionaries or teams of mercenaries.

Note that I'm not suggesting that you put your engineers on a pedestal. They are ordinary people like the rest of us. But I am suggesting that you treat them like the first-class members of the product teams they need to be.

Just consider the breakthrough innovations you use and love every day. Odds are that innovation originated from an empowered engineer working in an empowered team.

I will warn you that, in too many cases, your product managers will resist this. You will hear: "My engineers are not interested in anything but coding."

This is by far the most common excuse from people that don't understand empowered teams. I have heard it countless times, mostly when I ask a product manager or product designer why their engineers aren't participating in the product discovery work.

The first thing I should acknowledge is that occasionally this is true, and I'll come back to this situation later. But in my experience, this is the exception.

Whenever I hear this objection, I insist on speaking to the engineers directly. Much more often than not, this is not at all what the engineers say. In fact, the most common complaint I hear from the engineers is that they are not included until it's too late, and they are forced to deal with the consequences.

What's usually going on is that the product manager doesn't want the engineers to be included because she would rather the engineers spend their time coding. So, in this case, the issue is an overzealous product manager—thinking much more like a project manager than a product manager—either hearing what she wants to hear, or not caring enough to even ask.

However, sometimes the engineers do tell me they don't really care much about discovery. They prefer to code and are fine building "whatever." In this case, I ask them to tell me the last time any of the engineers were able to personally visit with a customer. The answer is usually between "a very long time ago" and "never."

But, as I said above, sometimes not even a single one of the engineers has any desire to do anything other than code. In this case, my discussion moves to the head of engineering, and I explain that she has mercenaries and not missionaries, and why she needs to raise the bar on hiring engineers. At a minimum, she needs at least one true tech lead on each product team, and discovery is one of the big responsibilities of the tech lead.

If as a product leader, you do nothing else other than this, you will have meaningfully moved forward on your use of technology, on your path to empowered product teams, and on giving yourself a real chance at continuous innovation.

81

The Destination

If you recall, I opened this book by describing the situation I so often encounter in companies. Now that we've discussed the work necessary to transform, I'd like to revisit this list, this time with where I hope your transformation will take you.

The Role of Technology

Your company understands the critical and essential role that technology plays in enabling your business, and the experience you provide to your customers.

When new technologies emerge that you believe have the potential to be relevant, you immediately designate some engineers to learn that technology and to consider how it may be able to help solve problems for your customers in ways that are just now possible.

This goes far beyond using technology for operational efficiencies. You understand that technology allows you to reconsider what's possible and reimagine every aspect of your existing business.

You view your product managers, product designers, engineers, and data scientists as absolutely core to your business. You would no sooner consider outsourcing them than you would outsource your executives.

Coaching

You have developed and embraced a culture of coaching. Every single member of a product team has at least one manager that is committed to helping her reach her potential. You have built a reputation as a company where ordinary people who are competent and have good character can develop into a member of an extraordinary product team.

Staffing

Your hiring managers know that they are personally responsible for recruiting candidates, ensuring a strong interview and hiring process, and then onboarding these new people and ensuring they are successful. Strong staffing has become a core competency for your managers.

Product Vision

You have an inspiring and compelling product vision that unites the various product teams from across the organization in a common purpose that is meaningful to your customers. This vision will likely take you between 3 and 10 years to fully realize, but you are consistently making progress on this vision, quarter by quarter.

Team Topology

You have designed your team topology to optimize for empowerment and autonomy. The people on your product teams feel real ownership over a meaningful piece of the larger whole, and they understand how and when to work with their colleagues on other teams to collaborate on larger problems.

Product Strategy

You are executing on a product strategy that focuses on the most important goals and is powered by insights that come from your data and your ongoing interactions with customers. The result is that you know the most impactful problems that you need your teams to solve.

Team Objectives

These *problems to solve* are assigned to specific product teams with *team objectives*. Those teams then use product *discovery* techniques to figure out the tactics that can actually solve the problems, and product *delivery* builds that solution to bring it to market.

Relationship to Business

Today, the relationship between the product teams and your business leaders and stakeholders is one of mutual respect and true collaboration. The product teams work closely with the stakeholders to come up with solutions that customers love, yet work for the business. Both the teams and the stakeholders understand and embrace this.

Empowered Teams

Most important, the product teams are empowered to come up with the best solutions to the problems they've been asked to solve, and they are accountable to the results.

The engineers are constantly looking to apply new technology in new ways to better solve customer problems. The designers are continuously working to provide the necessary user experience. The product managers take responsibility for the value and the viability of the solutions.

The teams are inspired and proud to be working collaboratively with skilled colleagues on meaningful problems. They have a strong sense of ownership and define their success by their consistent contributions to customers and the company.

The state I'm describing here is still not easy—you will always have strong competitors that covet your customers—but now you are equipped to not just fight back, but to grow and thrive by continuously innovating on behalf of your customers.

Final Thoughts

My deep hope is that the many product leaders out there who were never fortunate enough to receive serious coaching will now have a resource to help them raise their game—and hence raise the level of their people.

Even beyond that, I am especially hopeful that the next generation of leaders will read this and understand what they need to do to be the leader their people and company deserve.

I am hopeful that you'll all go off and become exceptional product leaders.

I hope you will be able to work in a company that knows how to utilize your talents.

Finally, I hope you will use your talents and your energies for good.

Acknowledgments

This book is based on the lessons learned from a career spanning nearly 40 years, exclusively working on technology-powered products and services. As such, there are countless people who have influenced me along the way.

So many managers and leaders took the time and made the effort to coach and develop my skills, and to show me what strong leadership looks like.

So many colleagues in engineering, design, and product showed me what it means to work on a strong product team.

And so many companies have invited me into their offices to sit down with their teams to get to know them and share what I've learned and, in every case, helped me to build my knowledge of strong teams and companies.

This book benefited in particular from the insights of a set of proven product leaders and discovery coaches that I admire and respect: Holly Hester-Reilly, Teresa Torres, Gabrielle Buffrem, Petra Wille, and Felipe Castro each dedicated real time and effort to help me make this book worthy of its subject.

I would also like to thank the leaders that allowed me to profile them in this book. Besides being exceptional leaders, they also have in common a desire to shine the light on others rather than on themselves. I'm grateful they agreed to let me provide others a glimpse into their leadership style: Debby Meredith, Audrey Crane, Christina Wodtke, April Underwood, Judy Gibbons, Avid Larizadeh Duggan, Lisa Kavanaugh, and Shan-Lyn Ma.

Thanks also to my long-time editor, Peter Economy, and my publisher John Wiley & Sons, especially Richard Narramore.

Finally, I want to thank my SVPG Partners, starting with my coauthor Chris Jones, and then Martina Lauchengco, Lea Hickman, Christian Idiodi, and Jon Moore. These people are my partners precisely because I believe they are the best in the world at what they do, and each and every one of them contributed substantially to this book. I am proud to know and work with each of them.

Marty Cagan, June 2020

My point of view on these topics was forged by the leaders at Vontu: Joseph Ansanelli, Michael Wolfe, Doug Camplejohn, Steve Roop, John Donnelly, Ken Kim, Margie Mader-Clark, and many others. This crew walked the talk and showed me what genuine leadership and focus on the team could do. I still remember Michael Wolfe telling me, "Mark my words, you will spend the rest of your career trying to recreate this." Michael, consider your words marked.

I also want to thank the teams I've had over the years. I was fortunate to have so many amazing people on these teams. There's no way to list everyone, but I'd like to single out Rich Dandliker, Bruno Bergher, Jon Stull, Derek Halliday, Alex Bovee, Ayan Mandel, Shun Chen, and Conall O'Raghallaigh. You all pushed in your own ways. My collaborations with you are my most cherished career memories.

Thanks also to all the SVPG partners: Martina, Lea, Christian, Jonathan. What an amazing and diverse crew! I learn from you all every day. I want to give a particular shout out to Martina Lauchengco, who is not only an SVPG partner but also my life partner. Martina, you support me and challenge my thinking in the best of ways.

Lastly, I'd like to express my most sincere gratitude to Marty for believing in me and bringing me into the SVPG partnership. I continue to learn so much from you and cherish our collaboration across all aspects of SVPG. With all my heart, thank you!

Chris Jones, June 2020

About the Authors

Marty Cagan

Before founding the Silicon Valley Product Group to pursue his interests in helping others create successful products through his writing, speaking, advising, and coaching, Marty Cagan served as an executive responsible for defining and building products for some of the most successful companies in the world, including Hewlett-Packard, Netscape Communications, and eBay.

Marty began his career with a decade as a software developer at Hewlett-Packard Laboratories—conducting research on software technology and building several software products for other software developers.

After HP, Marty joined a then-young Netscape Communications Corporation, where he had the opportunity to participate in the birth of the internet industry.

Marty was most recently senior vice president of product and design for eBay, where he was responsible for defining products and services for the company's global e-commerce trading site.

During his career, Marty has personally performed and managed most of the roles of a modern software product organization, including product management, software development, product marketing, user-experience design, software testing, engineering management, and general management.

As part of his work with SVPG, Marty is an invited speaker at major conferences and top companies across the globe.

Marty is a graduate of the University of California at Santa Cruz—with Bachelor of Arts degrees in computer science and applied economics—and of the Stanford University Executive Institute.

Marty is also the author of the top-rated book *INSPIRED: How to Create Tech Products Customers Love*.

Chris Jones

Chris has spent over 25 years building and leading product teams that defined new product categories at startups to Fortune 500 software companies including Lookout, Symantec, and Vontu. A holder of multiple patents, he has discovered and developed new products in consumer and enterprise mobile, web, data, and platform services.

Since joining SVPG, Chris has worked directly with over 100 companies ranging from startups to very large enterprises across a wide variety of technologies, business models, and industries. Chris has worked directly with leadership and operational teams at these companies to better align their organization, process, tools, and culture with modern product best practices.

Before joining Silicon Valley Product Group, Chris was the VP of Product, Design, and Analytics for Lookout and the Head of Product for Vontu (acquired by Symantec). At both companies, Chris built the product organizations from the ground up and led the effort to discover and deliver multiple category-leading products.

Chris graduated from Stanford with a Bachelor of Science in computer science.

Learning More

The Silicon Valley Product Group website (https://svpg.com/) is designed as a free and open resource where we share our latest thoughts and learnings from the world of technology-powered products.

SVPG also holds occasional intense workshops for product managers, product teams, and product leaders—both online and in person (usually in San Francisco, New York City, and London). Our goal is to share the most recent learnings and to provide a career-defining experience (see https://svpg.com/workshops/).

For companies that believe they need dramatic and meaningful transformation across their technology and product organization to competitively produce technology-powered products, we also offer custom, on-site engagements.

Index